# GOLFING HEROES

# GOLFING HEROES

**Renton Laidlaw**

ALL-TIME GREATS PAST AND PRESENT

INTRODUCTION BY

**Sandy Lyle**

St Michael

*SPORTS EDITIONS LIMITED*

| | |
|---|---|
| *Managing Director* | *Richard Dewing* |
| *Art Director* | *Mary Hamlyn* |
| *Designers* | *Sandra Cowell* |
| | *Rob Kelland* |
| *Desk Editor* | *Leslie Smillie* |
| *Copy Editor* | *Mark Baldwin* |
| *Picture Research* | *Tony Graham* |

This edition published for
Marks and Spencer plc in 1989
by Century Benham Ltd
A division of Century Hutchinson Publishing Group
Brookmount House, 62-65 Chandos Place,
London WC2N 4NW



ISBN 0 7126 3429 0

Designed by Sports Editions Limited

Typeset in Palatino
by Pastiche, Clerkenwell Road, London

Origination by Optoscan, Kidderminster

Printed and bound in Spain by Graficas Estella, S.A., Estella, Navarra

*Cover photographs* (ALLSPORT/David Cannon)
*Front:* Seve Ballesteros, Curtis Strange, Sandy Lyle and Tony Jacklin.
*Back:* Bernhard Langer and Jack Nicklaus in the late evening sun at Augusta.

# CONTENTS

# *P R E F A C E*

## by Renton Laidlaw

Golf is a sport fortunate to have produced a long line of personalities who merit special status. Either by their great deeds and example, or by their attitude and sportsmanship, they have created and maintained the proud tradition of the Royal and Ancient game, while encouraging thousands more to play and enjoy the playing of it.

The reputation of any sport is only as good as the men and women who represent it at the highest level. Those in this book competed with pride and earned much success – many continue to do so. All have been fine ambassadors for a marvellous game.

I never expected the task of reducing that list of great names to 50 would be an easy one and inevitably my idea of greatness may differ from yours. It is a personal choice limited by the number of pages. I just hope that I have satisfied far more than I have disappointed!

Hopefully, whether or not you agree with the list, you will enjoy being reminded of the careers and personalities of the men who were the early pace-setters, the men and women who shaped the way the game would grow around the world. Sometimes the road to stardom was littered with disappointments and in some instances tragedy. Some achieved greatness only to let it slip again.

The pen portraits are not meant to chronicle to the last detail the careers of the greats. Using a bigger brush and a wider canvas, the idea is to remind you what kind of men and women the golfing stars have been since the middle of the 19th century. Already there are some notable younger players coming along who will undoubtedly achieve greatness. Jose-Maria Olazabal of Spain, for instance, has won the British Boys', Youths' and Amateur Championships and is doing so well as a professional that he looks like being a natural successor to his fellow Spaniard Seve Ballesteros ... but Jose-Maria's greatest days remain in the future.

I owe a debt of gratitude to Sports Editions' Managing Director Richard Dewing and Art Director Mary Hamlyn for all their professional advice and enthusiasm, and to three golf-writing colleagues who helped me to compile the book on a tight schedule.

In Australia, Geoff Roach of the *Adelaide News* has built up a reputation as a scrupulously fair and fearlessly unbiased reporter and is also much admired for his literary style. He has a deep understanding of the game he writes about and plays with deep affection. Geoff cooperated on the profiles of most of the players from 'Down Under'. He knows them better than most.

Bill Elliott, one of the team of sportswriters working for the *Daily Star* newspaper, has written a revealing book about Bernhard Langer. He managed to find time to write eloquently about some of the 'newer fellows'.

I thank too Richard Dodd, the knowledgeable golf correspondent of the *Yorkshire Post*, whose shrewd eye helped bring to life personalities such as Tony Jacklin and the late Dai Rees, whose enthusiasm for the game was infectious. He also organised the tributes to two great Irishmen, Christy O'Connor senior and Joe Carr. Thanks are also due to Donald Steel whose *Guinness Book of Golfing Records* was such an invaluable source of reference and to Audrey Adams for the thoroughness of her research.

In conclusion I dedicate this book to my father who has always been an enthusiastic supporter of both golf and of my own work.

Renton Laidlaw
Golf Correspondent
*Evening Standard* London

April 25, 1989

Sandy Lyle

# *INTRODUCTION*

## by Sandy Lyle

I have always felt tremendously privileged to be involved in the great game of golf. It is a game with superb traditions and a reputation for fair play and sportsmanship which is second to none around the world.

That is as it should be and everyone I have met around the world while playing golf agrees. There is much for us to protect – players, administrators and the fans, too, who come to encourage us wherever we are playing.

Today the game is graced by many magnificent players as standards continue to rise yet, for all that, there is still only a limited number of golfers who over the years have come, genuinely, into that superstar bracket.

It takes much more than just talent to be a superstar. You need to have personality, charisma and be something of a showman too, whether you like it or not. It has always been this way.

I often stand at the practice ground to watch some of my own heroes practise – men such as Jack Nicklaus, Lee Trevino and Arnold Palmer. I can learn so much from them – men who have had a great influence on the nature and growth of the game and maintaining the golfing traditions.

Sadly I am too young to have been able to watch Ben Hogan compete when he was at his best, but like every golfer I have enjoyed reading about him and why he has achieved a legendary reputation in the game. There have been others whose contribution has been quite remarkable for one reason or another and sometimes despite difficult circumstances.

From Tom Morris Junior a century ago to Severiano Ballesteros today, the game has been well served by men and women who have had much to give and have given it willingly. Their stories make interesting reading. Maybe you will learn something you did not know about one of the old-time greats, or even a modern star, by reading this book. I hope you enjoy it as much as all the great stars have enjoyed or enjoy playing and giving the golf fan so much pleasure.

# TOM MORRIS JUNIOR

The first Open Championship star Tom Morris Jun. was so successful that he caused the Championship to be abandoned temporarily 11 years after it had been started.

Tom Morris Senior and Junior

Young Tom Morris was the first of the golfing greats – but also the most tragic. Yet before he died at 24 he had won the British Open four times and become, as a 17-year-old in 1868, the youngest-ever winner. It is a feat never likely to be beaten.

When he won the Championship Belt three times in a row to earn it outright, he brought the Championship sharply to a halt just 11 years after it had been started. Officials had not banked on this sort of domination and were so uncertain of how to handle the situation that it took them a year to sort the matter out. There was no Championship in 1871 and when Prestwick, the club that had initiated the Open in 1860, the Royal and Ancient Golf Club of St Andrews and the Honorable Company of Edinburgh Golfers got together to produce the perpetual Cup which is still played for today, the Open was then staged at these three venues on a rota basis.

No doubt suitably embarrassed at the gap in the proceedings, officials restarted the Championship in 1872. Morris merely continued where he left off, winning again for the fourth and what turned out, tragically, to be the last time. No one else since has won four times in a row and these days it seems an impossible feat.

The hiatus that followed Young Tom's third victory must be put into perspective. In those days the Open Championship may have been 'open to the world' but it carried little weight compared with, say, the R. and A. Club's autumn medal. In fact the Open was tagged on after the amateurs had played their competition. If the greens were less than perfect for the professionals it was hardly surprising. Of course in those days the professionals made most of their money competing in challenge matches, either with other professionals or with amateur partners, and Young Tom seems to have begun his professional career very early, winning money at an age most youngsters might have been content to caddie.

At the age of 13 he beat another boy in an exhibition match at nearby Perth and collected a £5 prize. Three years later, just a year before he began his domination of the Open, he won tournaments at Carnoustie and Montrose up the coast from St Andrews. Any talent spotter must have realised then that here was someone with a special gift for the game. He was a natural player and just failed to record the largest winning margin in the Championship when he took the 1870 title and the Belt by 12 shots. His father, Old Tom, later to become the R and A Club greenkeeper, had won by 13 shots in 1862.

Young Tom's winning margin at Prestwick was amazing, but not as remarkable as his score for three rounds of the then 12-hole circuit. He shot 149 or one over par – a score with a gutta percha ball which was never equalled by any of the great golfers who used the same equipment. He was one under 4's for his last 12 holes. The Belt he won was presented later to the Royal and Ancient Golf Club of St Andrews where it now rests in their museum, a memorial in some respects to a fine player cut off in his prime. Morris, broad-shouldered and with superb strength, was a giant of the time, incomparably better than his rivals. He revelled in the challenge the game afforded him. It was said he could squeeze his ball out of bad lies better than anyone else. And with hickory shafted clubs too! Needless to say he broke a great many clubs but they were easily repaired in the family shop!

At the time Young Tom was growing up there were two main golfing families to the fore – The Morrises in St Andrews and the Parks from Musselburgh near Edinburgh. There was Willie Park, the man who won the first Open, his son Willie Jun. and Mungo, a sailor who did not play so much golf as his brother Willie. In the early years the Parks won the Open seven times while the Morris family had eight wins to celebrate, evenly divided between father and son. It was during a challenge match between the Parks – Willie and Mungo – and the Morrises at North Berwick that the news that was to break Young Tom's heart arrived by telegram.

It was September 1875 and the Morrises had just gained their revenge over the Parks when, coming off the last green, Young Tom was handed the news which had been kept from him until the game was over. It said that his wife of just a year was in trouble at the birth of their first child and that he should get back home as quickly as he could. There being no trains at that time, someone immediately put a yacht at the Morrises disposal in order that they might sail back up the coast to St Andrews with all haste. No time was lost in putting to sea but before the ship had cleared the mouth of the harbour another telegram arrived to say mother and child had both died. It had a devastating effect on Young Tom and within three months he had died probably of consumption although often more romantically described as 'a broken heart'.

He was so distraught that he hardly ever played golf again but his final match against a Mr Molesworth from Westward Ho over three rounds in the snow at St Andrews saw him triumph by 9 and 7. It was, however, a hollow victory. As a golfer Young Tom had few, if any, weaknesses and the memorial erected in his name at his grave in St Andrews is a measure, too, of the respect in which he was held.

## *CAREER RECORD*

### Victories

| | |
|---|---|
| 1868 | British Open |
| 1869 | British Open |
| 1870 | British Open |
| 1872 | British Open |

### Did you know...

1. Tom Morris Jun. won the Open four times and came second, third, fourth and ninth in the only other Championships in which he played before his death at the age of 24.
2. On his gravestone in St Andrews, the inscription reads "Deeply regretted by numerous friends and all golfers, he thrice in succession won the Championship Belt and held it without rivalry and yet without envy, his many amiable qualities being no less acknowledged than his golfing achievements".
3. Tom Morris Jun. won the 1870 Open by 12 strokes but this was still one shot outside the record set by his father in 1862.
4. The Championship Belt which Tom Morris Jun. won outright causing a one year gap in the playing of the event until the organisers worked out how to handle the situation, is now the property of the Royal and Ancient Golf Club of St Andrews.

**Tom Morris** and the championship belt he won outright – much to the consternation of the Championship officials

# *HARRY VARDON*

The golfer who holds the record of six Open Championship wins using the famous Harry Vardon grip did not, in fact, invent the grip with which he is universally associated.

The capture of six British Open titles around the turn of the century secured a place for Harry Vardon among golf's 'Hall of Fame', but he rubber stamped his passport to sporting immortality by popularising the overlapping grip, which is destined to be taught to students of the game for as long as it is played.

Using this grip, an open stance, an upright swing and a graceful rhythm Vardon established himself as the leading member of the Great Triumvirate. Vardon, James Braid and J. H. Taylor enjoyed a domination of the game's spoils before World War One which bordered on gluttony. Between them they won 16 Open championships in a 20-year spell, Braid and Taylor having to be content with five apiece while Vardon set the yardstick of six by which modern golfers still measure their achievements. Peter Thomson of Australia and American Tom Watson have each, in turn, moved within touching distance of Vardon's record only to remain in his shadow, albeit in the illustrious company of Braid and Taylor. However, all four might have shared the distinction of winning the most Opens in history had Vardon's career – which was heading up a gardener's path – not been redirected by his employer, a Major Spofforth, when Vardon was 17.

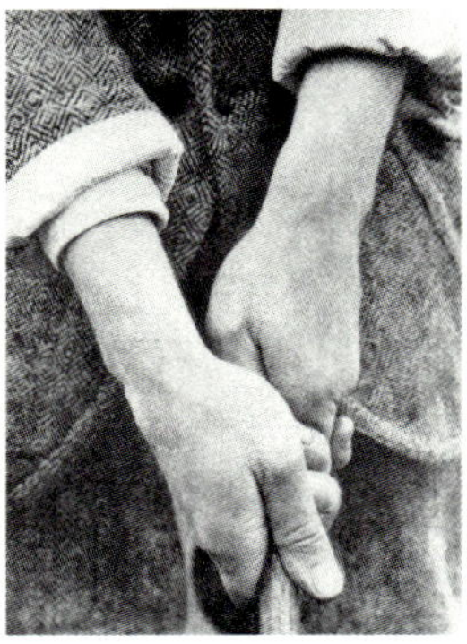

The famous Vardon overlapping grip

Born in Grouville, near St Helier in Jersey, young Vardon had played a crude form of golf with a few friends, their clubs manufactured from blackthorn and oak, their balls made of a local marble known as 'taws' and their course four 50-yard holes which the boys smoothed as best they could on local bumpy terrain. Yet his interest in golf was not nurtured through his teens to the extent of considering a career as a professional – until he joined Major Spofforth's staff as an apprentice gardener. The Major's all-consuming passion was sport, golf in particular, and he took Vardon with him for the occasional round, loaning his employee an old, yellow driver and an iron with which Vardon laid down the foundations for a swing that would shape golfing history. But even with the Major's assistance, Vardon had still only played, by his own reckoning, less than a couple of dozen or so rounds when he entered a Working Men's Club competition and won the only prize – a vase.

When his brother Tom became a professional at St Anne's-on-Sea, it must have sown a similar seed in gardener Harry's head, but it was only when Tom came second in a tournament in Scotland, win-

ning what was then a staggering sum of £12 10s (£12.50), that the idea blossomed into reality. Harry Vardon took the plunge and secured his first professional golfing post, at Ripon and, later, Bury.

In those days there were few tournaments but a circuit of head-to-head exhibition matches enabled him to use his talent. Playing stalwarts such as Sandy Herd he learned quickly. In 1896, after five years at Bury, Vardon moved on again, this time to Ganton near Scarborough in Yorkshire. He quickly marked his arrival by a crushing 8 and 6 victory over the then Open title holder J. H. Taylor in a special challenge match. His illustrious career had begun in earnest.

With the Great Triumvirate thus into its embryonic stage, Vardon kept himself active during the winter months in a manner which today's professionals would be far too wary of imitating – playing centre forward for his local soccer team. Common sense eventually prevailed and Vardon, captain of the side, confined himself to the somewhat safer occupation of goalkeeper. He took the first three of his half dozen Open championships – in 1896 (at Muirfield), 1898 (Prestwick) and 1899 (Sandwich) – while professional at Gan-

Vardon on the tee, watched by James Braid (above) and about to find his way on to the green (left)

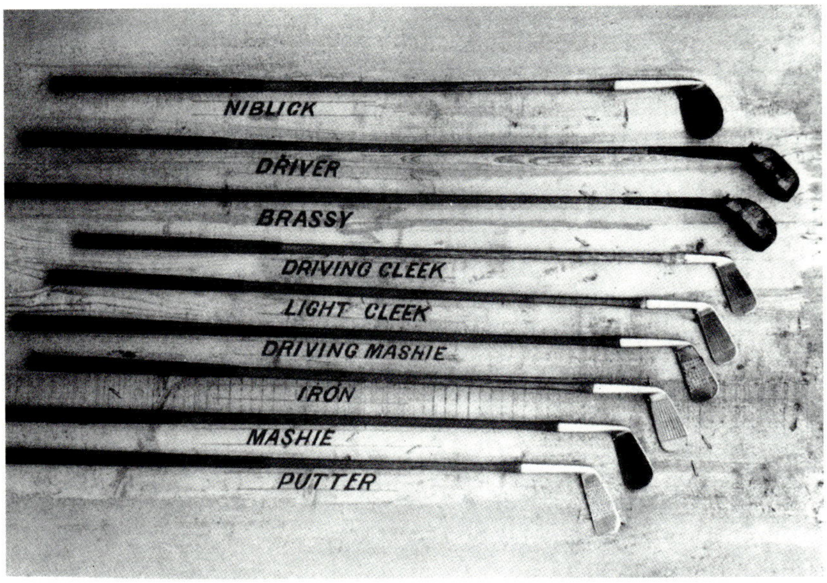


The clubs which won six Open Championships

ton and, for good measure, was runner-up on another three occasions, but he had gained a reputation that stretched beyond Britain. On the other side of the Atlantic, where interest in the game was growing steadily, he was in demand. In 1900 Vardon travelled on what was to be the first of several tours to America and won the United States Open title by two shots from J. H. Taylor, the rest of the field finishing a further eight shots distant.

Two years later a golfing revolution took place, one which Vardon was initially determined to resist. The gutty ball was usurped by the introduction of the rubber-cored one, known then as 'The Haskell' after its inventor, American Coburn Haskell. Vardon was sceptical and went into the 1902 Open at Hoylake saddled, by his own choice, with the handicap of playing the gutty. John Ball, who in 1890 had become the first amateur winner of the Open, persuaded Sandy Herd to use 'The Haskell' at Hoylake. With the extra distance and precision the ball afforded him Herd won the title – by just one shot from Vardon. Converted eventually, to 'The Haskell', Vardon won the 1903 Open at Prestwick despite suffering the initial effects of a bout of tuberculosis which was to see him spend long spells in sanatoriums throughout the following decade. Despite its debilitating effects Vardon won the Open in 1911 at Sandwich and three years later triumphed at Prestwick to complete his record six wins. In 1913 he tied with another Jersey golfer, Ted Ray, for the U.S. Open title but both were beaten in a play-off by a 20-year-old amateur, Francis Ouimet. It was front page news!

Although the victory did not end British domination of golf on both sides of the Atlantic it marked the turning of the tide in favour of America. The intervention of the 1914-18 war, and the consequent suspension of tournament play, was another factor which ensured his victory at Prestwick was Vardon's last major success. Yet, at the age of 50, he still managed to finish second to Ray in the 1920 U.S. Open, and much of his latter years, before his death in 1937, he spent teaching at the South Herts club in North London where he was professional for 34 years. His teaching also helped cement his reputation as the perfector of the overlapping grip. Although John Laidley had used it to win an amateur title before Vardon came along, and J. H. Taylor used it too, it was Vardon's use of it that somehow captured everyone's imagination.

## *CAREER RECORD*

**Harry Vardon** in typical pose in 1909

### Victories

| | |
|---|---|
| 1896 | British Open |
| 1898 | British Open |
| 1899 | British Open |
| 1900 | U.S. Open |
| 1903 | British Open |
| 1911 | British Open |
| 1912 | British Open |

### Did you know...

1. Harry Vardon popularised the over-lapping golfing grip: Although he did not invent it, he was so successful with it himself that it is known universally today as the "Vardon grip".
2. Harry Vardon is the only golfer to have won the Open Championship in Britain six times. He won his first Open in 1896 and his last in 1914 when he was 44. He might have won more but for contracting tuberculosis.
3. Harry Vardon was one of the first international superstars, travelling to America several times to take part in exhibition matches and major Championships.

# J. H. TAYLOR

The most articulate of the Great Triumvirate who shaped the pattern of golf at the turn of the Century, J.H. Taylor was a founder member of the Professional Golfers' Association.

J.H. Taylor, in his heyday, poses for the cameras

John Henry Taylor is one of golf's immortals. A member of the great triumvirate with James Braid and Harry Vardon, he won five Opens in that 21 year spell from 1894 when the trio together won 16 of the Championships.

J. H. Taylor started his roll of victories when, appropriately, he became the first English professional to win the Championship the year it was played in England (at Royal St George's) for the first time. He was born and died in the village of Northam in North Devon but throughout most of his 91 years he was an influence on the game either as a player or an administrator. He was the main driving force behind the formation of the Professional Golfers' Association in 1901 and throughout his life designed many golf courses, including Royal Birkdale.

Taylor worked hard to raise the status of the professional and, with Vardon and Braid, achieved much of which the modern professional can be justifiably grateful, yet he was not well educated. He left school at the age of 11 and, when others his age were learning Latin verbs or brushing up on their history and geography, the somewhat frail J. H. was building himself up physically by working variously as a caddie at Westward Ho, the club that was so dear to his heart, a boot-

Spy's view of J.H. Taylor in *Vanity Fair*

Blasting clear of a bunker in 1906

boy, a gardener's apprentice and a mason's labourer. It was not until he joined the greenkeeping staff of Westward Ho that he began to think seriously about golf as a career. Any hopes he had had of making a career for himself in the army or navy had been shattered because his eyesight was not good enough, so it was logical to stick to golf.

By the age of 19 he had turned professional at Burnham and hit the headlines by having the temerity to beat the famous old Scottish player Andrew Kirkaldy in a challenge match. Kirkaldy may have been teased about this defeat but he impressed upon his friends that Taylor had a future in golf and proposed him as his successor at Winchester. It was an ideal stepping stone for Taylor who moved later to Wimbledon and then to Royal Mid-Surrey where he stayed for more than 40 years.

Taylor had almost created a major upset in Scotland in the 1893 Open when he fired a Championship best round of 75 at Prestwick but in the end he had been out-gunned and out-manoeuvred by wiser, more experienced Scottish competitors. Taylor, had, however, learned a thing or two which enabled him to land the Cup the following year when he conquered a Royal St George's course which put a premium on long carries. The Open was for the first time a test not only of ability but also strength and Taylor passed the examination with flying colours. Helped by the good fortune that he missed a last day thunderstorm which killed several player's hopes, Taylor won in the end by five shots with his mentor Kirkaldy third a further stroke back.

Just to prove that his first victory, at a venue now happily restored to the regular Open Championship rota, was no fluke Taylor won again at St Andrews a year later despite opening with an 86. Midway through the third round Taylor trailed the leader Sandy Herd by nine shots but picked up two shots at the short eleventh where Herd ran up a 6 after being bunkered. He completed the last seven gruelling holes in 29. In the final round Herd had moved five clear again after four holes when the weather suddenly worsened. The wind blew strongly and it rained heavily – conditions ideally suited to Taylor's robust game. Nothing about his swing was graceful but it was extremely effective and by the turn Taylor had drawn level. In the end he won comfortably enough by four shots.

Arguably the finest of Taylor's victories came in 1913 at Royal Liverpool, a brute of a test when the wind blows and it rains. It did just that. Indeed the conditions were quite appalling. After the first two rounds, in which Taylor was one shot off the lead, the players turned up to battle in a wind so strong that tents were blown away and rain so heavy the greens were flooded. Helped by the fact that he was not a big man but very stocky Taylor, the king of bad weather golf, shot the only sub 80 round that day, a 77 in the storm, and triumphed, in the end, by a massive eight shots. That win made the tally of titles five-a-piece for the Triumvirate. There had to be a showdown.

There were rumblings of war about to break out but the 1914 Open at Prestwick was played before hostilities began. As for the golf, Taylor and Vardon ended up battling it out on the final day for the title. History revealed that Vardon captured his sixth title, still a record today, after Taylor, in the final round, ran into a sticky patch at the fourth. He drove into a new bunker put there to tighten up the hole by James Braid, took a disastrous 7 and, still seething, ruined his chances even further at the fifth by four-putting. Although he was a tough opponent with a more than ample share of determination in his character, Taylor was also a sensitive, emotional man and that defeat by Vardon irritated him for the rest of his life.

Taylor always adopted a most business-like approach to golf, according to the late Henry Cotton. He was involved in every aspect of the game – course-building and club-making. He always hit boldly up to the pin and in particular pioneered the use of the Mashie or seven-iron which he invented for approach shots. He did not give up playing until he felt he really was not able to give a good account of himself. Certainly at the age of 53 he was still good enough to finish fifth in the 1924 Open won by Walter Hagen.

J. H. Taylor may have lacked height compared to many but he towered above most in the contribution he made to the game. Bernard Darwin, the famous golf essayist, perhaps put it best of all when he wrote of Taylor: 'For innumerable years he was the head of his profession. It is due to him, more than to any other man, that the professional has climbed so far above its old unsatisfactory condition. He is a natural speaker, a natural fighter, a natural leader who would have made his mark in any walk of life.'

He made it in golf.

Receiving the Open Championship Trophy at Hoylake in 1913

# CAREER RECORD

**Victories**

| | |
|---|---|
| 1894 | British Open |
| 1895 | British Open |
| 1900 | British Open |
| 1909 | British Open |
| 1913 | British Open |

**Did you know...**

1. J. H. Taylor scored his first Open win in 1894 when the Championship was played for the first time in England at Sandwich. All previous Opens (since 1860) had been staged in Scotland.
2. J. H. Taylor was so powerful a hitter he built up a reputation as a bad weather performer. This was underlined when he won the 1913 Open by eight shots at Hoylake in rough conditions.
3. J. H. Taylor was never out of the top ten in the Open in Britain in the period between 1894 and 1909. During that period he won four times and was runner up five times including four in a row from 1904.
4. J. H. Taylor was the founder of the Professional Golfers' Association.

**Taylor** sporting his medal after his first Open Championship

# JAMES BRAID

One of the game's most accomplished professional golfers and course designers, James Braid's father never wanted him to take up the game.

James Braid joined golf's Great Triumvirate last of all. Harry Vardon, who had made such a dramatic impact with the new over-lapping grip that was to become so universally popular and John Henry (J.H.) Taylor had each won three Open titles before the tall Scot from the Fife fishing village of Elie and Earlsferry won the first of his five Championships in 1901.

Braid then dominated the Championship in the next nine years, and became the first man to take the title five times, justifiably taking his place as one of the game's most notable, well-liked and hugely-talented golfers and, later, course architect.

James Braid as seen by Spy in *Vanity Fair*

It would have been strange if Braid had not played golf coming from where he did. He may have had to ingeniously fashion out clubs for himself from old heads and shafts but he was always going to play the game. Rather like Sandy Lyle more than 80 years later, Braid remembered having a small club put into his hands at the tender age of four! He said he recalled playing with it not long after he had learned to walk.

All the lads at Elie played on the pleasant little course which tests in the most gentle way. Their style was frankly aggressive. They went for everything, took calculated risks and enjoyed their golf. Braid did too but he had an advantage over the others in that he balanced his aggression with a calm temperament. He never looked flustered and never was. He took reversals in the same way as he handled success. It helped, of course, that this tall erect man enjoyed playing the game so much that he always considered it fun, sometimes serious fun but always enjoyable.

Someone once wrote in later years that they wished they could be as intelligent as James Braid looked. He was an impressive figure who remained loyal over the years to the club that had been so loyal to him – Walton Heath in Surrey. He went there in 1903 when the club was founded. He had gone south, initially one suspects, against the wishes of his ploughman father. Never a golfer himself and therefore unsympathetic to the game, James' father would have preferred his son to have remained a craftsman joiner and amateur golfer.

On the first tee with a crowd of admirers

Having won everything there had been to win in Elie, Braid had moved on to Edinburgh where he had conquered new opponents off his handicap of three. Then one day, a friend suggested that he might like to consider the post of clubmaker at the Army and Navy Stores in London. He jumped at the chance to earn a shilling (or five new pence) an hour there but missed the outdoor life which was why he was delighted to be offered a job at first at Romford in Essex and then at Walton Heath, south of the capital. He remained there for almost 50 years and never once regretted it. Latterly he was an honorary member of the club and a highly-respected advisor, friend and confidant of many of the well-to-do members, some of whom were Government ministers.

He first sprang to public notice in 1895, the year after he had made his inglorious debut in the Open by shooting a 91, although that was not as bad as it looks in those days. All that was forgotten a little later when he halved a match he played with J.H. Taylor, the then Open champion, holing a putt to square on the last. Yet it would be six years before he achieved his crowning ambition and won the Open at Muirfield.

He had played well just before the Open in 1901 when taking the Musselburgh title with what was then a fantastic 36-hole total of 140 – the finest performance of his career helped by a new putter. He had ditched an old wooden putter and a wristy putting stroke in favour of a slow, much smoother take-away with a new aluminium club. The switch transformed his golf as dramatically as the much-publicised overnight 'miracle' that saw him go to bed a short driver and get up a long one. In fact he had changed his clubs and there was no mystique about that at all! Yet he began that 1901 Open at Muirfield indifferently, almost badly. He drove out of bounds. With a round to go, however, he had built up a five shot lead on Vardon and went on to win by three shots despite the fact that the head came off one of his clubs as he played an approach to the last green. He had 'arrived' and quickly made up for lost time.

He won again at St Andrews in 1905 and then at Muirfield for a second time in 1906. In 1908 he took the title at Prestwick by eight shots and in 1910 at the home of golf became the first five times Open winner, a distinction he shares today with J.H. Taylor, Peter Thomson of Australia,

A startling action shot of Braid with an old hickory-shafted club

# CAREER RECORD

James Braid in 1901

**Victories**

| | |
|---|---|
| 1901 | British Open |
| 1905 | British Open |
| 1906 | British Open |
| 1908 | British Open |
| 1910 | British Open |

**Did you know...**

1. James Braid's father never wanted his son to become a professional golfer.
2. James Braid won his five Open Championship titles in a brilliant ten year spell from 1901. During that period he was second three times and fifth equal on the other two occasions.
3. Curiously James Braid, the first man to win five Opens, never won that title in England where he lived for most of his life.
4. James Braid was one of the original "Big Three". He, J.H. Taylor and Harry Vardon were all born within a 13-month period between February 1870 and March 1871.

and Tom Watson of America. Only Harry Vardon has done better than that with six wins. Braid's triumphs were well received by the Scots who had been only too well aware of the English domination of the Championships since Willie Auchterlonie's win of 1893. Braid was a hero at home but remained a man of few words, unaffected by his successes.

In retrospect the 1914 Open at Prestwick was the last time the triumvirate contested together for the title and with all of them now having won the title five times there was even greater interest than normal in the clash of the Titans of their time. Braid was quickly out of the title hunt, but, curiously, he played a significant part in the eventual victory Vardon scored over Taylor. Braid had been asked to 'toughen up' Prestwick and had tightened up the fourth hole by putting in a new bunker that caught Taylor's ball and cost him a title-shattering 7.

As a second string to his bow and no doubt with some of the knowledge he learned from his father who had worked on a farm, Braid became an accomplished golf course architect with the ability to lay out, in his own mind, a circuit that would drain properly even in the heaviest rain. He was as much a genius in this sphere as he had been on the golf course in that remarkable nine-year spell which began in 1901.

Braid was the last player to win an Open with the old gutta percha solid rubber ball which made way for rubber-cored Haskell-ball at the turn of the century in what was another great golfing revolution. He also shot two rounds in the low 70's just before he died at the age of 80, well-satisfied that he had done the right thing by giving up carpentry the job his father would have preferred him to do.

He was universally known and liked, a man whose character was summed up in three words by his great rival J.H. Taylor. James Braid, he wrote was 'sincere, trustworthy and loyal.'

# *WALTER HAGEN*

He never wanted to be a millionaire but extrovert American golf champion Walter Hagen made sure that he did well enough to live like one.

Walter Charles Hagen, the first professional golfer to win and spend a million dollars, was one of the game's most flamboyant characters. He was the super showman who in his career won four Open Championships, five U.S.P.G.A. Championships and two U.S. Open titles in 15 years from 1914. Only Bobby Jones and Jack Nicklaus have won more.

Of German stock – his father was a blacksmith – Hagen was always determined never to be treated as a second-class citizen at a time when golf professionals frequently were. He set new standards which benefited everyone who followed him. When Hagen made one of his last public appearances at a function in Michigan in 1967, two years before he died, Arnold Palmer told him: 'If it were not for you this dinner would be downstairs in the professional's shop rather than up here in the ballroom.'

Hagen gave the professional golfer a proper status in society by highlighting social injustice. He hoped to embarrass those golf officials at Princes, who in 1920 refused to allow the professionals into the clubhouse, by parking his hired Rolls-Royce outside the front door and changing there. It was a typical gesture of a man who changed the pattern of professional golf. Three years later when runner-up to Arthur Havers at Troon, he declined to enter the clubhouse for the presentation ceremony having not been allowed in earlier. Instead he and his cronies went off to a local public house.

Everything he did he did with flair. He dressed colourfully. He lived stylishly. It was impossible to be neutral in one's view towards him. You either liked him a lot or disliked him intensely because of his super-confident approach, the impudence and at times arrogance of his behaviour. Most people, however, enjoyed being around when he played. Things happened. At the peak of his career he was so popular with the fans that they would watch him even when he was playing poorly. None of the great stars hit more bad shots than Hagen . . . and no-one played more dramatic recoveries. He was a crowd puller who commanded huge appearance fees for exhibition matches – most of them arranged by his manager

Walter Hagen – always a big favourite with the fans – did much to make the golf professional a respected figure

Bob Harlow who took away the cash in notes in a small suitcase!

While some golfers remain sullen and silent on the course, anxious less they break their concentration, Hagen was quite different. He chatted with the fans as readily as Lee Trevino does today and they loved it even if his opponents did not. Yet Hagen was never guilty of bad sportsmanship, just a little gamesmanship from time to time. Once, in 1919, it was alleged he called on Mike Brady to come out of the clubhouse to watch him hole a 15-footer to tie him for the U.S.

Hagen (right) steps out with Gene Sarazen and the 'Silver Scot' Tommy Armour

Open at Brae Burn in Massachussets. Hagen holed it all right and beat Brady the next day in the play-off by a shot. It was a close run thing but Hagen was a master of play-offs. No one ever beat him in one. When 'The Haig' said 'Who's going to be second?', he meant it!

When he was making a winning speech at the 1937 Ryder cup at Royal Birkdale, he said how delighted he was to be captain of the first American team to win on home soil. 'You mean foreign soil,' said a well-meaning fan in the crowd. 'Maybe,' answered Hagen, 'but can you blame me if I feel at home over here!' He helped and fostered Anglo-American relations not least by his remarkable participation in the Ryder Cup in which only one man, George Duncan, ever beat him. That was in 1929 and Duncan's victory was decisive. Hagen lost by 10 and 8 after having boasted the night before that having arranged to meet the British captain the following day it was a point in the bag for America. Had Hagen won the match would have been drawn!

One of his critics said of Hagen that he would never fail as a result of an excess of modesty. He was just a natural extrovert who more than perhaps any of the other great stars got more fun out of the game. He loved playing golf and enjoyed being dramatically outrageous at times, but it would be wrong to attribute his huge success and his tremendous influence to his warm, out-going personality alone. He was also a great competitor, no more so in match-play which was the way the U.S.P.G.A. Championship was decided in the old days. He won four titles in a row and went 22 36-hole matches against the best in America without losing. He could shrewdly assess an opponent's weakness and play on it until the fellow cracked!

He was also the first American-born winner of the British Open and the first man to win the Open titles on both sides of the Atlantic. On that first visit to Britain as American champion in 1920 he finished well down the field but promised he would be back to try again. He came back seven more times, won on four occasions, was second once and never finished worse than sixth. The 1920 event was the first Open after the First World War and Britain was only just recovering when Hagen blew in with his wardrobe of colourful clothes. He had multi-coloured sleeveless pullovers, immaculate plus fours creased down the side and magpie shoes. Golf fans in Britain could not believe their eyes.

His supporters could not believe what was happening to him in 1928 when he lost a £500 72-hole challenge match to Archie Compston at Moor Park by a humiliating 18 and 17. Two weeks later, having got all his bad shots out of his system against Compston, he won his third Open at Sandwich...and retained the title the following year at Muirfield. It took Hagen 25 years to complete the transformation from a ten-cents-a-round caddie into the highest paid professional. At a time when $40 was a lot of money he was charging that for an hour's lesson at his Florida base. He charged $400 for a lesson and the opportunity to play a round with him. Wealthy amateurs flocked to book up with him. In exhibition matches (and he played 1500 of them in 11 years), he used not 14 but 22 clubs. Cynics said that this was because the manufacturer paid him $500-a-year for every club he carried. Not that Hagen was ever greedy. Others have been far more motivated by money than he was but he made plenty.

He, more than anyone else, realised the commercial possibilities in golf and exploited them. In the booming 20's he was earning and spending 100,000 dollars a year. Even his annual trips to England cost him 10,000 dollars by the time he had hired the Rolls and paid his bill at the Savoy for himself and his retinue. Once, when booking in there with Tommy Armour, he had a case of gin, a case of whisky and a case of brandy sent up. Armour was shocked but Hagen waved his hand and said, simply: 'There are bound to be people coming to call.' 'Sir Walter', it was once said, was the nearest a professional golfer has come to being royalty – with whom he often played and sometimes even kept waiting on the tee!

He certainly enjoyed living like a millionaire and must have been delighted that he took the decision early in his career to concentrate on golf rather than baseball in which, apparently, he was a more than useful pitcher. He enjoyed shooting, hunting and fishing, often going off on an overnight expedition when well-placed to win a tournament. Few could have produced as low scores as he did with such woefully inadequate preparation. When returning early in the morning during a tournament, he was chided by a friend about the fact that Leo Diegel, his rival for the golf title, had been in bed for hours. Hagen retorted quickly: 'Maybe, but he is not sleeping!' That was typically Walter Hagen, once described by the late Pat Ward-Thomas in *The Guardian* as the W.C. Fields of golf. Hagen once told Fred Corcoran, the top American manager in the days before Mark McCormack: 'Don't worry, don't hurry. We are only here a little time so never forget to stop and smell the flowers'.

He was a legend in his own lifetime and Ben Hogan said that Hagen had the greatest mental approach to golf of anyone. He knew that it was essential to relax, to stay loose in order to cope with the pressures of tournament golf, and he did so his way. Henry Longhurst, writing in the *Sunday Times*, shortly after Hagen's death, commented on the fact that there had been three major golf explosions. The one set off at the turn of the century by Harry Vardon, the one prompted by the arrival of televised golf and Arnold Palmer, and the one sparked off so dramatically by Hagen. He was a cancer victim at the age of 76 and the whole world of golf mourned the passing of a larger-than-life personality whose contribution to the game was beyond calculation.

## CAREER RECORD

### Victories

| | |
|---|---|
| 1914 | U.S. Open |
| 1919 | U.S. Open |
| 1921 | U.S. P.G.A. Championship |
| 1922 | British Open |
| 1924 | British Open, U.S. P.G.A. Championship |
| 1925 | U.S. P.G.A. Championship |
| 1926 | U.S. P.G.A. Championship |
| 1927 | U.S. P.G.A. Championship |
| 1928 | British Open |
| 1929 | British Open |

**Hagen** with his first major trophy – the 1914 U.S. Open

### Did you know...

1. Walter Hagen was the Lee Trevino of his day. He chatted regularly with the fans as he played round.
2. Hagen revolutionised golfing dress with his colourful rig-outs.
3. He was the first American-born winner of the Open in Britain in 1922.
4. Hagen often said that he did not necessarily want to be a millionaire, just to live like one.
5. In the 1920's Hagen was earning 100,000 dollars a year. He was the first to realise the commercial possibilities of the game.
6. Hagen sometimes had 22 clubs in his bag in exhibition matches. This was because he was paid 500 dollars a year per club played!

# *BOBBY JONES*

By the time he was 28 Bobby Jones had achieved all he could in golf including victories in the Amateur and Open Championships of America and Britain in the same year.

It was golf's impossible dream but, against all the odds, Bobby Jones – or indeed Bob Jones as he himself preferred to be called – made the dream a reality. In 1930 he won the Open titles of both Britain and America and also the Amateur Championships of both countries to complete the first and only Grand Slam.

The effort took so much out of him that at the age of 28, when most golfers have not reached their prime, he retired from the international scene. There were no other golfing worlds to conquer. He had achieved what no golfer will ever do again. Today the so-called Slam no longer includes the two Amateur titles. They have been replaced by the U.S.P.G.A. Championship and, appropriately enough perhaps, the U.S. Masters tournament which remains a permanent memorial to Jones. It was he who, with the help of Alister Mackenzie, designed the now famous National course at Augusta on what had been a fruit farm and who with Clifford Roberts began the Augusta National Invitation better known today as The Masters', a title, incidentally, Jones never liked.

Bobby Jones at Sunningdale in 1926, where he had to pre-qualify before going on to win his first Open

No golfer dominated the world of golf so completely in the eight years from 1923 as he did, modestly and in a manner which epitomised the proud reputation of the game for sportsmanship. Four times in major Championships he penalised himself for infringements no-one else could have seen.

In his golden period Jones won thirteen of the 21 National championships in which he competed – an incredible performance for an amateur who played probably fewer than 100 rounds a season and who devoted less than three months to golf each year because of his many business interests. He was a true golfing genius, a man with a natural talent and a swing which really did merit the use of the now hackneyed phrase 'poetry in motion'. Yet he never had a formal lesson in his life, although he was guided by Stewart Maiden, the Scottish professional at the East Lake Club in Atlanta where the Jones family initially had a summer house before, fortunately for Bobby, moving to it permanently.

Jones tees off on the 14th at Royal Lytham and St Anne's in the 1926 Open

Jones, respected by everyone in the game including the professionals, was winner of five U.S. Amateur Championships and was runner-up once. Many of the records he set in the 20's still stand today. He was American Open champion four times and four times runner-up, while in Britain he won one of the three Amateur Championships in which he played and three of the four Opens at a time, remember, when the journey from America could only be made by boat and took more than a week. Just how massive a talent he had and why he was considered the most complete athlete in any sport can be judged from one amazing statistic. Against the top professionals of the day Jones, the part-time amateur, won seven of the last 12 National Opens in which he played and was runner-up in the other five. It was little wonder that he became a golfing legend.

The one occasion in four when he did not win the Open in Britain was in 1921 when the Championship was played at St Andrews and Jones was in the country as a member of the U.S. Walker Cup team. It was that week that Jones did something he would regret for the rest of his life, something quite out of character for him in later years. It must be said that despite his later deserved reputation for restraint and sportsmanship he did have a fiery temper which he had to keep well under control at Championships after being involved, as a teenager, in an incident during the U.S. Amateur that prompted officials to warn him that he would face a ban if he did not stop... throwing clubs! What had brought things to a head was Jones, who had been playing in the U.S. Amateur at the age 14, throwing one of his hickory clubs so carelessly in frustration that it hit a spectator!

He stopped such impolite gestures in National Championships overnight and became a paragon of golfing virtue but in 1921, aged just 19, he was still not in total command of his at times volatile nature. When he received the rare honour of being elected a Freeman of St Andrews in 1958 Jones said that if he had to choose one course over which he would want to play for the rest of his days it would be the most famous stretch of golfing links in the world. But in 1921 he was less enamoured with the course on that first occasion he tangled with it. On 152 after two rounds, records show that he took 46 for the front

nine, dropped two more at the tenth and then, after being bunkered and taking five shots to get on to the green at the short eleventh tore up his card. It was a gesture for which he never forgave himself.

For Jones golf was never more than a game. He never ever entertained the thought of turning professional to play full-time for money although after his retirement, which came as such a shock to everyone in golf but which he himself had pre-planned for two years, he made instructional films in Hollywood and wrote instructional articles for money when that kind of thing did not infringe

The young Bobby Jones – not long after hitting a spectator by throwing his club away in frustration!

the amateur status rules. Essentially, however, he remains the greatest amateur of all times. When born in 1902 he was not given much of a chance to live. There was something wrong with his digestive system but, showing the determinaton he would later show on the golf course, baby Jones came through the crisis. Because the family home was close to the East Lake club, it was natural that Jones, from an upper middle class family – he never was as exceptionally well-off as people imagined – should spend much time at the golf course. At nine he was the club's junior champion, shooting scores under 100 and by the time he had reached the age of 12 he was scoring in the 70's with a swing he imitated from Maiden – a swing unmatched for its tempo. Later, golfers playing adjacent fairways to him would stop their own games just to admire his swing.

At 13, in a match he never forgot, he won the Club Championship by beating his father Robert P. Jones and a year later he made his National Championship debut. Although he was a finalist in the U.S. Amateur at 17 he did not play his first U.S. Open until 1920 when he finished tied eighth behind British pro Ted Ray who that year beat a group of golfers which included Harry Vardon by a shot. Three years later Jones scored his first U.S. Open triumph, beating pro Bobby Cruickshank by two shots in a play-off. He was runner-up for the next two years in that event but compensated by winning the U.S. Amateur, in which he would build up such a reputation. In his five U.S. Amateur victories between 1924 and 1930 his average win in semi-finals and finals was 9 and 8!

In 1926 he came to Britain for the Walker Cup, in which he scored a 12 and 11 success over Cyril Tolley, and to try to land the Amateur Championship. But a little known Scot beat him in the sixth round and, although he had not planned to play in it, he was persuaded to stay over and compete shortly afterwards in the Open. The Open that year was at Royal Lytham but in those days there was a regional pre-qualifying test as well and Jones was assigned the pleasant task of having to play at delightful Sunningdale. The 66 he shot there, which stood for many years as the Old Course record, has been described as the nearest he could have got to playing a flawless round. He was once bunkered, and single-putted just once. He hit every green in regulation bar one.

When he went to Lytham he battled past Al Watrous on the final day to win by one stroke, helped by a fantastic second shot from a sandy lie over a bank of gorse at the seventeenth which is remembered today by a commemorative plaque. Curiously, between rounds on the final day,

Jones had nipped back to his hotel for a sandwich. On returning he realised he had left his badge in the locker room and the truculent security man at the gate did not believe he was a competitor. To avoid any fuss, Jones paid to come through the turnstiles. He was no prima donna. He returned to a New York ticker-tape welcome and when he won the U.S. Open at Scioto in Ohio, where later Jack Nicklaus would learn his golf, he had become the first man to hold the Open titles of both countries in the same year, a portent of the greatness yet to come.

The following year, 1927, he won another U.S. Amateur and the Open again, helped by a record 68 at St Andrews of all places. He was the U.S. Amateur champion once more in 1928 and collected another U.S. Open title in 1929 by 23 shots in a play-off with luckless Al Espinosa. Then came his most remarkable year, 1930, the year he won everything that mattered, the year that only emphasised his greatness. Jones was a longer than average hitter of the ball, brilliant with his approach play and so deadly on the greens that he broke course records regularly in exhibition matches. But golf was essentially a pastime. He had graduated from school at 16 and had earned a degree in engineering at Georgia Tech. and one in English literature at Harvard where he also studied French, German and European literary history. By 1926 he had also completed two years at Emory University studying law and, although cutting short his studies, qualified to practice. It is a wonder he had time for golf!

Yet Bobby, named after a grandfather who considered the game a waste of time, had his eye on the possibility of winning a transatlantic double-double and knew 1930, Walker Cup year, was the year to have a go at it. Despite his immense talent he was never comfortable during those Championship weeks. He chain-smoked on the course, could not eat and frequently lost as much as a stone in weight, so it is not difficult to imagine just what he went through that year as he took the four major titles. After all, in 1926 when he had won at Lytham, he had needed to hold his celebratory glass of whisky in two hands he was shaking so much at the end!

In 1930 everything worked out fine, yet he almost fell at the very first hurdle – the Amateur in Britain, again at St Andrews. He knew that despite a first round bye, he would be required to win eight matches to take the title but in the third round against Tolley, who had not forgotten the way Jones had destroyed him in that 1926 Walker Cup, it was tight. Jones had to hole from eight feet to stay level with one to play and Tolley missed a putt on the eighteenth from 12 feet that would have killed the Grand Slam bid stone dead. A relieved Jones won at the first extra hole. Then he had a narrow squeak against American Walker cup col-

Jones receives his third Open trophy at Hoylake in Grand Slam year 1930 (above) and poses to have his portrait painted (left)

league Jimmy Johnston before surviving at the last, and he came back from two down with five to play to beat another American George Voigt on the home green. But, in the final, he had a comfortable 7 and 6 win over Roger Wethered. Jones, over 36 holes, was virtually unbeatable.

After a holiday in Paris with his wife Mary, he moved on to Hoylake and, despite what he himself later regarded as 'sloppy' golf, he led from start to finish. He beat Macdonald Smith and Leo Diegel by two shots and became the first man since John Ball in 1890 to win the Amateur and Open titles in Britain. The first Double complete, the action moved to America and first to Interlachen in Minneapolis in July where in a heat-wave of more than 100 degrees fahrenheit and near 100 per cent humidity and on a course with knee-high rough, Jones won again with a one under par 287. Nobody had scored that well before! It might have been a lower aggregate had he not lost a ball at the short seventeenth despite having 20,000 people look for it for five minutes. He finished in style, however, holing a 40 footer up hill. Three down and just one to come, the U.S. Amateur at the course where he had made his Championship debut 14 years earlier, Merion in Pennsylvania in September.

Charles Price, in his excellent book *A Golf Story* which is all about Jones, Augusta and the Masters, recalls that the weeks between the third and fourth legs of the Grand Slam were not uneventful for him. In August, at East Lake, Jones narrowly missed being hit by lightning and, as he ran for cover, passed beneath a double chimney of the clubhouse which was hit and exploded showering bricks and mortar 300 yards. Jones' shirt was ripped off his back and his shoulder badly gashed. Then, in Atlanta, he was nearly hit by a runaway car, jumping clear at only the last second and at home only days before the Championship he unthinkingly tried to catch a blade that had slipped from his razor. Luckily he only scratched his hand!

Dozens of reporters converged on Merion despite the fact that the enormity of the task he had set himself was not fully appreciated by most people. Even after Jones won the pre-qualifying medal with a record low score and had strolled to victory with five wins – the closest of which was 5 and 4 – some papers did not even mention Grand Slam, a description coined by Jones' life-long biographer O.B. Keeler for the four-wins-in-one-year achievement. His dream realised, Jones wanted only to slip quietly into the background and enjoy his golf again without the glare of publicity. Although initially uncertain whether he would give up playing competitively or not he sent a note to the U.S.G.A. in November 1930 saying he was retiring completely. The story made banner headlines.

Donald Steel, in his *Guinness Book of Golf*, ends his piece on Jones with an epitaph penned by great American golfing essayist Herbert Warren Wind. It deserves repeating here. About Bobby Jones, Wind had this to say: 'As a young man he was able to stand up to just about the best that life can offer, which is not easy, and later he stood up, with equal grace, to just about the worst.'

## *CAREER RECORD*

The British Amateur champion in 1930

### Victories

| | |
|---|---|
| 1923 | U.S. Open |
| 1924 | U.S. Amateur Championship |
| 1925 | U.S. Amateur Championship |
| 1926 | British Open, U.S. Open |
| 1927 | British Open, U.S. Amateur Championship |
| 1928 | U.S. Amateur Championship |
| 1929 | U.S. Open |
| 1930 | U.S. Open, U.S. Amateur Championship, British Open, British Amateur Championship |

### Did you know...

1. Bobby Jones won seven of the last 12 national championships in which he played such was his mastery of the game and his domination of the scene.
2. Bobby Jones, noted universally for his superb sportsmanship, was warned as a youngster that if he did not behave himself on the course he might not be allowed to compete in U.S. Championships. This followed a club throwing incident in which he hit a spectator.
3. Bobby Jones was named after his grandfather who considered golf was a waste of time.

# GENE SARAZEN

Winner of all four Grand Slam titles, Gene Sarazen, who changed his name because he thought his real one was too artistic, played a shot in 1935 that was heard around the world.

The gallery are obviously impressed with this one!

When Eugene Saraceni, better known to golfers around the world as Gene Sarazen, won the U.S. and British Open championships in 1932 he became the highest paid sportsman in the world.

In the days when top baseball hero Babe Ruth and the President of the United States Franklin D. Roosevelt were both receiving the princely sum of $15,000 a year, Sarazen signed a contract to be managed by publicity man Raymond McCarthy for a guaranteed annual figure of $25,000 for two years. Still easily recognisable today in his plus fours, Sarazen, little more than five feet five inches in height, has been a giant in a game renowned for it characters and larger-than-life personalities.

There was a romance and glamour about Sarazen's rise to fame and his subsequent winning of no fewer than seven majors. He was the first man to win all four of the so-called Grand Slam titles, although he was unaware of the enormity of his feat at the time. Arnold Palmer

Still going strong in 1973 (right) and (below) trying to coax the ball into the cup in 1956

invented the idea of the Slam much later. Known for almost his whole career as 'The Squire', Sarazen has made headlines with two of the most publicised shots ever played in golf. The first occurred at Augusta in 1935 when he holed a four-wood second shot for an albatross at the water-guarded 15th en route to his only U.S. Masters win.

Only a handful of people saw that golden moment in golfing history but millions saw his other shot to remember. It happened in 1973 at Royal Troon's Postage Stamp short hole – the 8th, where Sarazen, celebrating the 50th anniversary of his appearance in the Championship and playing with two other former winners Max Faulkner and Fred Daly, holed in one with a five-iron. The following day, incidentally, he holed from off the green for a birdie two! Yet Sarazen might never have turned to golf at all had he not been given a crudely-made hockey stick as a ninth birthday present. He was fond of hockey but the stick was so crudely made that it was virtually unusable for hockey. The head was far too small so Gene called it, instead, his golf club and became so proficient with it that it was obvious he would want to have a go with 'the real thing'.

His parents were Italian immigrants, his father having failed in a bid to become a priest. Instead he turned to carpentry and with young Gene's added income from selling papers, or picking fruit or even lighting gas lamps, the family was able to survive just above the poverty line and no more. Times were hard and when Gene contracted pneumonia and pleurisy at the age of 15 he was not expected to live. He did, but it was suggested that he give up his role as apprentice carpenter (a job for which he had no aptitude) for a healthier outside occupation to aid his recuperation. His father, who had been no supporter of his son's liking for what was then an elite game, changed his mind and agreed to Gene becoming an assistant pro at the local club. From that day Sarazen (who changed his name because he felt Saraceni was too much like that of a violinist) never looked back.

Two years later he had moved to sunny Florida and, incredibly, within three years was American Open champion, winning the title at Skokie near Chicago. He had so little money and was such an outsider that year that he lived in a dormitory with some of the other contestants. Yet by the end of a week in which he pipped John Black and the legendary Bobby Jones by a shot, the pawky, likeable, impish Sarazen had made it and become a household name.

Never short of confidence, Sarazen proved that first Open win was no fluke when, later that same season, he won the U.S.P.G.A. Championship – then decided by match-play – and threw down the gauntlet to Walter Hagen, who had won the Open that year at Sandwich. They played over 72 holes for the World Championship and the cocky Sarazen won. As a result of his success in the States he made his first foray across the Atlantic in 1923 determined 'to show the British a thing or two'. In rough conditions, unlike any he had experienced before, he caught a chill, suffered the humiliation of taking an eight at a short hole, and failed to qualify. But Sarazen promised he would be back to win and did, although not until 1932.

Sarazen had lost the 1928 Open to his great friend Hagen at Royal St George's but with Hagen missing in 1932 and Bobby Jones having retired, he was favourite. He was also helped by the fact that he had signed up Hagen's experienced caddie 'Swankie' Daniels to work for him.

Daniels had promised Sarazen a win and together they strode to an impressive five shot victory. Sarazen's winning total that year of 283 stood as the low aggregate record until 1950. Winning the American Open title a few weeks later at Fresh Meadow puts him in that very elite category of golfers who have achieved the double in the same year – Bobby Jones in 1926 and 1930, Ben Hogan in 1953, Lee Trevino in 1971 and Tom Watson in 1982.

Always concerned with the inadequacy of his bunker play, Sarazen is credited with having invented the sand-wedge without which no-one would start a round these days. The club has revolutionised the game although it did not help Sarazen win the 1933 Open at St Andrews in which he was bunkered at the eleventh on the second day and at the fourteenth in the last round, failing by several strokes each time to make par.

In 1934, as a stop-off for the professionals heading north from their winters in Florida to their summer club jobs, Bobby Jones instituted the Augusta National Club Invitational, now better known as the U.S. Masters. It was in the second year of this event that Sarazen played the shot which has been talked about around the world ever since. Craig Wood, holding a three shot lead, was in the clubhouse being feted as the winner. Sarazen needed to birdie three of the last four holes to force a play-off. Not impossible but highly improbable. In fact he parred the last three but only after hitting his second shot into the cup for what the Americans call a double eagle at the fifteenth to catch the stunned Wood. Sarazen, always a complete enthusiast, won the play-off the next day by five and is still a regular visitor to Augusta – being proudly involved each year in the ritual nine hole past champions match.

The game has benefited hugely from Sarazen's contribution and not just as a player. He became an accomplished commentator, and as compere of the famous Shell Wonderful World of Golf films – which pitted the best players in competition in some of the world's most beautiful spots – he further helped to popularise the game.

# *CAREER RECORD*

**Victories**

| | |
|---|---|
| 1922 | U.S. Open, U.S.P.G.A. Championship |
| 1923 | U.S.P.G.A. Championship |
| 1932 | U.S. Open, British Open |
| 1933 | U.S.P.G.A. Championship |
| 1935 | U.S. Masters |
| 1936 | Australian Open |
| 1954 | U.S.P.G.A. Seniors |
| 1958 | U.S.P.G.A. Seniors |

**Did you know...**

1. Gene Sarazen made golfing history when he sank a 4-wood second shot for a rare albatross 2 at the par 5 fifteenth in the second U.S. Masters at Augusta in 1935. He went on to beat Craig Wood.
2. Gene Sarazen, who suffered pleurisy and pneumonia as a child, was allowed to take up golf as a method of restoring himself to full health.
3. Gene Sarazen is one of only four golfers who have had victories in all four majors. The others – Ben Hogan, Gary Player and Jack Nicklaus.
4. Gene Sarazen changed his name from Saraceni because he felt that that name sounded as if he was an Italian violinist rather than a professional golfer.
5. Gene Sarazen, aged 71, played in the Open Championship at Royal Troon in 1973 and holed in one at the short eighth (The Postage Stamp).
6. It has been a constant regret of Gene Sarazen that he never ever captained the American Ryder Cup team. Walter Hagen was always favoured for the post.
7. Gene Sarazen, Byron Nelson and Sam Snead now hit off each year to signal the start of the U.S. Masters.

**Gene Sarazen** – The 1932 Open Champion

# HENRY COTTON

No golfer did more to raise the status and prestige of the professional golfer than Sir Henry Cotton who won three Opens, one of them, appropriately, in front of King George VI.

The many friends of the late Henry Cotton campaigned for several years to gain official and national recognition of his great achievements in golf by securing for him a knighthood. Although in earlier years Cotton had been awarded an M.B.E. for his services to the Red Cross, the Prime Minister and the Queen were regularly urged to offer him the title of Sir Henry for his services to golf. It was felt that the delay in conferring a knighthood on Cotton was because he lived mainly in Portugal, although he always insisted the reasons for this were climatic and nothing to do with easing, in his case, a heavy tax burden.

A very dapper Henry Cotton on his way to his first tournament win

It was sad, therefore, that Henry Cotton died at the age of 80 – in London – a few days before it was announced he was to be knighted. He had been told of the honour some weeks earlier and confided the news to his step-daughter just before he died. Sir Henry Cotton would have enjoyed the 'handle' for he was a man of great style. Everything he did was in the first class mould, from hand-made shoes and shirts to champagne and caviar in the fridge. Once, by mistake, he gave the cat the expensive caviar instead of Whiskas! 'The best is always good enough for me,' he used to say. It suited the cat too!

Cotton could afford the best because he was hugely successful in more than 60 years of professional golf. He loved life, loved golf and loved being a star. It suited him admirably. He came from a well-to-do Cheshire family, went to a public school, where he excelled at all sports, and turned professional when he was 17. It is an undisputed fact that Henry Cotton improved the lot of professional golf in Britain and was largely responsible for forcing golf clubs to open their doors to professional golfers.

Cotton's career began in the days when professionals were not admitted into any clubhouse under any circumstances, a fact he resented and declared he would change. This he did by refusing to use the changing tents provided at professional tournaments. Instead, he parked his enormous limousine as close as possible to the first tee and while changing his shoes served champagne to his friends and followers. Such flamboyance and his obvious sense of style

impressed golf club members wherever he played; they warmed to him and invited him into their clubs. Thus the doors were finally opened and the standing of professional golf and golfers has since gone from strength to strength.

Cotton was born at Holmes Chapel, in Cheshire, when his mother was 41 years old. 'I only just caught the bus,' he once said mischievously. Such was Cotton's style that when he decided to try his luck in America in 1928 – just as today's top players like to do – he travelled first class on the *Aquitania*. He had with him £300, almost his entire fortune, and vowed to stay as long as the money lasted. Needless to stay, he spent five months playing in American tournaments and returned with his £300 intact. 'I could be said to have bought my experience cheaply,' he later wrote. He satisfied himself that he needed to practise even harder to succeed and that if all went well he could play better and possibly win the Open championship. He had seen, too, that big money could be made out of golf and saw no reason why he could not do as well as the Americans. In fact, Cotton did all three. He won the Open championship – three times – made big money out of the game and did just as well as the Americans.

Winning the Open championship is every golfer's ambition and it took a good deal of patience before Cotton finally succeeded. His first Open appearance was in 1925 but, after several near misses, it was

At Walton Heath for a challenge match in 1952 (top), top of the bill at the Coliseum in 1938 (above) and showing off his swing for the cameras (left)

In the sand, at Sandwich, en route to his first Open Championship

1934 before he finally won, scoring 283 at Sandwich to equal the then Open record set by Gene Sarazen. It was during this Open that Cotton scored a 65 in the second round proper prompting Dunlop to produce a new golf ball to recognise the feat. The Dunlop 65, as it was called, is still manufactured today. The last man to win a pro event in Britain using hickory shafts, Cotton won the Open again in 1937 at Carnoustie in atrocious weather. He called it his greatest victory at a time when he was one of the dominant figures in world golf. There is no telling how many titles he might have won had the Second World War not interrupted his career.

He served in the RAF, obtaining a commission, and resumed his title-winning golf after the war, including a third Open championship success at Muirfield in 1948. His second round of 66 that year, a course record, was watched by His Majesty King George VI and Cotton went on to take the title with five shots to spare. Henry Cotton was more than just a golfer, he was also an entertainer. He appeared on the London stage many times, often topping the bill with his display of trick shots and ready wit. When he finally decided to play fewer tournaments, he turned to writing books, a newspaper and magazine column and designing golf courses. He produced many masterpieces, including the lovely Penina Hotel course on Portugal's Algarve, where he and his wife Toots made their home.

Henry and Toots were generous hosts and entertained lavishly in their white-painted villa beside Penina's first tee. Henry played golf daily on the course he built, often just nine holes with friends. Afterwards all would retire to his villa and, naturally, talk golf. His caddie, in those later years, was an old donkey called Pacifico, who was known to bray on cue as an opponent of Henry's lined up a vital putt. Over the years, Cotton's many achievements were widely acclaimed. He was twice captain of the Professional Golfers' Association and, possibly the highest accolade, was elected an honorary member of the Royal and Ancient Golf Club of St Andrews, the game's governing body.

The knighthood came too late for him to enjoy but he died a contented man, having more than fulfilled his tremendous potential and maintained to the end a crowded schedule. Henry Cotton's name is revered by all professionals. His behaviour gave the professional much-needed status and his performances on the course were inspirational.

## CAREER RECORD

**Henry Cotton** – the 1948 Open champion

### Victories

| | |
|---|---|
| 1930 | Belgian Open Championship |
| 1931 | Dunlop Southport Open |
| 1932 | British P.G.A. Match-play Championship, Dunlop Southport Open |
| 1934 | British Open Championship |
| 1935 | Yorkshire Evening News Tournament |
| 1936 | Italian Open Championship, Dunlop Metropolitan Open |
| 1937 | British Open Championship |
| 1940 | British P.G.A. Match-play Championship |
| 1945 | News Chronicle Tournament |
| 1946 | French Open Championship, British P.G.A. Match-play Championship, Spalding Tournament |
| 1947 | French Open Championship, Yorkshire Evening News Tournament, Dunlop Tournament |

### Did you know...

1. Henry Cotton was the last golfer in the 1930's to win a British tournament using hickory-shafted clubs.
2. When Henry Cotton shot a brilliant 65 in the Open at Sandwich in 1934, the Dunlop manufacturing company produced a ball to commemorate that feat.

# JOYCE WETHERED

In her short career Joyce Wethered, one of the longest, straightest hitters of a golf ball, was likened to Bobby Jones for her sportsmanship and dominance of the game in Britain.

Joyce Wethered – five successive English Amateur Championships and four British titles earned her the respect of the entire golfing world

Joyce Wethered, who became Lady Heathcote-Amory when she married in 1926, was in a class of her own in the 20's. She won five English Amateur Championships in a row and took the British titles four times to earn the respect of everyone who played golf. The great Bobby Jones, having played with her, commented after the round with true sincerity: 'I have never played with anyone and felt so outclassed'.

Henry Cotton, who knew her well and played many times with her, also had nothing but admiration for the way she played the game indicating that he could not remember anyone, except perhaps six-times Open champion Harry Vardon, who hit the ball so straight so often as she did. The praise heaped upon her was well-deserved. She was so accurate through the green and so deadly on it that one spectator was heard to say at St Andrews when she won the last of her four British titles in 1929 against the great American Glenna Collett: 'This lady has no mercy'. She certainly did not when competing, but off the course she was charming with never a hint of the prima donna in her. As a result she was hugely popular. An article published in *The Observer* in 1948, the year she and her husband failed at the final hurdle to win the Worplesdon Foursomes, described her this way: 'There could be no more kindly nor more popular person than Joyce Wethered. She has never queened it on the tee although she would have had a perfect right to do so with her record. Whether she is playing among the silver birches of Blairgowrie during her holidays at her Scottish home at Glenfernate or golfing on more familiar territory at Worplesdon in Surrey or Devon, she plays without fuss and purely for fun.

Although she and her husband lost that 1948 final at Worplesdon, she was something of a course and competition expert – winning no fewer than eight times with seven different male partners including her brother Roger, the talented amateur champion who lost a 36-hole play off for the Open to Jock Hutchinson in 1921. So powerful was her psychological superiority, so strong her game, that her form in her heyday would have earned her a place in the men's Walker Cup team at number three or number four. She hit straight, far, further than all her contemporaries and with pin-point accuracy. She had an impressive pivot. Her rhythm, her tempo, her balance were incredible. When she made contact with the ball she was on her toes with her hands moving like lightning on impact. Her concentration was legendary. Once when asked whether the train that had passed by as she putted on the seventeenth green at Sheringham had distracted her she answered: 'What train?' The remark has become part of golfing folk-lore even if she is often quoted as having said it at one of half a dozen other venues!

Another wonderful shot keeps the gallery happy

Her Championship career was really a comparatively short one. She won her first English title in 1920 and her last British in 1929 and managed to squeeze in a three-year break from competition in between. Indeed she was only coaxed out of retirement in 1929 because the Championship that year was being played at St Andrews and Glenna Collett, then the leading American, was going to be there. While some golfers might admit to a certain rustiness if they were suddenly shot back into top line competition it did not worry Joyce Wethered. She duly reached the final with Collett and produced probably the most dramatic of all her victories for the crowds who came to watch. She was five down after eleven to the American who was four under 4's but had fought back to two down at lunch. By the time they reached the turn in the afternoon Wethered had turned that two hole deficit into a four hole lead. In the end Wethered clinched victory at the Road Hole – the famous seventeenth, and, mission achieved, called it a day as far as Championships were concerned.

She had, of course, won five English titles in a row from 1920, the year she burst on the scene as an unknown teenager and had the temerity to beat the then top player Cecil Leitch with whom she was destined to have several notable matches. During her domination of the English event she won 33 ties in a row. To have won all six British events in which she played she would have had to win 43 games in a row. She won 38. So in 11 Championships appearances she won 71 of the 76 games she played. She was in a different class. Leitch gained her revenge for that English defeat in 1920 by beating Wethered for the British and French titles the following year but it was level pegging again after Wethered beat her 9 and 7 in the British in 1922. Wethered won again over her great rival in the last final in which they met at Sandwich in 1925.

Having given up Championship golf she became golf manager in the Fortnum and Mason store in London – a move that brought into question at the time the matter of her amateur status. She kept it but one imagines it was the subject of much discussion in the long room at St Andrews and in the headquarters of the Ladies Golf Union. The controversial issue was neatly resolved when she announced in 1935 that, after having turned down several invitations to play in America, she had decided to visit the States for a series of exhibition matches with top amateurs and professionals. She told an *Evening Standard* reporter that she had decided she would like to play some of the best courses in America and would probably earn £40 a round and a share of the profits! She made an estimated £4000 – an amazing sum in those days – and played with Babe Zaharias (who was just beginning her career), Gene Sarazen and Walter Hagen. On returning to Britain she resumed her job in London, but as a professional.

In 1954 Joyce Wethered, who has been described as the greatest woman golfer of her time, became President of the English Ladies' Golf Association and was re-instated as an amateur. At the time she was 53 and no longer competing in tournaments. She had no need to re-apply for amateur status but the Royal and Ancient Golf Club of St Andrews decided she should be one once again in order to fulfil her E.L.G.A. duties. Now 88, she lives in Devon modestly proud of the legacy she has left in golfing history. The manner in which she played and dominated those marvellous days sixty years ago is a lesson to every youngster who takes up the game.

Passing on putting tips to a crowd of youthful admirers

# CAREER RECORD

**Victories**

1920 English Ladies' Championship
1921 English Ladies' Championship
1922 British Ladies' Championship, English Ladies' Championship
1923 English Ladies' Championship
1924 British Ladies' Championship, English Ladies' Championship
1925 British Ladies' Championship
1929 British Ladies' Championship

English Amateur Champion – again!

**Did you know...**

1. Joyce Wethered was such a straight hitter and solid golfer that she would have easily earned a place in the men's Walker Cup side!
2. In eleven Championship appearances Joyce Wethered won 71 out of 76 matches she played.
3. Joyce Wethered earned an estimated £4000 when she went to America to play a series of Challenge matches against Gene Sarazen and Walter Hagen.
4. When Joyce Wethered became the President of the English Ladies' Golf Association, the Royal and Ancient Golf Club of St Andrews decided she should be re-instated as an amateur.
5. Joyce Wethered was known in her heyday as the Bobby Jones of British women's golf – a rare tribute.

# *BEN HOGAN*

Even a near fatal crash could not stop champion Ben Hogan whose dedication and determination remain unmatched by any other golfer over the years.

Ben Hogan is a golf legend. Maybe the game's only cult figure. A man who drove himself into being a great player, survived a horrific car crash and then showed supreme courage to make a gloriously successful comeback. And since his playing days his decision to withdraw from public life and work quietly at his Texas home running his golf club manufacturing company has created a mystique about a man who, at his prime, was the closest you could come to being unbeatable in a quirky game like golf.

He was a perfectionist to beat all perfectionists. He was seeking that golfing impossible – to hit every shot perfectly and became obsessed by that. There is a story once that Hogan, after a fine round which had included a fistful of glorious birdies, made off tight-lipped to the practice ground. His playing partner that day urged him to relax, pointing out how well he had scored and reminding him that it was not possible to birdie every hole. Hogan never stopped walking but turned and rapped out: 'Why not?'

Ben Hogan – he defied the medical experts and fought his way back to the top

Hogan won four American Open titles, the greatest of which was his 1950 triumph just over a year after being involved in a near-fatal crash. He twice won the U.S. Masters, was twice the U.S.P.G.A. Champion and, on the only occasion he played the Open in Britain, he won the title at Carnoustie in 1953. He had arrived in Scotland over a week before the Championship to begin his meticulous preparation. He promised to come back and defend but never did.

That 1953 season was, for him, a record-breaking year. By winning the Masters and U.S. Open as well he collected three of the four titles now considered the Grand Slam. He probably would have won all four but for the fact that the U.S.P.G.A. Championship that summer was played directly against the Open – a decision for which the P.G.A. of America deserved to be roundly criticised. Hogan, at least, got his priorities right.

Cold-eyed and, unlike Sam Snead and Byron Nelson, a slim 10 stone, Hogan always believed that the game was maybe as much as 20 per cent technique but certainly no less than 80 per cent in the mind. No-one had a tougher mental approach than him. His concentration was so ferocious he had no time for the niceties of being a showman too. There were no pleasant asides to the galleries. He was so

Ben Hogan demonstrates his remarkable balance with this drive

wrapped up in a cocoon that he was even known to ignore a fellow competitor's hole-in-one. He preferred to let his clubs do the talking although he could rap a stinging response if annoyed.

Like the time at the 1967 Ryder Cup match at Houston when he was captaining the USA and there was a dispute about which size ball would be used – the bigger American version or the smaller one used in Britain. No less a star than Arnold Palmer queried, at a team meeting, the size of ball Hogan wanted him to use. 'What makes you think, sir, you will be playing tomorrow,' was the icy response from a man whose coolness at all times earned him the nickname 'The Iceman'.

Then there was the time a young Gary Player, for whom Hogan has always been a hero, telephoned the great man to ask his advice. 'Mr Hogan,' said Player with due deference, 'you cured the hook and I believe with a little help from you I could cure my hook.' There was a silence at the other end. Player hastily went on to explain how hard he had practised, how he was shaping out his career when Hogan interrupted. 'Are you affilliated with a club manufacturer? Call Mr Dunlop,' he said curtly before hanging up.

Brutal treatment perhaps, but there is a background to the story that few people ever recount. Player had been given a

An older Hogan – still looking impressive on the practice range

Hogan driver less than a year earlier, and, much to Hogan's displeasure, had painted it black to match the other clubs in his bag. Hogan's sharp attitude on that later occasion is, perhaps, more understandable.

Some people argue that his reputation as a cold fish is unwarranted but Hogan, so determined to remain in the shadows that he now seldom turns up at the U.S. Masters, fosters the legend. Maybe with a more open-hearted approach his contribution to the game would have been even greater than it has been but no one would deny that whenever or wherever golf is talked about these days, the name of Ben Hogan crops up!

Hogan was born the third child and second son of Chester and Clara Hogan in Dublin, Texas in 1912 and never had it easy. He was only nine when, in bizarre and quite unnecessary circumstances, his father, a car mechanic, committed suicide leaving Clara to bring up the family. Ben sold papers to make a buck or two and caddied, along with Byron Nelson, at the Glen Garden Club. Later he took a job as a croupier, a bank-teller, a waiter and a petrol-pump attendant before deciding his future lay in golf. He turned professional when he was 19, knowing that to succeed as a tournament player he needed to hit the ball a long way and knowing, too, that he would have to create a swing that compensated for his slender frame.

He did create it, and people use his instruction manual *Five Lessons. The Modern Fundamentals of Golf* as their bible. Some professionals carry it permanently in their luggage. He worked for hours perfecting a swing with a long wide arc and a follow through longer than anyone else. He had a wide stance to help him generate the power but success was frustratingly slow in coming. Many might have opted for a lesser goal in life but Hogan, his grey eyes burning with ambition, refused to back down. He wanted to be a great champion. He wanted to be a golfer people would look up to and admire for his skill, his determination, his courage and his technique.

His chum Byron Nelson had made his mark long before Hogan made his own first breakthrough by winning the U.S.P.G.A. title in 1946 at the age of 34.

But he really shot to prominence two years later when, with what we know today as impeccable 'course management', he went back to the Riviera course in Los Angeles, where he had won the 1947 and 1948 L.A. Opens, and became what he had always dreamed of becoming – the American champion.

Hogan had played so brilliantly there on the two previous occasions that the course was already being referred to as Hogan's Alley and club members who had watched him tie the course record 66 in 1947 and shoot a four round aggregate of 275 in 1948 – a record that would stand for 25 years – fancied he would do well in the Open. They recalled a 270-yard approach fired through the wind to three feet at the 560-yard eleventh hole making even the Sphinx-like Hogan smile. He was Championship material. He won shooting an average of 69 – a new record.

In that golden year of 1948 he collected the U.S.P.G.A title again and the stage seemed set for him to dominate the game. But dramatically fate dealt a low blow. Some thought his career not only shattered but brought prematurely to an end when he was involved in a road accident with a Greyhound bus which had moved out to pass a lorry in thick fog.

Hogan and his wife Valerie, whom he had tried to save by flinging himself across her, had to be cut out of the wreckage. The whole of his lower body had been torn apart, the car engine having been pushed into him by the force of the crash. If he lived, said the experts, it was unlikely he would ever walk again because his legs were so shattered. His career, they told him, was over. They did not bank on the willpower of Ben Hogan. He proved them wrong and delighted the golfing world when he not only came back but, after his return, incredibly went on to win six more majors and take his final tally to nine. Only Jack Nicklaus, Bobby Jones and Walter Hagen have won more major titles.

Hogan always had near-monastic self-discipline, and that he used to good effect as he clawed his way back to fitness and golf again. He relied, he said, on muscle memory as he began the painful, tough rehabilitation process. He walked initially a few yards, then 100 yards, then a quarter of a mile and then a mile. He kept his wrists strong by squeezing a rubber ball. Then came the day when he was ready to get back out on the golf course. Less than a year after the accident he was ready for Los Angeles again. He promised at first only 'to be present' but the man who had been battered so badly played, and nearly won. He lost a play-off to Sam Snead as much because of tiredness as anything else.

Even more amazing, just months later at Merion and again after a play-off, he won his second U.S. Open. One legacy

A player of legendary concentration Hogan was not one to play to the gallery

of the crash was a dodgy knee. It was still difficult for him to play those uphill and downhill shots and there was, of course, a need to play 36 holes on the last day in the Open. Everyone waited for Hogan, his face set in a mask-like manner to hide the agony of the pain, to falter. With one hole to play and watched by 20,000 engrossed fans, Hogan needed a par 4 to tie Lloyd Mangrum and George Fazio. Under pressure and suffering terrible pains in his legs, he hit a 200-yard one-iron shot to the plateau green and two putted from 38 feet. The next day he won the play-off.

He won the Open again the following year at Oakland Hills and also took the Masters title which he had twice missed by a shot. In 1953 he won the U.S. Open at Oakland overwhelming Sam Snead by six shots, the Masters and the Open at Carnoustie when, despite a chest cold, and some of the worst of Scotland's so-called summer weather, he earned the reward of having painstakingly prepared. He won by four shots with a then record aggregate of 282 and returned to a ticker-tape parade in New York with President Eisenhower leading the cheers. He was back in Britain in 1956 to win the World Cup at Wentworth with Sam Snead but never again played the Open and, strangely, never ever played the Old Course at St Andrews. He won his last tournament in 1959 in Texas at the age of 47 and last hit the headlines as a player when he trimmed Augusta's back nine to 30 to catch Gay Brewer with a round to go in the 1967 Masters. On the final day Brewer fired 67, Hogan 77.

Looking back on his career it is fair to point out that for a decade he was as close to being invincible as is humanly possible. Pat Ward-Thomas, the late lamented golf writer for *The Guardian*, summed Hogan up this way:

'Only the directness and economy of speech and the unwavering regard of those cold, grey eyes might have suggested that here was an exceptional person. There are in Ben Hogan qualities similar to those that make men millionaires, dictators, destroyers or great creators. Probably it is as well that he turned to golf'.

# *CAREER RECORD*

His greatest triumph? – the U.S. Open Champion, only one year after his horrific car crash

## Victories

| | |
|---|---|
| 1938 | Hershey Four-ball |
| 1940 | North and South Open, Greensboro Open, Asheville Open, Goodall Round Robin |
| 1941 | Asheville Open, Miami Four-ball, Inverness Four-ball, Chicago Open, Hershey Open |
| 1942 | Asheville Open, North and South Open, Los Angeles Open, San Francisco Open, Hale America Open, Rochester Open |
| 1945 | Nashville Open, Portland Open, Richmond Open, Montgomery Open, Orlando Open |
| 1946 | U.S. P.G.A. Championship, North and South Open, Goodall Round Robin, Miami Four-ball, Inverness Four-ball, Phoenix Open, San Antonio Open, St Petersburg Open, Colonial National Invitational, Western Open, Winnipeg Open, Golden State Championship, Dallas Open |
| 1947 | Miami Four-ball, Inverness Four-ball, Chicago Open, Los Angeles Open, Phoenix Open, Colonial National Invitational, International Open |
| 1948 | U.S. Open, U.S. P.G.A. Championship, Inverness Four-ball, Los Angeles Open, Western Open, Motor City Open, Reading Open, Denver Open, Reno Open, Glendale Open, Long Beach Open |
| 1950 | U.S. Open |
| 1951 | U.S. Masters, U.S. Open, World Championship |
| 1953 | British Open, U.S. Open, U.S. Masters, Colonial National Invitational, Pan-American Open. |

## Did you know...

1. Ben Hogan was a man of great will and determination – less than a year after suffering multiple pelvic fractures, shattered ribs, a broken collar bone, a smashed ankle and a minor heart attack he was runner-up to Sam Snead after a play-off in the Los Angeles Open.
2. In 1953 he won three Grand Slam titles – and was denied a chance to win the fourth as the U.S.P.G.A. clashed with the U.S. Open!
3. Henry Cotton ranked Hogan as one of golf's three all-time greats with Vardon and Jones.

# BYRON NELSON

He set up records that are unlikely to be broken on the American Tour, but the pressure of doing so forced him in to early retirement.

Byron Nelson, who won three of golf's so-called majors – the Masters, U.S. Open and U.S.P.G.A., in a four year spell from 1937, would have had an even more glittering career but for the Second World War. Nelson was unfortunate that he hit the peak of his game at just the wrong time yet he achieves greatness because of his incredible consistency in 1944 and 1945.

In 1944 he won 13 of the 23 tournaments in which he competed and the following year 19, one of which was 'unofficial'. He won 11 of those 19 tournaments in a row and that season averaged 68.33 strokes for 120 rounds but, because of war time regulations, was denied the Vardon Trophy awarded each year to the golfer on the U.S. Tour with the lowest scoring average. No-one has come close in the past 43 years to matching Nelson's scoring prowess in what was truly his golden period. At one point he shot 19 rounds in a row under 70 and in 1945 was estimated at the end of the season to have been an incredible 320 under par.

Byron Nelson at Augusta in 1986 – 49 years after winning his first Masters!

During the 1940's, when the pay-out of prize money sometimes only went down to as little as twelfth place, Byron Nelson went 113 tournaments without being out of the money. He always wanted to be the best at whatever he was doing and at that time no-one was better. Nelson had been excused army service because of a blood problem. His blood took nearly 12 minutes to congeal, compared with the normal two and a half, and the army was not prepared to take a chance with him. Instead Nelson stayed home and re-wrote whole chunks of the American golfing record book.

His great talent was always shot-making. He could make the ball do anything. There was not a shot or shape of shot he could not execute with ease and, rightly, is bracketed with Sam Snead and Ben Hogan as the great mid-20th century triumvirate. The ability to manufacture shots in the old days, of course, was much more vital than it is today. The greens and fairways were not kept in the condition they are now. Nelson and the other players of that time did not have the luxury of consistently good greens. In the late 30's and throughout the 40's, before green-keeping became a sophisticated science, the putting surfaces were patchy. There were hard and soft bits on them. Knowing just where to land the ball to get near enough to make a birdie was something of a science ... and the clubs were not quite the precision items they are today.

Originally Nelson had a wristy swing, ideal in his early days when playing with hickory-shafted clubs. The old hickories were so porous they could be affected by the humidity and so whippy that they twisted on impact. With the advent of more reliable steel shafts Nelson was forced to change his swing to maintain his power, especially off the tee. The new swing, with a revolutionary one-

Still with a huge following in the 1980's

piece take-away at the start of the back swing and incorporating fuller use of the legs, was as major as the surgery Nick Faldo used more recently to get more consistency and length. He had to be patient but persevered and, despite a dip and a sway, the new swing won him the Masters in 1937 when, on the final day, he picked up six strokes in two holes on Ralph Guldahl in the final round.

His great thrust that week came round that stretch of the course down at the bottom of the hill where Rae's Creek can be so troublesome and where the wind gusts and whistles round the tall pines with frustrating uncertainty. The stretch just after the turn is now known as Amen Corner and there is a suggestion that it was Nelson who so nick-named it. For the record, Nelson made a birdie 2 to Guldahl's 5 at the short twelfth where the green slopes away into the creek and then eagled the long, testing, dog-leg thirteenth where Guldahl took 6. That year Nelson had two shots to spare over the runner-up but in 1942 he beat Hogan for the same title by just one shot.

Nelson also took the U.S. Open in 1939 when Sam Snead closed with an 8 when he had the title virtually in his pocket, Nelson played off with Densmore Shute and Craig Wood with whom he was still tied after 18 extra holes. They had to play another 18 and Nelson triumphed, helped by a holed one-iron for an early eagle! But in 1946 he lost a U.S. Open play-off to Lloyd Mangrum when he should have won outright. He had been penalised at one point because his young caddie inadvertently kicked his ball in the rough. He also won two U.S.P.G.A. titles but played only twice in the British Open, finishing fifth in 1937. His other appearance, in 1955, was without much distinction at St Andrews, but the 43 year-old part-timer did travel to La Boulie that year for the French Open before returning home. It was the last big event in which he played and he won it.

Remarkably, both he and Hogan had started caddying at about the same time and at the same golf club near their homes in Texas. There always was great rivalry between them even if Nelson's career was, by his own choice, ending at just the time Hogan was returning from war service to re-establish his authority. In 1946 however Hogan won their duel when, in a season in which they dominated the tournaments, he won 13 times to Nelson's 10. Nicknamed 'Mr Golf' by the headline-makers on the Texas newspapers (one fancies much to Hogan's dislike), Nelson had by then almost had enough and retired shortly afterwards to his Texas ranch to contemplate what might have been but certainly not to brood. He was only 34.

'People,' the big six-footer once said, 'say it is too bad I won all those events when the prize money was so small but I am not envious. You can only beat the competition that is around at the time and you can only compete when you feel well enough to do so. It was fun when I played, much more fun I fancy than it is now.' Some say he gave up because of what playing the circuit was taking out of him. For someone with a blood problem he simply could not have maintained the schedule for much longer than he did. It was far more punishing for him than it would have been for someone who was completely fit. Instead he involved himself in television commentating and teaching. His most famous pupil is Tom Watson, the five times No. 1 money-earner in the States and for a time in the late 70's and early 80's the most dominant figure in the game. Watson never starts a season without flying down to Nelson's Texas ranch for a swing check-up.

The friendship began at Winged Foot, New York State in 1974 when Watson, who for a time had the reputation as a choker in major events, blew the lead in the U.S. Open. Nelson, impressed by Watson's game and attitude, introduced himself and suggested he might be of some help to the young man. Watson needed no second asking and a firm friendship was established. Today one of the most important things in Nelson's life is Tom Watson and his career. Undoubtedly he helped Watson cope with pressure so well that the pupil went on to win two U.S. Masters, a U.S. Open at Pebble Beach when he pipped Jack Nicklaus and five Opens in Britain. If he could somehow sort out Watson's putting he might yet see his protege equal Harry Vardon's six Open wins. Ironically putting was Nelson's own main weakness.

When Mrs Nelson was taken ill with a stroke in their 51st year of marriage, Watson flew down from Kansas more than 20 times to visit her and keep Nelson company at the farmhouse his wife had completely rebuilt. The lovely story goes that it was she in 1944 who inspired Nelson's great scoring run. She agreed with him that it would be nice to have a ranch but insisted they should not use the capital they had in the bank for the job. She suggested he should go out and earn what they required and he did. They bought their ranch in 1946 and Nelson went into semi-retirement.

Nelson, now remarried, politely and hardly surprisingly refused all invitations to involve himself in the Senior circuit in recent years. It would have been tough to try to come back 40 years on and impossible to recapture his former magic.

# *CAREER RECORD*

## Victories

| | |
|---|---|
| 1935 | New Jersey State Open |
| 1936 | Metropolitan Open |
| 1937 | U.S. Masters, Belmont Match-play Championship, Thomasville Open |
| 1938 | Hollywood Open, Thomasville Open |
| 1939 | U.S. Open, Phoenix Open, North and South Open, Western Open |
| 1940 | U.S. P.G.A. Championship, Texas Open, Miami Open |
| 1941 | Miami Open, Greensboro Open, World Championship |
| 1942 | U.S. Masters, World Championship, Oakland Open |
| 1944 | World Championship, San Francisco Open, Knoxville Open, New York Red Cross Tournament, Golden Valley Invitational, Nashville Invitational |
| 1945 | U.S. P.G.A. Championship, Phoenix Open, Greensboro Open, World Championship, Knoxville Open, Corpus Christi Open, New Orleans Open, Miami Four-ball, Charlotte Open, Durham Open, Atlanta Open, Canadian Open, Philadelphia Inquirer Invitational, Chicago Victory Open, Esmeralda Open, Seattle Open, Glen Garden Invitational |
| 1946 | San Francisco Open, New Orleans Open, Chicago Victory Open, Los Angeles Open, Houston Open, Columbus Invitational |
| 1951 | Bing Crosby National Pro-Am |

## Did you know...

1. Byron Nelson and his great rival Ben Hogan started off as caddies at the same golf club!
2. Byron Nelson helped Tom Watson to win several majors after first offering his advice in 1974.
3. In one season Byron Nelson shot an amazing sequence of 19 consecutive rounds below 70!

Yet another victory speech for Byron Nelson

# *CHRISTY O'CONNOR*

For shot-making artistry and skill Ireland's Christy O'Connor Sen. stands tall among the great golfers of this century.

Peter Thomson may have won the fourth of his five Open Championships at Royal Lytham in 1958 – but there are many in Ireland who would claim that the title rightfully belonged to their own national hero, Christy O'Connor. The man himself agrees it was his greatest chance to win a major, and failure caused him anger and irritation and cost him the crowning glory on his standing as Ireland's greatest golfer.

O'Connor stood on Lytham's last tee needing a birdie three to win and a par four to tie with Thomson and Welshman Dave Thomas, who had finished just in front of him with aggregates of 278. The hole measured 379 yards and O'Connor knew he could get home comfortably with a drive and wedge. But, with the crowd encroaching onto the fairway and leaving little room, O'Connor decided to take a three wood and play short of the left bunkers. In those days the final two rounds of the championship were played on the same day and O'Connor had led at the half-way stage on 135, the lowest aggregate since Henry Cotton's 132 at Royal St George's in 1934. He was out in the last two ball on the final day with the Argentinian Leopoldo Ruiz.

There was a long wait on the tee as the stewards tried to marshall the crowds into some kind of order but the Irishman nevertheless struck his three wood well. 'I was happy with it. I could not see the ball finish because the crowd had blocked my view but someone shouted "great shot Christy. You're short of the bunkers". But when I got to the ball it was not only in the sand but lying poorly'. The record shows that O'Connor took 5 and finished a shot outside the play-off. Thomson beat Thomas by four shots the following day leaving a disappointed and angry O'Connor to brood on what might have been.

His anger stemmed from what he claims was the inordinately slow play by the men in front of him, Thomson and Thomas. He had complained three times to Royal and Ancient officals and indeed to Thomson himself at lunch between the third and fourth rounds but no penalties were imposed and Christy allowed the situation to irritate him so much he lost his tempo and concentration. He never did win an Open championship. In 26 attempts between 1951 and 1979, he finished second, again to Thomson, in 1965,

The gallery look on anxiously as Christy hits to the green – this time in the 1961 Ryder Cup

was twice third and had seven other top ten finishes – but the title remained elusive.

If greatness is measured by major championship victories, then the great Christy is not Ireland's best golfer. That accolade would go to Fred Daly, who won the Open in 1947, but O'Connor believes that the consistent winning of tournaments over a protracted period is a more genuine guide. In a career that spanned more than three decades he did practically everything else except win the Open. He won 25 events on the European Tour and 31 titles at home; he made a record ten consecutive appearances in the Ryder Cup, taking part in the 1957 victory at Lindrick and the 1969 tied match at Royal Birkdale; he played in 15 World Cups, winning once with Harry Bradshaw in Mexico City in 1958.

Because of a problem over his registration with the Irish PGA, he was a late starter on the tournament circuit. He was already 27 when he played his first major event in 1951, and Bradshaw and Daly were already well established as the power men of Irish professional golf. He

The Ryder Cup again – at a chilly Muirfield (above) and another glorious drive in the Open at Hoylake (left)

A rather damp Troon in 1973

was soon to form a great relationship with Bradshaw, who O'Connor said was not just a friend but a father figure. 'We had great times together and made a good team. I was something of a sleeping partner when we won the Canada Cup in 1958. Harry played quite magnificently and tied for the individual tournament, only to lose in a play-off'. Christy was soon to take over as Ireland's top player but it annoys him when people call him a natural player. 'I never had a natural swing. I worked long and hard over in the West of Ireland to cultivate my swing. I learned a lot from watching others and used it to develop my own game. Hours and hours on the beaches taught me how to hit a driver off the fairway. You have to hit it cleanly off the surface and flick it up'. Hence, the tag Wristy Christy.

It has been said about him that most Irishmen he met wanted to buy him a drink and most of them succeeded. That, of course, is an exaggeration, like many other stories about O'Connor, who was born close by the first green at Galway Golf Club. He would never deny his liking for 'a jar in the bar' with friends.

Christy O'Connor retired from the PGA European Tour in the early 1980's but still swings as sweetly as ever and is still fit enough to take a punt or two from the unwise. When he became a senior golfer in 1976 he won the PGA title six times in the first eight years.

## *CAREER RECORD*

Another smile for the cameras from Christy

### Victories

| | |
|---|---|
| 1953 | Ulster Professional Championship |
| 1954 | Ulster Professional Championship |
| 1955 | Swallow-Penfold Tournament |
| 1956 | Dunlop Masters Tournament, Spalding Tournament |
| 1957 | British P.G.A. Match-play Championship |
| 1958 | Irish Professional Championship |
| 1959 | Dunlop Masters Tournament, Daks Tournament |
| 1960 | Ballantine Tournament, Irish Hospitals Tournament, Irish Professional Championship |
| 1961 | Carling-Caledonian Tournament, Irish Professional Championship, Irish Dunlop Tournament, Gleneagles Pro-am |
| 1963 | Martini Tournament, Irish Professional Championship |
| 1964 | Martini Tournament, Jeyes Tournament, Carrolls International Tournament |
| 1965 | Senior Service Tournament, Irish Professional Championship, Irish Dunlop Tournament |
| 1966 | Carrolls International Tournament, Gallaher Ulster Open, Irish Professional Championship, Irish Dunlop Tournament |
| 1967 | Carrolls International Tournament, Irish Dunlop Tournament |
| 1968 | Gallaher Ulster Open, Alcan International |
| 1969 | Gallaher Ulster Open, Southern Ireland Professional Championship |
| 1970 | Bowmaker Tournament, John Player Classic, Sean Connery Pro-am |
| 1971 | Irish Professional Championship |
| 1972 | Carrolls International Tournament |
| 1975 | Irish Professional Championship |
| 1976 | Southern Ireland Professional Championship, British P.G.A. Seniors Championship, World Seniors Championship |
| 1977 | British P.G.A. Seniors Championship, World Seniors Championship |
| 1979 | British P.G.A. Seniors Championship |
| 1981 | British P.G.A. Seniors Championship |
| 1982 | British P.G.A. Seniors Championship |
| 1983 | British P.G.A. Seniors Championship |

### Did you know...

1. Christy O'Connor Senior played ten times for Great Britain and Ireland in the Ryder Cup matches from 1955 to 1973.
2. Christy O'Connor Sen has finished second, third and sixth in the British Open. His nephew Christy O'Connor Jun. has finished second and fifth in the Championship.

# D A I R E E S

His enthusiasm was infectious, his determination was tremendous but Welshman Dai Rees died without ever having won the Open in Britain.

Dai Rees at 45 – 40 years after his first golf stroke!

One of golf's great enthusiasts was without any doubt Dai Rees, a mercurial little Welshman whose zest for golf was matched only by his zest for life. Like many men of small stature, he learned to be tough both outwardly and inwardly and those ingredients carried him to the top of his chosen career as a professional golfer.

There was never much doubt that Dai Rees would become a professional because he was brought up on a golf course. His father, also known as Dai, was a club professional in Wales and his mother was for many years a club stewardess. David James Rees was born in Fontygary, a small village just outside Barry in Glamorgan, and he vividly recalled his very first golf shot. He was five years old and was sitting behind the eighteenth green at The Leys club watching the club champion, a scratch golfer by the name of R. J. Middle, holing out a succession of four and five yard putts. The champion suddenly handed his putter to the tiny boy and said: 'See if you can knock the ball into the hole, Dai bach.' He did. A few days later, Middle took little Dai's hand and walked him to the nearest hole to the clubhouse, the twelfth, teed up a ball five inches high on a pile of wet sand and told the boy to hit it. 'Believe it or not,' Rees later wrote, 'I covered that first hole of my life in bogey, holing out

Dai at his peak and (below) with Arnold Palmer and H.R.H. Prince Philip at the Ryder Cup

with my fourth shot – a sixty-yard approach.'

From that moment, the golf bug had well and truly bitten and Dai Rees lived for the game for the rest of his 70 years. He played with an odd assortment of clubs in his early days and his first proper set of hickory-shafted clubs was delivered by Father Christmas when he was 13. Rees was expecting the delivery and as soon as was opportune, he switched on the bedroom light to admire his present. Before first light that Christmas morning, he was at the golf club and ready to play.

Rees joined the professional ranks in unusual circumstances. He had entered the Welsh Boys' Championship when he was 15 but his entry form was returned by sour officials with a note which said: 'Being the son of a professional, and obviously earning money from the game, it is considered that you are not an amateur.' So it was that a bitterly disappointed youngster abandoned the amateur game and joined his father as an assistant professional, a decision he never once regretted in later life.

Rees became an outstanding golfer, winning a string of titles between the 1930's and the late 1960's, including four British P.G.A. Match-play championships and also the British P.G.A. Seniors. Victory in the Open championship, however, eluded him although three times he finished runner-up – to Ben Hogan in 1953 at Carnoustie, to Peter Thomson in 1954 at Royal Birkdale and to Arnold Palmer in 1961, also at Royal Birkdale. But as a Ryder Cup player – and a Ryder Cup captain – Rees excelled. He played in the event nine times, his first in 1937 at Southport and Ainsdale.

On his Ryder Cup debut, Rees partnered Charles Whitcombe to a halved match in the 36-hole foursomes against two former Open champions, Denzil Shute and Gene Sarazen; and in his 36-hole singles the next day, he sensationally beat Byron Nelson who, at the time, was one of the best golfers in the world. But there was no fairy-tale ending on that occasion because the Great Britain and Ireland team, as it then was, lost 8-4.

Rees, were he alive today, would tell you his greatest triumph in golf was captaining the Great Britain and Ireland Ryder Cup team to victory at Lindrick, near Sheffield, in 1957. Although the home side trailed three matches to one after the opening day's foursomes, thousands upon thousands of spectators turned up at Lindrick the next day to watch the deciding singles. By 11.30am, the gatemen had run out of tickets and it was later estimated that at least 5,000 people saw one of Britain's greatest sporting triumphs for nothing. Rees, who was the previous day's only winner, in partnership with ex-Marine Commando Ken Bousfield, played himself at number five in the singles and made short work of former U.S. Open champion Ed Furgol, winning 7 and 6 and then charged back onto the course to cheer his team to victory.

The exuberant little Welshman was the toast of Britain. He was named Sportsman of the Year, was awarded the CBE in the New Year Honours List and took the Ryder Cup proudly to official golf dinners. He captained three more Cup teams, but was an observer in 1969 when countryman Brian Huggett played his heart out at Royal Birkdale.

When Huggett holed a vital putt on the final green to halve his match against Billy Casper, he thought he had secured the winning point for the home side. Huggett wept tears of emotion and one of the first men onto the eighteenth green to comfort him was Dai Rees. Although his playing days were drawing to an end by 1969 – but only just – Rees loved the game of golf so much that he continued to visit as many tournaments as possible. Sometimes he joined the radio commentary teams and was an eloquent expert.

Rees was always cheerful, always full of encouragement and advice for the younger players and extremely popular among the old and young, amateur or professional. He was elected an honorary member of the Royal and Ancient Golf Club of St Andrews in 1976, of which he was immensely proud, and never lost his zest for the game. Later in his career he played in occasional tournaments and, at the age of 60, finished third in the 1973 Martini event at Barnton.

A great Arsenal supporter all his life, Rees was slightly injured in a car crash on his way to a match one Saturday, and never quite fully recovered. He died, aged 70 in 1983, leaving the golfing world to mourn a great personality.

# *CAREER RECORD*

## Victories

| | |
|---|---|
| 1935 | British Assistants' Championship |
| 1936 | British Match-play Championship, British Assistants' Championship |
| 1937 | Sunningdale Foursomes |
| 1938 | British Match-play Championship |
| 1939 | Yorkshire Evening News Tournament |
| 1946 | Silver King Tournament |
| 1947 | Daily Mail Tournament, News Chronicle Tournament, Penfold Tournament |
| 1948 | Irish Open |
| 1949 | British Match-play Championship |
| 1950 | British Match-play Championship, Yorkshire Evening News Tournament, Dunlop Masters |
| 1951 | Yorkshire Evening News Tournament, News Chronicle Tournament, New South Wales Open (Australia) |
| 1952 | Yorkshire Evening News Tournament, Wisemans (New Zealand) Open |
| 1953 | Daks Tournament |
| 1954 | Egyptian Open, Belgian Open, Yorkshire Evening News Tournament, Spalding Tournament, Southern England Professional Championship |
| 1956 | Swiss Open, Yorkshire Evening News Tournament |
| 1959 | Swiss Open, British P.G.A. Close Championship |
| 1962 | Dunlop Masters, Daks |
| 1960 | Gleneagles Pro-Am, Teachers Seniors Championship |
| 1963 | Swiss Open |
| 1966 | Southern England Professional Championship |

## Did you know...

1. At the age of 5 Dai Rees completed his first ever hole of golf in bogey – holing out from 60 yards!
2. Dai Rees played in a total of seven Ryder Cups – his greatest triumph came when he captained the winning team in 1957.

1957 – and a jubilant British captain holds aloft the Ryder Cup for the first time in 24 years

# *PETER THOMSON*

Noted for his graceful style Peter Thomson from Melbourne in Australia won five Open Championship titles in Britain then dominated the Senior Tour in America just as effectively.

Peter Thomson is the father figure of Australian golf who has won fame and fortune by his mastery of the British Open. His influence on every aspect of golf in his native Australia is overwhelming. As a player, Thomson collected Championships with astonishing consistency, consummate ease and a minimum of flourish and fuss. As a spokesman and model for his sport he has been exemplary, his charm and intellect helping to shape and sustain the increasingly more lucrative Australian Tour through his role as President of the Australian Professional Golfers' Association.

He has been and remains a course architect of renown, a lucid, entertaining commentator, a gifted writer and speaker able to converse and explain the intricacies of subjects as diverse as Australian football, international theatre and traditional opera. And his sense of fun and humour is as legendary as the uncomplicated swing and tungsten-tipped nerves which made him such a relentlessly successful competitor. Thomson's abiding fame, however, will always centre on his acquisition of five British Open championships, the same number as Tom Watson and only one less than the record tally of Harry Vardon.

The father of Australian golf – Peter Thomson

From 1951 – when, at 21, he played his first Open at Portrush and finished sixth – to 1979, when 27th in his last appearance, at Royal Lytham, he walked the Open courses like a quiet colossus. His first victory came at Royal Birkdale in 1954 and when repeated at St Andrews in 1955 and Hoylake in '56, he had created a hat-trick unprecedented in the modern game. Though Bobby Locke's putting wizardry would halt the sequence next year at St Andrews, Thomson triumphed again at Lytham in 1958, by four shots in a 36-hole play-off with Welshman, Dave Thomas, after earlier setting a qualifying record low score of 63. And finally, in 1965 back at Birkdale where it all started, he claimed what he regards as his greatest Open win, turning back challenges from Jack Nicklaus, Arnold Palmer, Gary Player and Tony Lema to pull clear by two at the finish. That year the competition was stronger than in any of his previous winning years.

Though Great Train Robber Ronald Biggs chose the same day to make his daring prison escape, Thomson's fifth title earned him equal billing on newspaper front pages the next day! Such was his influence on the Open and mastery of British conditions that he also finished three times second, once third and nine

Warming up at Sunningdale

times in the top 10 over that 29-year unbroken span. Thomson's secret, if there is such a thing, lay in the simplicity of his method and approach. He could never understand the need to complicate instruction. Indeed, Henry Longhurst once suggested they collaborate on a teaching book. But after two half hour sessions together at a St Andrews hotel, Longhurst abandoned the project. 'Thomson's lessons are so simple they spoil the book,' he declared. 'He reduces all the standard chapters to one line. The grip, for instance, ought to be good for 20 or 30 pages. Thomson simply says if you get set up right then you won't need to worry about the grip. It will all come naturally.'

Certainly it all came naturally for Peter William Thomson, born in the Melbourne suburb of Brunswick, one of four sons of Arthur and Grace. Though his earliest sporting prowess was as a dashing left-handed batsman in cricket, Thomson started golf on nearby Royal Park public course at 12 and by 15 had already won the club championship. Progression to a Melbourne sandbelt club was a natural move and on March 12, 1946, the fresh-faced youngster was admitted as a member of the august Victoria Golf Club. Within two years he had won the Australian foursomes title with clubmate Doug Bachli – who would go on to win the British Amateur in 1954, the same year Thomson collected his first Open – and then the Victorian Amateur Championship by beating Bachli 6 and 4, shooting 13

1954 – on his way to the British P.G.A. Match-play Championship

three's in 32 holes in the final at Woodlands. And when, in 1948, the youngster finished low amateur in an Australian Open won by Ossie Pickworth over Jim Ferrier, it was obvious his future lay in the professional game.

By then he had completed a diploma of applied chemistry and had started a career as an industrial chemist with employment as a rubber technologist for sporting goods manufacturer, A.G. Spalding. His major golfing sphere of influence had come from Harry Young, who also caddied for him, but now the dynamic professional Norman von Nida emerged to guide his career path. The Von had become a dominant figure in Australian and British golf with his superb play, explosive temperament and supreme confidence. Between 1946 and 1953 'The Von' won 12 tournaments in Britain, three Australian Opens and four Australian PGA titles. And then, as now, he was more than willing to assist a young Australian with talent in any way.

Von Nida had instant rapport with the quiet, ambitous Thomson. 'He led me out of the amateur ranks like a farmer leads a donkey out of the barn with a carrot in front of his nose. In my case the carrot was a promise of money and at 19 years of age nothing looked sweeter,' Thomson would write later. After two mandatory years as an assistant to the same George Naismith who later took on another promising youngster called David Graham, Thomson was ready to tackle the world and victories in the 1951 Australian and New Zealand Opens relieved him of any financial anxiety. By the time he reached Royal Birkdale in 1954 he was bubbling with confidence and enthusiasm, having already proved himself as a rookie on the U.S. Tour. He then would make two decisions which proved vital. First, he discarded the clubs he had used for the past six months and took a new set from the rack. Then he removed the driver from the bag, confident he could get enough length with a three wood on fairways bone dry from a summer's drought. Then he set about winning the Open. Here's how he described it:

'By lunchtime of the last day I had a feeling I was going to win and instead of lunching in the clubhouse I rushed back to my hotel for a tie and jacket. I played the last round with the American, Frank Stranahan, and while waiting for him to putt out during the last round I saw a figure in a cap and green flying jacket running full pace towards the green. It was Norman von Nida, who had finished earlier and come out to guide me in. He beseeched me to keep calm and told me I had it in the bag and I thought at the time he was a lot more nervous than I was. But his presence gave me a lot of strength. In any case, everything was going so well I had no fears of letting it slip.

The Thomson era had begun and championship after championship fell to his immaculate driving, superbly controlled iron shots and adequate putting. He won all over the world, at stroke, team and match play, forging an immense reputation for his golf and demeanour. He pioneered the Safari circuit in Kenya and Zambia, was a strong force in establishing the Far East circuit and the Japanese Tour. And though he would turn his back on American golf, dismissive of the big ball and contemptuous of American course preparation which so favoured target golf, he won the Dallas Centennial Open in 1956 over Gene Littler and Cary Middlecoff and finished fourth in that year's U.S. Open after leading for two rounds. Almost 30 years later, Thomson resigned himself to big ball dominance in the game and returned to America to dominate the Seniors Tour through a golden 1985 in which he won nine tournaments and almost one million dollars in prize money. Yet he might never have played there had he been successful in State politics. Ironically he got involved only because for one of the few times in his life he failed to achieve an objective. In 1982 he stood for State parliament as a Liberal candidate and failed by only 1395 votes to win the seat.

In recent years a chronic wrist injury has hampered his performance and Thomson is poised to walk away from golf competition for the final time. Among other interests he now designs golf courses with Mike Wolveridge and his reputation in this respect is as great as was his golf.

## *CAREER RECORD*

### Victories

| | |
|---|---|
| 1950 | New Zealand Open |
| 1951 | Australian Open, New Zealand Open |
| 1951 | New Zealand Open, New Zealand Professional Championship |
| 1954 | British Open, British P.G.A. Match-play Championship |
| 1955 | British Open, New Zealand Open |
| 1957 | Yorkshire Evening News Tournament |
| 1958 | British Open, Dunlop Tournament, Daks Tournament (tied with H.R. Henning) |
| 1959 | New Zealand Open, Italian Open, Spanish Open |
| 1960 | Yorkshire Evening News Tournament, Daks Tournament, Bowmaker Tournament, New Zealand Open, Hong Kong Open, German Open |
| 1961 | British P.G.A. Match-play Championship, Yorkshire Evening News Tournament, Dunlop Master, Esso Golden, New Zealand Open |
| 1962 | Martini International |
| 1963 | Indian Open |
| 1964 | Philippines Open |
| 1965 | British Open, Hong Kong Open, New Zealand Open, Daks Tournament, Piccadilly Tournament |
| 1966 | British P.G.A. Match-play Championship |
| 1967 | British P.G.A. Match-play Championship, Alcan International, Australian Open, Australian Professional Championship, Hong Kong Open, New Zealand Caltex Tournament |
| 1968 | Dunlop Masters |
| 1970 | Martini International (tied with D. Sewell) |
| 1971 | New Zealand Open |
| 1972 | W.D. and H.O. Wills Tournament, Australian Open |

On top again

### Did you know...

1. Apart from winning the Open five times Peter Thomson finished second three times, third once and in the top ten on nine other occasions!
2. Thomson's fifth Open victory shared front-page billing with news of the escape from prison of Great Train Robber Ronald Biggs.
3. Henry Longhurst thought that Peter Thomson would be an ideal candidate to work on a teaching book but after hearing Thomson's advice on the grip – 'If you set up right it will all come naturally' – decided to abandon his plans!

# *'BABE' ZAHARIAS*

She won gold medals at the Olympics and when she turned to golf she was equally brilliant but the one battle supreme champion Babe Zaharias could not win cost her her life.

There could have been no greater tribute paid nor one more richly deserved than the headline in *The Guardian* the day following the tragic death of Babe Zaharias at the age of just 42. It simply read: 'Death of the world's greatest sportswoman'.

The sporting world was stunned at the death so young of a sportswoman who excelled at so many different disciplines but who, after coming late in life to golf, created such an interest in the women's game. In the late 30's, 40's and early 50's she was what Walter Hagen had been to the men's tour in America in the 20's. She revelled in the showmanship aspect of the game. She was refreshingly extrovert and although her reign in the professional ranks was short compared to the wonderful achievements of Mickey Wright and Kathy Whitworth in America, it is 'The Babe' who etched herself and her personality indelibly on the minds of everyone who knew her or were lucky enough to watch her exciting play.

1947 – and 'Babe' becomes the first American to win the British Women's Amateur Championship

She was born one of seven children of Norwegian parents. Her father was a sailor used to battling with the roughest of seas round Cape Horn – he was shipwrecked on one voyage and stayed alive only by clinging one-handed to a lifeboat. He held a colleague in the other hand. The determination shown then by her father, that refusal to give up, was clearly an inherited characteristic of young Mildred. She enjoyed life yet loved to win but, in the end, even her great spirit could not help her beat the cancer that gripped her athletic body before she was 40 and attacked her ruthlessly and persistently from the inside.

Babe Zaharias, who earned her nickname because she was so good at baseball the other kids in the street dubbed her their equivalent of the then top star Babe Ruth, was mightily strong in physique yet not manly in her movements. Her mother was the best skier and skater in their district and Babe's gracefulness was inherited from her mother. Money was short in the Didriksen household but there was a family commitment to personal fitness and no question that savings should be made elsewhere in the budget in order to send 15-year-old Babe to the National Athletic Championships in nearby Dallas. She went and was an outstanding success.

She set two records for javelin throwing and basketball throwing and followed that up with victories in the long jump, the pole vault and the shot putt. She was as sharply competitive on the tennis and

'Babe' Zaharias – winner of over 80 titles before losing her fight against illness at the age of only 42

basketball courts and in the swimming pool where, not surprisingly, her prowess raised speculation that she might try one day to swim the English Channel. In fact she never did. She was a good discus thrower, high jumper, sprinter and few could beat her at the bowling alley either. She was a sporting phenomenon. Her all-round expertise was such that she was her club's only representative in the National Club Championship meeting in Chicago in 1932. It meant a tough schedule of events for the irrepressible Babe who loved hectic pace and the drama of it but the proof of her incredible superiority can be seen in the scoreline that sunny afternoon. She took part in seven events, won five outright, tied one, was placed in the other and single-handedly won the team event!

She was an accomplished diver and it is even said she had to be persuaded to give up boxing after taking on and beating some of the fellows of her own age and weight. Asked to be a guest pitcher for the St Louis Cardinals against Brooklyn she impressed immensely. She was a more than average roller-skater and in basketball made the All-American team three times. She was incredible. She was a natural who revelled in the challenge of 19 different sports.

In the 1932 Olympics in Los Angeles, when she was still only 18, Babe set two world records in the javelin and 80 metres hurdles and tied the record in the high jump with what was then an unorthodox method. Olympic rules allowed her to compete in only three events. She won two golds and a silver! Earlier that year she had won eight out of ten events she entered in the American National Championships. Later Babe was voted the leading athlete of the first half of this century.

When someone suggested she have a go at golf, she went out and bought a set of heavy men's clubs. Gripping the driver the way she was used to holding the baseball bat, she hit her first tee shot 210 yards and, at that moment, was hooked. Stung by the golf bug, she determined to become the best. She practised for hours on end, blistering and causing her hands to bleed. Having taped them up with the American equivalent of elastoplast she continued to hit shots until the tape was oozing blood.

Never the golfing sophisticate, Babe had taken up golf at the age of 21 three years before she married Texan wrestler

George Zaharias. She played her first full event within a year and won the second professional event in which she competed. Ruled a pro for a time because of her baseball earnings, she regained her amateur status in January 1943 and very quickly made her mark. She won 17 events in a row in 1946 and 1947 including the American and British championships. She won the latter at Gullane in Scotland where she shocked officials by wearing short pants!

Turning professional again in 1947, and instantly earning $75,000 for ten instructional films, she won 31 of the 128 events in which she competed on the U.S. L.P.G.A. Tour of which she was a founder member. She was No. 1 earner for four years in a row at the time of the Tour was being established. She captured the US Women's Open three times in 1948, 1950 and in 1954, just a few months after the first of her cancer operations when she won by no fewer than 12 strokes.

Her fightback to fitness matched that of Ben Hogan after his near fatal car crash. She astounded her doctors, some of whom had felt when she was first struck down in 1951 that she would never play again. The realisation that she had cancer had come as a devastating blow especially since it was the most virulent form of it and was diagnosed far later than it should have been. Busy Babe had just not had time to go for a check-up.

Winning that third American title was her last great effort. She could beat everyone on the course but even Babe could not beat the disease that was destroying her and, in 1955, she won the last professional event in which she played.

In her career she won over 80 titles. Her massive length off the tee – she was as long as a man – and her ability to recover brilliantly from the most difficult spots made her the darling of the crowds. Extrovert, warm hearted, friendly, enthusiastic and simply a vibrantly brilliant superstar, Babe Zaharias latterly bore her illness with good humour and remarkable fortitude. Despite the pain and the anguish of it all, she never forgot how to smile and no one will ever forget her. The Babe really was very special indeed.

## *CAREER RECORD*

'Babe' Zaharias – winner of over 80 titles before losing her fight against illness at the age of only 42

### Victories

| | |
|---|---|
| 1940 | Western Open, Texas Woman's Open |
| 1944 | Western Open |
| 1945 | Western Open, Texas Woman's Open |
| 1946 | U.S. Amateur Championship, Texas Woman's Open |
| 1947 | British Amateur Championship, U.S. Woman's Titleholder Tournament |
| 1948 | U.S. Open |
| 1950 | U.S. Open, U.S. Woman's Titleholder Tournament, Western Open |
| 1951 | Tampa Open |
| 1952 | U.S. Open Titleholder Tournament |
| 1954 | U.S. Open |

### Did you know...

1. Babe Zaharias won 17 amateur tournaments in a row in 1946 and 1947.
2. Babe Zaharias won 31 times out of 128 pro events she competed in her eight year career.
3. In 1932 Babe Zaharias created three world records in the 1932 Olympics before she turned to golf.

# FRED DALY

Six British golfers have won the Open in the past 50 years and Northern Ireland's Fred Daly remains one of the most popular.

Fred Daly on the first tee in the Irish Open at his beloved Portrush

Fred Daly was already a veteran golfer by the time he became headline news in 1947 by winning the British Open Championship at Hoylake. Born in County Antrim, he was first introduced to the game by his father, an artisan member of Portrush Golf Club who encouraged his son to take up golf by giving him a set of cut-down clubs as a three-year-old.

By the time he was nine Daly was working as a caddie at the club and his intimate knowledge of the links making him, even at that tender age, a much sought-after worker. Like all young caddies he honed his own talent for golf by spending endless hours chipping and putting in his spare time, learning how to hit different shots with the same club because he only had one! It is a classic route to a career in golf and like many players before and after him, Daly ended up knowing more about the golf swing than any of the modern players who use a full set of clubs and whose formative years are spent on golf scholarships at American colleges.

His tough apprenticeship meant he

An admiring gallery (above), shoulder high after his Open victory at Hoylake (right) and turning on the style at Worthing (below)

was ready to turn professional by the time he was 17, and although the outbreak of war in 1939 interrupted his career, Daly returned after it with his appetite sharpened for a different and more pleasureable sort of combat. Even so it came as a surprise when he won at Hoylake. Until then he had always been regarded as a good player but hardly a man capable of taking the most glittering prize in golf – a prize won in the past by Cotton, Vardon, Hagen, Sarazen and Snead.

Daly's reputation at the time revolved around his prowess in match-play rather than stroke-play events, and with the great Henry Cotton the biggest star of the day, Fred was relegated to bit part status when the 1947 Open began. Four rounds later he was the star. In those days the Open not only finished on a Friday, it climaxed with 36 holes. When he began his penultimate round that Friday morning Daly was four shots clear of the field but a nervous 78 halved the gap between him and the chasing pack. The pressure, the pundits felt, would tell in the end, and Daly would crack! He did not. Instead Fred had a tremendous stroke of luck. Out early in the afternoon, he missed the worst of a sudden gale that swept in from the Irish Sea and by the time everyone had finished, his last round 72 had been good enough to give him the title by one stroke from Reg Horne and the American Frank Stranahan. Fred pocketed a cheque of £250 for his achievement and set off immediately for Belfast for what he promised would be a party to remember. Unfortunately he arrived home to find a National Day of prayer and every pub in town was closed. But the party, he explained later, was only slightly delayed.

If there were any doubts about the quality of this shock Open champion, Daly buried them later the same year when he won the Match-play Championship and followed that up with a series of exhilarating displays in the next few Open Championships. In 1948, at Muirfield, he came second to Cotton, and in 1950 was third after closing rounds of 69 and 66. Then in 1951 he was fourth behind Max Faulkner at his beloved Portrush and followed that up with a third place in 1952. It was quite a record of consistency and underlined that what happened in 1947 was no fluke. During the same period Daly also won two other match-play titles and took part in four Ryder Cups before a combination of age and ill-health forced him away from the tournament scene. His absence from what passed as a European Tour in those days was much lamented for Daly was a quiet, charming Ulsterman with a sense of humour so impish that his was the first name down on most party lists.

These days he still manages a few occasional holes at his adopted club, Balmoral, in Belfast, where only his trophy room survived a blaze which gutted the clubhouse. His championship medal is still proudly on display back at Portrush and Daly turns up every year at the Open to run a jaundiced eye over the new heroes of golf. With an Open first prize climbing steadily towards the £100,000 mark today's stars lead a different and ritzier life to the one Daly enjoyed. There was good money to be made back in the late 40's and early 50's but it was still 'peanuts' compared to the modern gravy train.

'I'm not jealous,' he says. 'Well maybe just a bit. In my day there was no chance of becoming a millionaire or of buying a Rolls. I got my first car, for example, when I was 46 and it wasn't a Roller. But it's been a great life. I've met a lot of wonderful people and I am still asked for my autograph from time to time. My one great disappointment came the year after I won the Open. I was runner-up to Cotton at Muirfield. The King was there one day and met Henry but he did not come near me and I was still the champion'. Official thoughtlessness left a sour taste in his mouth. Fred was always down to earth, and more than deserves his name on the famous silver claret jug held aloft by the winner of the Open each year.

## *CAREER RECORD*

### Victories

| | |
|---|---|
| 1936 | Ulster Professional Championship |
| 1940 | Ulster Professional Championship, Irish Professional Championship |
| 1941 | Ulster Professional Championship |
| 1942 | Ulster Professional Championship |
| 1943 | Ulster Professional Championship |
| 1946 | Irish Open Championship, Irish Professional Championship, Ulster Professional Championship, Irish Dunlop Tournament |
| 1947 | British Open Championship, British P.G.A. Match-play Championship |
| 1948 | British P.G.A. Match-play Championship, Dunlop Southport Tournament, Penfold Tournament |
| 1950 | Lotus Tournament |
| 1951 | Ulster Professional Championship |
| 1952 | British P.G.A. Match-play Championship, Irish Dunlop, Daks Tournament, Irish Professional Championship |
| 1955 | Ulster Professional Championship |
| 1956 | Ulster Professional Championship |
| 1957 | Ulster Professional Championship |
| 1958 | Ulster Professional Championship |

### Did you know...

1. Between 1936 and 1958 Fred Daly was the Ulster Professional Champion on no fewer than eleven occasions.
2. Before his tenth birthday Daly was in great demand as a caddie at the Portrush Golf Club!
3. Daly's greatest disappointment came the year after his Open triumph. The King was at Muirfield as a spectator and chatted with Henry Cotton while ignoring the then reigning champion – a snub that was to leave a bitter taste for several years afterwards.

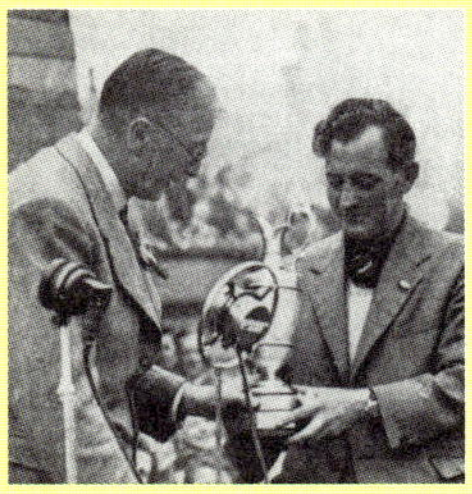

The 1947 Open Champion

# *BOBBY LOCKE*

His distinctive style was not one many wanted to copy but Bobby Locke, who hooked his way to many Championship wins, was so successful in America he was banned.

Bobby Locke survived the Second World War as a distinguished bomber pilot before exploding on to the world of golf with four British Open titles in nine years from 1949. Born Arthur D'Arcy Locke (the Bobby was a name used in childhood which stuck throughout his life) in a small town in the South African Transvaal, he found himself in a country perfectly suited to golf. The country had a superb climate and a life-style centred on the great outdoors which provided Locke with the ideal backdrop to develop his golf game in the lazy, hazy days before the War changed everything. Yet if this was the bonus for Locke, the disadvantage was that South Africa was a long way from most of the golfing action and the fortunes to be made. Then, as now, Europe and America were the places to test your talent and make your name.

Bobby Locke at Carnoustie in 1975, 40 years after his first South African Open Victory

Locke, to his credit, never hesitated. He could have remained in his homeland as a pampered local hero, but he chose instead to spend his life forever travelling the sporting world, a trail-blazer on a path to be followed later by Gary Player. His first appearance in Britain hinted at the great things to come when he took the Amateur medal in the 1936 Open Championship – and already he was making his reputation as one of the greatest putters the world has ever seen. His confidence on the green was marvellous to see unless, of course, you were his opponent at the time. In 1946, for example, he played a series of challenge matches against the great Sam Snead in South Africa. The established star and the young Locke played 14 times that winter, Locke winning 12 of them much to Snead's consternation. 'I go for the flagstick every time with my approach shot and then take two putts, Bobby just seems to go for the green and then takes one putt. That's the difference,' said Snead afterwards.

Throughout his career Locke used the same old, hickory-shafted club with a discoloured steel blade, never allowing the face to open on his back swing so that some experts maintain that he actually hooked his putts into the hole. Whatever the truth of that, Locke, who began his career with a gentle fade off the tee, developed into one of the fiercest hookers of all time. The right-to-left flight of his ball was

so pronounced that he used to line up at least 45 degrees to the right of his intended target so that his ball usually flew out over the rough only to swing violently back and end up in the middle of the fairway. The crowd loved it and Locke would tug at the white cap that became his trade-mark as they applauded.

By the time the Second World War ended Locke was well on his way to becoming a genuine star. He had by then won five South African Opens as well as making an impact on the international scene with victories in the Irish, Dutch and New Zealand championships. Now, however, the world was safe to travel again and Locke set off on an odyssey that was to propel him to the most exalted ranks of the game.

After defeating Snead in their series of exhibition matches he was persuaded to go to America and promptly won four of the five events he had entered. He won three more tournaments that year and in 1948 added three more victories. It was sensational stuff. No foreigner has ever achieved so much so swiftly in the States either before or since, but the Americans,

Checking the borrow on another vital putt (above) and on his way to setting up another birdie (left)

On the way to another Open Championship

unhappy at being beaten, changed the rules to make it more difficult for him to play there. Actually he did not mind. His first love as far as golf was concerned was Europe and, in particular, Britain. Returning to the United Kingdom in 1949 Locke began a series of assaults on the Open Championship that was to establish him as one of the all-time greats.

In 1949 he won his first Open Championship after a 36-hole play-off against Harry Bradshaw at Sandwich. Twelve months later Locke successfully defended his title at Troon with an aggregate score of 279 for 72 holes, an Open record at the time. In 1952 he won yet again but this time he finished with a new rival, Australia's Peter Thomson, just a stroke behind. Thomson won three times in 1954, '55 and '56, but Locke never gave up and got his reward when, in 1957, he won his fourth Championship, this time at St Andrews, leaving the Australian ace three sweet strokes behind.

His victory was not without drama, however, for some eye witnesses maintained he had not replaced his ball on the same spot on the last green, after having marked it to let someone else putt. A film proved the point. Locke had moved his marker to one side at the request of his playing partner and then, in the excitement of the moment, he had forgotten to move it back a club-head length before replacing his ball. He had not, however, moved his ball nearer the hole and officials adjudicating on the matter were aware that in any case he could have taken three putts and still won. The Royal and Ancient rules committee decided that under the equity rule no action should be taken. The result would stand but, curiously, Locke was never quite the same player again.

The fuss at the time quite clearly took something out of him.

Then a bad car crash shortly afterwards affected his eyesight so that the trusty putter was no longer the wizard of old. Perhaps his time simply had gone. The charisma, however, never diminished. He remained throughout his life a character who appealed to the golfing public all over the world and his death in 1987 at the age of 70 at his home in South Africa produced an avalanche of affectionate obituaries.

What he did inspired Gary Player to a large extent. Bobby Locke was a tremendous ambassador for the game and for his country.

## *CAREER RECORD*

The Open Champion again – for the fourth time – here at the home of golf, the Old Course, St Andrews

### Victories

| | |
|---|---|
| 1935 | South African Amateur Championship, South African Open |
| 1937 | South African Amateur Championship, South African Open |
| 1938 | South African Open, South African Professional Championship, Irish Open, New Zealand Open |
| 1939 | South African Open, South African Professional Championship |
| 1940 | South African Open, South African Professional Championship |
| 1946 | South African Open, South African Professional Championship, Yorkshire Evening News Tournament, Dunlop Masters |
| 1947 | Canadian Open |
| 1949 | British Open |
| 1950 | British Open, South African Open, South African Professional Championship, Dunlop Tournament, Spalding Tournament |
| 1951 | South African Open, South African Professional Championship |
| 1952 | British Open, French Open |
| 1953 | French Open Championship |
| 1954 | Dunlop Masters, Dunlop Tournament, German Open, Swiss Open, Egyptian Open |
| 1957 | British Open, Daks Tournament, Bowmaker Tournament |
| 1959 | Bowmaker Tournament |

# KEL NAGLE

Australian Kel Nagle foiled Arnold Palmer's bid to win all four major titles in a year when he pipped the American for the Centenary Open title at St Andrews in 1960

Whenever Peter Thomson is asked which of his century of tournament victories most excited him, the answer is always the same. 'Winning the Canada (now World) Cup in both 1954 and '59. They meant most because I was playing for Australia – and playing with a very fine fellow,' says Thomson. That very fine fellow is Kel Nagle. The finest, many Australians would insist. Certainly the most amiable and modest. And perhaps, as he continues to compete on the Seniors Tour in his 69th year, the most durable.

From Paris to Paraparan, in Hong Kong, Switzerland and Canada, Kel Nagle has won Open golf championships and the hearts of the galleries with his superb short game and ever-present smile. Overall, he has captured 57 four-round tournament victories. And who knows how that list might yet expand because Nagle has always been the classic late developer among golf's elite. He was 39 and seemingly past his best when he captured his first and only Australian Open championship, by four shots at The Australian Golf Club, in 1959. Then, a year later, Kel went one enormous step better, capturing the Centenary Open championship at St Andrews by holding off a classical Arnold Palmer charge in the final round and setting a then record Old Course low score of 278.

Kel Nagle now playing the Seniors circuit after a long and fruitful career

It was an epic performance and clearly, as Nagle told the thousands who cheered him at the presentation on the clubhouse steps, the most wonderful moment of his life. He had been a 100-1 outsider and ignored by the cognoscenti even when he opened with rounds of 69 and 67 to trail Roberto de Vicenzo by two at the halfway point. He was not ignored, however, by his friend Thomson. They had finished third together in the Canada Cup at Portmarnock the previous week where Nagle had employed a new driver to devastating effect. He had found it among a box of clubs in a pro shop in Fort Worth, Texas. Right away he sensed it was perfect for him. 'You're putting it on a sixpence with that driver. I'll have a bit on you at St Andrews,' Thomson told him on their way back from Ireland.

Nagle was not so confident however. The little finger on his right hand was beset by tendonitis and he feared he was starting to lose some of the length from the tee which had marked his early tour

Another cracking drive straight down the middle

Playing the Esso Golden tournament at Moor Park in 1961 – Nagle went on to take the trophy in 1963

nament career. But on soft, yielding greens that were a legacy of a soggy Scottish summer, Nagle's putting was devastating. Time and again key putts disappeared as he carded a third round 71 to overhaul de Vicenzo and post a two shot lead. No sooner had he holed out on the eighteenth than a massive deluge descended on the Old Course. Nagle could enjoy a leisurely lunch and a fretful dinner. The fourth round would be postponed until the next day. The Open would finish for the first time on a Saturday.

Ignoring the pain from his finger, Nagle calmly set about his task next day and seemed assured of a comfortable victory when he drove safely on to the Par 4 Road Hole – the famous seventeenth where the elevated green drops down at the back on to a road – with his two shot margin intact. Ten minutes later, however, he was staring down the line of a wickedly-breaking, right to left eight footer for his par. And up ahead, at the eighteenth, a huge roar signalled a closing Palmer birdie to slice the margin to just one. Nagle's nerve and his old Bullseye putter were equal to the task. The putt was in from the time he touched it. Now a par would suffice for victory.

A long, straight drive and a perfect pitch left him just three feet from the cup. Two careful putts later Kel Nagle had crowned his career and become only the second Australian, behind Thomson, to capture the Open. Quickly borrowing Thomson's coat, for he had forgotten his own in the tension of the morning, Nagle accepted the Trophy, a replica, a cheque for £1,120, a gold medal and a gold money clip in which was set a watch and the inscription 'Centenary British Open winner'. Then he went to celebrate with his usual cup of tea! He has never been a drinker or a smoker.

Kel Nagle was born at North Sydney in 1920 and can recall simulating golf as a seven-year-old, using sticks as clubs and old cigarette tins as the balls. But he did not play seriously until his 15th birthday. Within a year he became apprenticed to Tom Popplewell at Sydney's leafy Pymble course. The Second World War interrupted his career and Nagle, father of four strapping sons, did not play his first professional tournament until he was 26! A long driver (if not always a straight one) Nagle's strength was his wonderful short game. It was his ally wherever he played around the world. He travelled extensively, winning tournaments in Europe, Asia, the United States and the Pacific including the 1964 Canadian Open, 1961 French Open, the New Zealand Open nine times, the 1961 Hong Kong and Swiss Opens, six Australian P.G.A. crowns and nine New Zealand P.G.A. titles!

Just half an inch prevented him becoming the first Australian to win the United States Open. It was at feared Bellerive, Missouri in 1965 and Nagle and Gary Player had the issue between them. Birdies at the tenth and twelfth in the final round took the Australian ahead. Then a disastrous double bogey at the fifteenth seemed to have cost him his chance. But up ahead Player faltered, and when Nagle's birdie putt at the seventeenth disappeared, a birdie on the last could win for him. It was not meant to be: the putt for victory hung agonisingly on the edge but would not fall. The pair went to an 18 hole play-off next day. It was never a contest after Player birdied two of the first three holes and Nagle twice struck a woman with shots at the fifth. Player's 71 was three shots better, but Sam Snead said soon after: 'If I had Kel Nagle's putting stroke, nobody would ever have beaten me.'

What few knew is that Nagle played for much of his prime with severe back pain and tendon injuries in his hands which eventually required extensive surgery. At the Bi-Centennial Classic in Melbourne in 1988 he completed four rounds despite painfully arthritic feet. Yet he was never heard to complain or to offer excuses and still doesn't as he competes against his old mates on the U.S. Seniors Tour and pursues his love for fishing, harness racing and his host of grandchildren.

Nagle will always be remembered for his Centenary Open triumph and his short game skill. But equally he has been revered for his character, charm and sincerity. 'A prince among men,' is how Bruce Devlin describes him. It is more than apt.

## *CAREER RECORD*

### Victories

| | |
|---|---|
| 1949 | Australian PGA Championship |
| 1953 | McWilliams Wines |
| 1954 | Australian P.G.A. |
| 1955 | New Zealand Open, New Zealand P.G.A., New South Wales Open |
| 1958 | Australian P.G.A., New Zealand Open, New Zealand P.G.A. |
| 1959 | Australian Open, Australian P.G.A., Ampol Open |
| 1960 | Centenary British Open, New Zealand Open, Caltex Open (NZ), New Zealand P.G.A. |
| 1961 | Hong Kong Open, Irish Hospitals Open, French Open, Swiss Open |
| 1962 | New Zealand Open |
| 1963 | Esso Golden Tournament (U.K.) |
| 1964 | Canadian Open, New Zealand Open, Caltex Open (NZ) |
| 1966 | Wills Masters, B.P. Tournament, Caltex Open (NZ) |
| 1967 | Victorian Open, New Zealand Open, Esso Golden Tournament |
| 1968 | New Zealand Open, Australian P.G.A., B.P. Open (NZ), New South Wales Open |
| 1969 | New Zealand Open, Caltex Open (NZ), Garden City Open |
| 1970 | New Zealand P.G.A., Otago Charity Classic |
| 1971 | Volvo Open (Sweden), World Seniors Championship, British Seniors Championship |
| 1973 | British Seniors Championship, New Zealand P.G.A. Championship |
| 1974 | New Zealand P.G.A. Championship |
| 1975 | New Zealand P.G.A., British Seniors, World Seniors |
| 1976 | Otago Charity Classic |

### Did you know...

1. Following his win in the Centenary Open Kel Nagle celebrated in his usual manner – with a cup of tea!
2. Among his many victories are an amazing nine New Zealand P.G.A. titles!
3. Nagle did not play in his first professional golf tournament until the age of 26 and was 40 when he took first place in the Centenary Open.

The Centenary Open – **Kel Nagle** wins by one stroke from Arnold Palmer

# SAM SNEAD

Another golfing legend, sweet-swinging, long-hitting Slammin' Sam Snead found the U.S. Open was one Championship he just could not win.

The elegant Sam Snead can never look back on a glorious career without wondering why he never won the title every top American dreams of winning. It remains a mystery why 'Slammin' Sam – so called because he hit the ball a country mile – never ever landed the U.S. Open Championship, although he came close often enough. He was second four times between 1937 and 1949, twice managing to lose the title rather than have it snatched from him.

For him it is hugely disappointing, of course, but in the scheme of things his failure does not seriously tarnish his remarkable contribution to a game he only took up by chance because his older brother Homer enjoyed it. Sam turned out to be rather better than his brother!

Sam Snead displays his solution to the 'yips'

Today the name Sam Snead conjures up a picture of a golfer with a remarkable flowing, graceful swing and if, these days, the overall view is spoiled in some people's minds by a rather awkward-looking side-saddle, croquet-style putting method which other top stars with putting problems would probably shun, it has to be remembered that it was just that which helped keep him active when the dreaded putting twitch might have otherwise forced him to quit.

Snead was born in the backwoods – the Virginian backwoods – where his father ran a small farm that just did not provide enough to raise the family. He worked at the local hotel, too, just to help make ends meet. There was little for a lad to do in the tree-lined slopes of the Virginian mountains except hunt a little, fish a little, shoot a little and earn some valuable family dollars working as a caddie at the fashionable Spa resort hotel of the The Greenbrier at Sulphur Springs.

It was to the Greenbrier at the age of 24 that Snead went as an assistant. He did not know what lay ahead of him but he fancied himself as a golfer, self-taught, of course, with a natural right-to-left shot. Golf would be fine as a career, he thought, after he had injured his back and been forced to give up thoughts of playing football full-time. That back injury would trouble him the rest of his life yet he still remains one of the most resilient of golf stars with, even today, a classic swing which is the envy of golfers half his age. It is a swing that won him a record 84 events on the American circuit and, adding in his international successes, 164 titles worldwide. How many more might there have been had he had Hogan's single-minded-

ness. At times, because he always found the game so easy, he was inclined to be just a little lackadaisical. At times his putting let him down but his record shows not as often as some might suggest.

While his eyesight may not be as sharp today as it once was, his swing has hardly deteriorated. Of course he experiences now the aches and pains which restrict his backswing and follow through, but the tempo is still the same as it always was in the days when he was making his name in the Virginian Hills. He scored his first victory just two years after turning pro in 1934 and 40 years later at the age of 71 was finishing second in an American Tour event. He remains the oldest winner on the Tour having been two months short of his 53rd birthday when he won his eighth Greater Greensboro title. Sam loved it up there in North Carolina where the galleries are among the least sophisticated. And they loved him.

In 1979, the year he retired from playing the main circuit and two years before he helped found the Senior circuit, he shot 67 and 66 in the Quad Cities Open. He was 67 at the time and had, as a result,

Another huge gallery for 'Slammin' Sam (above) and (left) golf or fishing? (the 1986 Masters)

become the first man on Tour to shoot lower than his age. Despite that U.S. Open lapse, Sam Snead has had an incredible career which included three U.S. Masters victories, three U.S.P.G.A. Championships and a lone British Open victory at St Andrews in 1946 when he came over under sufferance and at the insistence of the golf club company to which he was contracted.

Sam – still enjoying the game as much as he ever did

Peter Alliss recalls that when Snead first saw the Old Course, he asserted that it must be the worst bit of real estate in the world, so bad that it would not be given away in the States. Of course before he headed back home he had changed his mind. It helped that he had the famous Open Trophy in his luggage! He came, saw, and conquered – helped by a string of birdies on the last nine despite having said he disliked seaside golf. He had played in the Open in 1937 as well, finishing joint 11th, and would play on only one other occasion – in the 1962 Open that was such a triumph for Arnold Palmer. That year he finished sixth but he missed all the rest. Frankly, he never really enjoyed playing in Britain where visiting he said was like 'camping out!'. It was a rich comment from a golfer who came from a relatively poor background and from a reasonably remote hill-billy area but the comment was typically Snead in the early days. He always had a 'say-it-as-it-is' down-to-earth, approach.

Snead, who had set off for his first event in 1936 with just nine ill-matched clubs, finished fifth after something of a scare. He very nearly did not get the chance to tee off on his debut at all after officials watched him hit his first two drives out of bounds. The first hole at Hershey was only 345 yards long but Sam hit his opening drive nervously into a sewage works and his second into a factory yard. Mightily embarrassed, he was on the point of repeating his 300-mile overnight journey to the course to drive back home when George Fazio, the professional who had suggested he should make up a four, urged him to hit another. He did and this time staggered the group by hitting the green 345 yards away down the hill. He was on the putting surface, too, with a driver at the 275 yards second at which everyone usually played safe because of the water in front of the green and was through the back of the 600-yards third in two! He shot a 67!

Short of finances, Snead needed to make a big cheque early in his career to help his cashflow and a low finish in Oakland in the fourth official tournament he played earned him a 1,200-dollar cheque. he used it wisely. In fact he has always had a reputation for meanness which in many instances was undeserved, but created in the early years of his career because he was seldom seen at the bar with the boys. He denies all stories that he buried much of the money he earned in the early years of his career in tin cans on the farm!

Not that his failure to appear in the hotel lounge was indicative of his being out practising. He hardly needed to, of course, with the swing he had been blessed with and he did not punish himself Hogan-style on the range. He found golf, compared to many of his contemporaries, remarkably easy – consequently, he was not always as razor sharp as he might have been in the clutch situations near the end of tournaments, although he himself denies he felt the pressure especially in the U.S. Open. Managed by that great old character the late Fred Corcoran, who also handled 'Champagne' Tony

Lema until his death in 1964 and for a time ran the U.S. Tour, Snead was favourite to win the American Championship in 1937 but lost by two strokes to Ralph Guldahl who shot a record low score 281.

Two years later at Philadelphia, in the days before huge scoreboards flashed the position of the leaders at any time to players on the course, he needed a par 5 to win. Sadly he did not know that. He played the hole more aggressively than he needed to and ended up taking 8. He did not even finish second. In 1947, Snead holed a curving down-hill 18-footer to force a play-off with Lew Worsham – then lost the play-off. And in 1953 he had to play second-fiddle to his great rival Ben Hogan with whom he teamed up to win the World Cup at Wentworth in 1956.

Sam Snead, eight times a member of the Ryder Cup team and once non-playing captain, liked nothing better than a golfing 'wager'. He loved to take on and beat a 'high-roller', an amateur with more money than sense. Sometimes with as much as 10,000 dollars on the line.

Two years ago Snead admitted that when it all started for him as a sometimes bare-foot caddie, he never dreamed he would be playing 250 rounds of golf a year at the age of 65 but that, he insists, is because he never has had a year off. He has played as much golf as he could within reason and in his late 70's remains the most enduring star of them all.

Always delighted to keep his stream of admirers happy

# *CAREER RECORD*

**Victories**

| | |
|---|---|
| 1936 | Virgina Professional |
| 1937 | St Paul Open, Miami Open, Nassau Open, Oakland Open |
| 1938 | Greensboro Open, Inverness Four-ball, Goodall Round-Robin, Chicago Open, Canadian Open, Westchester, 108 Hole Open, White Sulphur Springs Open |
| 1939 | Miami Open, St Petersburg Open, Miami Biltmore Four-ball |
| 1940 | Inverness Four-ball Ontario Open, Canadian Open, Anthracite Open |
| 1941 | Canadian Open, St Petersburg Open, North and South Open, Rochester Times Union Open, Henry Hurst Invitational |
| 1942 | St Petersburg Open, U.S. P.G.A. Championship, Cordoba Open |
| 1944 | Richmond Open, Portland Open |
| 1945 | Los Angeles Open, Gulfport Open, Pensacola Open, Jacksonville Open, Dallas Open, Tulsa Open |
| 1946 | British Open, Miami Open, Greensboro Open, Jacksonville Open, Virginia Open, World Championship |
| 1948 | Texas Open |
| 1949 | Greensboro Open, U.S. P.G.A., U.S. Masters, Washington Star Open, Dapper Dan Open, Western Open. |
| 1950 | Texas Open, Miami Open, Greensboro Open Inverness Four-ball, North and South Open, Los Angeles Open, Western Open, Miami Beach Open |
| 1951 | Miami Open, U.S. P.G.A. Championship |
| 1952 | Inverness Four-ball, U.S. Masters, Greenbrier Invitational, All-American Tournament, Eastern Open, Julius Boros |
| 1953 | Texas Open, Greenbrier Invitational, Baton Rouge Open |
| 1954 | U.S. Masters, Palm Beach Round Robin |
| 1955 | Miami Open, Greensboro Open, Palm Beach Round Robin, Insurance City Open |
| 1956 | Greensboro Open, Dallas Open |
| 1958 | Greensbrier Invitational |
| 1959 | Sam Snead Festival |
| 1960 | Greensboro Open, De Soto Open |
| 1961 | Sam Snead Festival, Tournament of Champions |
| 1964 | Haig and Haig Scotch Mixed Foursomes, U.S. P.G.A. Seniors, World Seniors |
| 1965 | Greensboro Open, U.S. P.G.A. Seniors |
| 1970 | U.S. P.G.A. Seniors, World Seniors |
| 1972 | U.S. P.G.A. Seniors, World Seniors |
| 1973 | U.S. P.G.A. Seniors, World Seniors |
| 1980 | Golf Digest Commemorative Pro-Am |
| 1982 | Legends of Golf (with Don January) |

Sam didn't want to make the trip across the Atlantic to the Old Course in 1946 – maybe he was glad he did!

# *MAX FAULKNER*

So confident was England's extrovert Max Faulkner of winning the 1951 Open Championship that he was signing autographs as champion after just two rounds at Royal Portrush.

Max Faulkner, a veritable peacock of the links, is an extrovert member of a very exclusive club: he is a British golfer who has won the Open in the last 40 years.

Most recently, Nick Faldo and Sandy Lyle have been modern-day winners of the most coveted crown in golf – but until their successes in 1987 and 1985 there had been a dearth of post-war British victories. Fred Daly from Belfast took the title in 1947, Henry Cotton, watched by King George VI triumphed at Turnberry in 1948 but between Faulkner's win at Royal Portrush in 1951 and Lyle's 1985 success at Royal St George's there was only the 1969 triumph of Tony Jacklin. With Britain just emerging from the post-war depression, 1951 winner Faulkner was just what was needed – a larger-than-life sporting hero in every respect...so confident that even after two rounds and with only a two shot lead at Portrush he was signing autographs: 'Max Faulkner – 1951 Open champion'. That kind of bravado usually ends up with the perpetrator very firmly on his backside and totally humiliated, but in Faulkner's case there was no such scenario. He did win.

Max Faulkner tees off in the 1946 Open at St Andrews

The fact is, of course, that Faulkner probably never gave it a second thought. He was on overdrive that week in Northern Ireland on the last occasion the Championship was played in Ulster. It was in the stars that no-one would or indeed could beat him.

A normally extrovert person attracted to wearing bizarre, or perhaps it might be more kindly to suggest, bold colours and plus fours, Faulkner kept his natural ebullience in check that week. No officials were ringing their hands at his antics not even when he stood on his hands and kicked his legs in the air after a putt on the last green for a third round 69 ran round the hole and stayed out. That was just high spirits. No one minded that. Henry Longhurst, writing in the *Sunday Times* after Faulkner's win, admitted he blanched and felt a chill run up his spine at one point during the Championship when Max, extending his arms out on either side of his body, told him with deep sincerity 'I shall never miss another of those.' The fact is he did not that week.

Resplendent in plus fours Max finds his way out of trouble

The gods were with him.

Every champion has to have some luck along the way en route to a major success. Faulkner had his in that he missed much of the bad weather, but to win needs more than just a share of luck, you also need the principle prerequisite of being a better-than-average golfer and competitor. Never let the reputation Faulkner had as something of golfing clown blind you from the fact that he was also a very good player, a solid striker of the golf ball and, as befits a man who for a time had been a Physical Training instructor in the RAF, always super-fit.

If he had a nagging problem it was with his putting and that week in Portrush he had a new club in his bag to replace not one but ten putters he had ritually snapped in a vice. They had not worked for him and they had to go. It was a daft gesture on a par with the man who 'punished' his clubs after a bad round by tying them to the back of his car and then driving 40 miles home with them bouncing off the road. Or like the man who coolly, calmly and in the most cold-bloodedly calculating way disposed of his clubs one by one as he travelled by train across the Forth Bridge! Faulkner was no half-measures man. The clubs had failed him. The club he gave the reprieve to that week was a lengthy but light-weight model with a 'pencil-slim' grip scarcely thicker than the shaft itself. He claimed it gave him additional feel and touch, so vital an ingredient in any Championship-

Safely out of the sand and on to the green

On the tee at the Matchplay Championship, watched by playing partner Peter Allis and (right) getting in some valuable putting practice

winning performance.

He did, in fact, putt beautifully – taking fewer than 30 putts in each of the four rounds. 'I played rubbish through the green but putted like a dream,' he said later. In the end and despite a last round 74, his worst of the Championship, he beat Antonio Cerda by two shots and on the final day held off a pack of hungry title hunters that included Bobby Locke, Peter Thomson, Harry Bradshaw, Fred Daly and Harry Weetman, that broad-shouldered gentle giant of man killed a few years later in a car crash. That win, despite the fact he was a long odds shot before the Championship began, and his triumph later that year in the Dunlop Masters, earned Faulkner the inaugural Golf Writers' Trophy award. It most assuredly was his year.

Faulkner was always a free spirit, not an easy man to pin down. He was at times outrageously extrovert but in an amusing and never vulgar way. He was a reporter's dream, always ready with a quick quote or a story that made a good headline. He was, it was said by a writer at the time, a lover of life with something of a Peter Pan in his make-up. Open champions usually are fine gentlemen but most have a sterner on-course side to their personality that is instrumental in helping them win. Faulkner did not fit the mould. He was warm, friendly and chatty on and off the course. The only person he ever got annoyed with at times was himself!

Born during the First World War at Bexley in 1916, Faulkner was brought up in a golfing atmosphere. He was encouraged to diligently stick at the game by his father Gustavus, who later made it easier for him to practise by buying the course at Selsey! Just after the Second World War he spent some time with Henry Cotton and his team at Royal Mid-Surrey but then was off again after a disagreement about which make of ball he should use. He competed for a time as 'unattached' thus underlining his naturally free spirit. He hated to be tied down.

Watching him play with all the confidence in the world and in eye-catching rigouts well ahead of their time, it was difficult to imagine how tense and nervous Faulkner always was inside. During the bigger tournaments, he once confided, he hardly got more than two hours sleep. He hated waiting around to tee off. he wanted to get on with the job. His two heroes were Locke, whose temperament he admired, and the pre-war Ryder Cup golfer Charlie Whitcombe who was his favourite when it came to style. He loved the way Whitcombe kept hitting so many straight balls arrow-like into the far distance. He often said that if he himself had had Locke's temperament, he might have won four or five Opens but in a way I am glad he did not have such control. He was what he was and everyone loved him for his eccentricities.

In later days he took to farming and fishing, owning for a time several boats which he hired out on the south coast. But he will be remembered for what he did one week at Portrush in 1951, winning a Championship a host of his contemporaries would have loved to win and probably deserved to ahead of him – but then golf was never meant to be a fair game.

## *CAREER RECORD*

### Victories

| | |
|---|---|
| 1946 | Dunlop Southport Tournament |
| 1949 | Dunlop Tournament, Penfold Foursomes, Lotus Tournament |
| 1951 | Open Championship, Dunlop Masters Tournament |
| 1952 | Spanish Open, Dunlop Tournament |
| 1953 | Spanish Open, British P.G.A. Match-play Championship |
| 1957 | Spanish Open |
| 1959 | Irish Hospitals' Tournament |
| 1968 | Portuguese Open, Pringle British P.G.A. Seniors' Championship |
| 1970 | Pringle British P.G.A. Seniors' Championship |

### Did you know…

1. Max Faulkner was so confident of winning the 1951 Open that after the second round, and holding only a two-shot lead, he was signing the autograph books as 'Max Faulkner' – 1951 Open champion'.
2. When his putt for a 69 at the end of the third round at the 1951 Open ran round the hole and stayed out his response was to stand on his hands and kick his legs in the air!
3. His 1951 triumphs in the 1951 Open and in the Dunlop Masters earned Max Faulkner the inaugural Golf Writers' Trophy.

The 1951 Open Championship Trophy – not to be presented to a British player again until Tony Jacklin in 1969

# CATHERINE LACOSTE

She retired at the age of 24 but by then the French amateur had made her mark on the world stage with a victory that left the American professionals open-mouthed in astonishment and awe.

Catherine Lacoste conquered the golfing world and then retired at the age of 24 unwilling to cope with the pressure that stardom inevitably brought her. 'It is difficult to keep playing all the time in the knowledge that if you win then that is what the spectators expect but, if you lose, you are on the way down,' said Mlle Lacoste shortly before she married Spaniard Jaime Prado y Colon de Carjaval, son of the Marquis of Castiglione, and gave up the big-time for good. Of course she had nothing else to prove having become in 1967 the youngest winner, the first European winner and the first amateur winner of the U.S. Women's Open. It was a monstrously outrageous performance. It caused the American professionals to blush with embarrassment! Catherine, a sturdy 5ft 4ins tall, took that victory in her stride but she was, of course, the daughter of two great sports personalities who knew all about winning.

Catherine Lacoste in action in 1967 – the year of her astonishing victory in the U.S. Women's Open

Her mother was the first French woman to win the British women's Championship in 1927 and her father was Rene Lacoste who won Wimbledon twice and was the first Frenchman to win the U.S. Open at Forest Hills. With that background it was no surprise that she was a competitor of quality, a young lady with an air of confidence that could sometimes be misunderstood. She was not popular with everyone but with most she got on well helped by the fact that she had a ready smile. In fact she had plenty to smile about when it came to reviewing what she did in a career even shorter than that of Bobby Jones! In 1963 at the age of just 18 she was the lynch-pin in the fabulous French victory in the Women's World Amateur Team stroke play competition for the Espirito Santo Trophy but she was a teenager with years of coaching behind her. In golfing terms she was far older than 18!

Her grandfather had founded the golf club at St Jean de Luz near Biarritz and it was there as a youngster that Catherine learned the rudiments of the game from M. Raymond Garaialde, father of Jean Garaialde, the doyen of French professional golf. St Jean de Luz is a hilly, wooded course that demands long, straight hitting and an ability to fashion shots off difficult side-hill lies. With father Rene making sure she knew all about the technique of the game, Catherine improved rapidly – so rapidly she won nearly all the juvenile competitions her

mother organised at the course in the summer no matter what her handicap. Undoubtedly learning to play the game on such a tough course helped her later when she won that American title at Hot Springs, Virginia, without her mother and father present to see her do so. She told them to stay away! She was if nothing else frank and to the point. They did not go. They did not see her thread the ball between the high pines and, when she did go off-line, recover with all the flair and panache of a Ballesteros. They missed a superb performance in which Mlle Lacoste proved that if you have a solid game and a massive belief in yourself it is possible, even as an amateur, to beat all the best American professionals.

She told a reporter from *The New York Herald-Tribune* after her victory that her opponents that memorable week were just people. 'If you play well you beat them and if you don't they beat you,' she said, making it all sound ridiculously uncomplicated. Yet it was a typical comment from a very independent young lady who was, during her short golfing career, affectionately referred to as 'The Crocodile Kid' – a reference to the fact that her father was France's tennis Crocodile!

Finding her way clear of trouble (above) and (left) in despair after missing a vital putt

She had a marvellously exciting golf game but complementing her technical prowess, and just as important an ingredient in helping her make history, was her calm, unruffled temperament. When she hit into trouble there were no tantrums, just a smile, and a shrug of the shoulders as she strode off to repair the situation. Another important ingredient in her make-up was a built-in tendency never to give in. So it was that, at the time she was playing, when Arnold Palmer and Jack Nicklaus were the common hero figures, Catherine Lacoste chose instead to heap her admiration on the other member of Golf's then 'Big Three', South African Gary Player – like her small of stature, incredibly determined and a man who has worked hard at the game to reap rich rewards.

In fact she decided at the age of 12 to devote more time to golf than tennis and won the French Junior Championship at the age of 19. That was in 1964. In 1965 she took the amateur prize in the U.S. Open – an omen of what was to come two years later. In 1967 she had won the French Championship with a resounding victory over an old (and older) rival Brigitte Varangot and was set to take on the world and in particular the might of American professionalism again. Forty years after her father had won the U.S. tennis crown, Catherine Lacoste travelled to Virginia Hot Springs for another crack at the U.S. Women's Open. Despite what she had achieved in the 1965 Championship, she was not given a chance. She may have been the French champion but she was ignored until she shot a 71 to be just one off the lead.

Peter Ryde, former golf correspondent of *The Times*, recalls in *The Golfers – The Inside Story* that the American press were caught napping but quickly made amends with zany headlines such as 'The Murderous Mademoiselle'. After Catherine shot a second round 70 that she said could have been a 63 to move into a five shot lead the headlines became even bigger! Ryde recalled significantly: 'She had the edge on the American professionals in one respect. Because golf was not her livelihood, she had never learned to play the percentage shot. Her game was attack, attack, attack all the way.' Heavy rain nearly cut the Championship short on the final day but they played and Catherine, feeling the pressure at last, took 40 to the turn. By the seventeenth her lead was just one shot. The American professionals were closing in like sharks. Catherine had the answer – a seventeenth hole birdie and a par at the last to win by two! She had to decline the 5000 dollars first prize. When she telephoned home her parents said simply: 'Bravo'. That five-letter word summed up their pride in what she had done. France was proud of her.

She always promised she would give up golf when she got married and she did, but not before winning, in 1969, the U.S. and British Amateur Championships, the latter a particularly poignant victory because she was emulating her mother. She won at her sixth attempt. She could have gone on winning but, true to her word, decided to call a halt when she announced her engagement. Her fiance did not want her to quit but she did, commenting in the same forceful way as she played her golf that it was not possible, in her opinion, to be a good amateur at both golf and marriage. How many records might she have broken? How many titles might she have won? The questions are superfluous. Catherine Lacoste's mind had been made up. When she quit the international scene at the tender age of 24 she had already done enough to ensure her immortality in the history of the game.

## *CAREER RECORD*

The 1969 British Amateur Champion

### Victories

| | |
|---|---|
| 1964 | French Junior Championship |
| 1967 | U.S. Open Championship, French Open Championship |
| 1968 | French Close Championship, U.S. Western Amateur Championship |
| 1969 | Spanish Women's Championship, French Close Championship, French Open Championship, British Women's Championship, U.S. Amateur Championship |

### Did you know...

1. French Prime Minister Georges Pompidou, who took a keen interest in Catherine Lacoste's record-making performances for France, used to invite her out to lunch.
2. Catherine Lacoste hit her 1-iron as far as most men helped by the fact that she trained so hard. She did not lift weights nor did she spend hours on the practice range but she did visit a Paris gymnasium during the winter to help her build up the right muscles for golf.
3. When Catherine Lacoste retired at 24 she told reporters that she had lost the urge to play at top level. "When you win you lose a little bit of your sensitivity," she said. That she felt was bad for a girl.

# *J O E  C A R R*

For a time Ireland's Joe Carr was the best amateur golfer in the world but the ebulient Dubliner never ever wanted to take to the professional ranks.

Joe Carr – winner of six Irish Amateur Championships and three British Amateurs

Joe Carr is one of the greatest golfers Ireland has ever produced, and also one of the most popular. When Joe was a young man, he won almost every tournament he entered. Yet to his great regret, his enormous trophy cabinet – it fills a complete wall of his Dublin home – is missing about 50 silver cups. He sold them when times were hard and has never been able to get them back.

Strenuous efforts over the years to trace those missing cups have always failed, much to his bitter disappointment. Why did he sell them? The genial, easy-going Carr explained: 'My father, who was the manager at Portmarnock Golf Club in Dublin, died towards the end of the Second World War. Money was very tight and I was earning only £2.58 a week as an apprentice in a wholesale warehouse. I sold every silver trophy I had to raise some money for the family. I got very little for them and every penny had gone by the next day because I went to the races and lost the lot! We Irish are great gamblers when we've no money. Then, when I became established in business, I tried to replace them but I couldn't remember which tournaments I'd won. I wrote to a lot of clubs in Ireland asking for help but most of them hadn't kept records. It was a sad business.'

Joe Carr never had any plans to turn professional, although he was easily good enough, and the amateur game gave him great enjoyment and made him many friends throughout the world. The high regard in which he is held can be measured by the fact that he is a member of no less than 31 golf clubs, although he pays

Joe in action at the 1967 Open

annual subscriptions to only two – the Royal and Ancient Golf Club of St Andrews and the Augusta National in Georgia, which stages the U.S. Masters each year, an event in which he regularly participated. The other 29 clubs to which he belongs made him an honorary member in recognition of his many golfing achievements and they are worth listing here: Sutton, Portmarnock, Milltown, Royal Dublin, Killarney, Lahinch, Royal Portrush, Macroom, Malone, Howth, Newlands, Youghal, Douglas, The Island, Malahide, Moate, Lucan, Tramore, County Cork, Dun Laoghaire, Skerries, Warrenpoint, Delgany, Ballina, Mullingar, Rosslare, Ballycastle, Portumna and Royal Lytham and St Annes.

Carr was born close to Portmarnock and also the nine-hole Sutton Golf Club, which was to become his second home. For many years, Carr owned a house overlooking the Sutton course and he brought the club worldwide fame because he always entered tournaments from there rather than from the more illustrious Portmarnock. Sutton, in those days, had nine criss-cross holes packed into a mere 24 acres by the sea and was only 300 yards across at its widest point but Joe loved it.

A scratch golfer by the time he was 15, Carr played off plus one when he was 17. For the next 30 years, incredibly, he retained a handicap of plus one or better, and because of his tremendous golfing deeds, Sutton became a breeding ground for good golfers. All the younger players wanted to emulate the great Joe Carr and the club was soon able to boast several Irish international players among its membership. Indeed, the tiny club once had an annual fixture against England's largest county, Yorkshire, and they were magnificent matches. Sutton, always captained by Carr, turned out all their international and inter-provincial players and, likewise, Yorkshire always played at full strength. The matches were the highlight of both Sutton's and Yorkshire's golfing year and ended only when Carr eased himself out of the competitive golf scene in the early 1970's having, by then, achieved almost everything available to him in amateur golf.

Joe still going strong twenty years later

His first major win in golf was the

East of Ireland Open Amateur Championship in 1941, a title he was to win on 11 more occasions. He was also West of Ireland champion 12 times, won the South of Ireland three times, the Irish Amateur Championship six times and the Irish Open Amateur four times. But his greatest achievements were in winning three British Amateur Championships. His first was at Hoylake in 1953 when he beat American Harvie Ward on the last green in the 36-hole final; in 1958, he beat the former English Champion Alan Thirlwell 3 and 2 at St Andrews and two years later at Portrush he crushed American Bob Cochran 8 and 7.

The list of his golfing achievements is impressive. He represented Great Britain and Ireland ten times in the Biennial Walker Cup matches against the United States, captaining the side twice, and represented Ireland in the home internationals 23 times from 1947 to 1969 without ever missing a year. Carr played with and against all the great amateurs during his quarter of a century at the top of the amateur golfing tree, including Jack Nicklaus before he turned professional, and is still known and revered throughout the world. As well as being a fine and exceptionally strong golfer, Carr was also one of the best-loved characters of the game and made an outstanding captain of both the Great Britain and Irish teams. Rodney Foster, another of the game's exuberant characters, recalls playing under Carr's captaincy in the 1964 World Amateur Team Championship in Rome. 'We were leading the world at the halfway stage and Joe promised us he would sing a song in the Hilton Hotel dining room at the end of the week if we won,' said Foster. 'We did – and Joe sang "Danny Boy" to a packed audience. He had a terrible voice but all the diners gave him a standing ovation.'

Perhaps Carr's greatest pleasure from the game was in watching his son, Roddy, play an heroic role in Great Britain and Ireland's historic Walker Cup victory over the Americans at St Andrews in 1971. Young Roddy was undefeated, winning three and a half points from a possible four, and his scalps included Lanny Wadkins. Tom Kite was also in that defeated American team. On that memorable and emotional day in May Roddy had provided Joe Carr with his happiest golfing memory. He told friends in St Andrews that night: 'Now I've seen it all.' It was at that point, at the age of 49, that Joe Carr decided to retire quietly from competitive golf.

1987 – 'The Grand Match' – former Walker Cup players against ex Ryder Cup men

# *CAREER RECORD*

**Victories**

| | |
|---|---|
| 1946 | Irish Amateur Open Championship |
| 1950 | Irish Amateur Open Championship |
| 1953 | British Amateur Championship |
| 1954 | Irish Amateur Championship, Irish Amateur Open Championship |
| 1956 | Irish Amateur Open Championship |
| 1957 | Irish Amateur Championship |
| 1958 | British Amateur Championship |
| 1960 | British Amateur Championship |
| 1963 | Irish Amateur Championship |
| 1964 | Irish Amateur Championship |
| 1965 | Irish Amateur Championship |
| 1967 | Irish Amateur Championship |

Joe smiling again – this time after a 64 at Gullane in the qualifying round for the Open

**Did you know…**

1. Joe Carr played 23 successive years for Ireland in the home internationals series, beginning his run in 1947.
2. At one time, with money very tight, Joe sold 50 of his silver trophies. To his eternal regret, and despite strenuous efforts, he has been unable to trace them since.
3. His happiest moment in golf came as he watched his son Roddy play a major role in the historic Walker Cup victory when Great Britain and Ireland beat the U.S.A. in 1971.

# ARNOLD PALMER

**Multi-millionaire Arnold Palmer's magnetic charm, rugged good looks and power golf game earned him worldwide admiration and sparked off the modern golf boom.**

His shirt still hangs limply over his shoulders, and his trousers continue to fight a losing battle to remain somewhere around his waistline, an intriguing tussle that has gone on now in full public view for 30 years and more. He is to professional golf what Elvis was to rock 'n' roll, Jimmy Dean to rebels and Marilyn Monroe to calendars. He is Arnold Palmer and the instant he steps out of his Cadillac at a golf course anywhere in the world, the word is passed on in excited, hushed, even reverential tones: 'Arnie's here'.

Despite being born in 1929, making him considerably closer to a free bus pass than the first blush of youth, Palmer remains firmly fixed in the American sporting consciousness as a giant of the game. He is simply a living legend and deservedly so. If he is no longer hitting the living daylights out of golf balls, Arnie remains a glowing, sun-tanned advertisement for the benefits of an outdoor life. The son of a greenkeeper, Palmer now owns the course which his father tended, and where he learned the game by slipping out to play when the members had gone home.

Arnie celebrates another birdie putt

Palmer is the focal point of the modern game. Jack Nicklaus has said that every pro should consider giving Palmer a percentage of his earnings. No one disagrees. Palmer brought an extraordinary talent out of a very ordinary background three decades ago and every professional has since reaped the benefits of Arnie's exploits.

Palmer's story is a case of the right man arriving in town at exactly the right time. In the late 60's television had just worked out the technology to cover golf properly and Palmer, with his chin-up, go-for-everything style, brought a new excitement sweeping into the sport. Housewives throughout the States stopped baking apple and blueberry pies when Arnie was on the screen slicing, hooking and hitting the ball with all his might. His attraction was two-fold: first he seemed to swing like an amateur but scored like a pro. Secondly, the familiar, chiselled face always told you what was going on inside the man.

Almost overnight Palmer became a national hero, a man who never knew when to give up and who seemed to symbolise America's romantic idea of itself. A hundred years earlier, or so the fans believed, Palmer would have been using

those same Popeye-like forearms to heave an axe and clear a site for a house in a virgin forest somewhere. To them he was, and still is, Davy Crockett, John Wayne and Audie Murphy rolled into one.

To be fair, Arnie has never let the fans down. He remains a man of the people despite a lifestyle that would fit more closely into Dallas or Dynasty than Downtown America. His is one of the best known faces in the States and one of the most loved. He has an image that has never been even slightly rolled in the dirt, so the biggest corporations in the land queue to get him to endorse their products. It means that his face is pushed at you from every magazine, every subway advert in the U.S.A. Watches, swimming pools, cars, oil business machines, all have Palmer as their advocate and, of course, he is responsible for selling more golf equipment to the masses than any other player in history. Even when he sleeps he makes big money on sales of endorsed products.

And as the money continues to roll in like some relentless tide, Palmer enjoys

The gallery ready to cheer Arnie yet again and (left) blasting clear of the sand in the World Matchplay

Playing a left-handed shot to find his way clear and (right) 'Ouch! How did that one miss?'

spending it. For years now he has owned and flown his own private jet, indulging in the occasional victory roll as he arrives at Augusta for the U.S. Masters or at some other point on the seemingly never-ending U.S. Tour. He once earned a rebuke from team captain Ben Hogan when he did a roll before a Ryder Cup match! These days it is the Seniors Tour that grabs most of his attention and he is still capable of putting together an outstanding round, still as competitive as ever.

Still the fans remain loyal to this ex-Marine who still wears the look of a man anxious to establish a beach head on some distant shore. In the old days there were so many fans and they were so partisan to his cause they were soon nicknamed 'Arnie's Army', a noisy supportive group who were worth at least a shot a round to their man. Once the connection was made between their desire and his adrenalin, Palmer simply exploded into action.

His career started in earnest in 1954

when he became the United States Amateur Champion. The next year he turned professional and won the Canadian Open in his rookie year. Between then and 1973, when his eyes began to let him down on the putting green, Palmer won an astonishing 61 titles in America. These included four U.S. Masters and one U.S. Open. Curiously he never won a U.S.P.G.A. Championship. Abroad he has won 19 titles and dramatically rejuvenated the British Open in the early 60's. He won the Open in 1961 and 1962 but it was his mere attendance at our Open that once more lifted the Championship to the very forefront of world golf. Before Palmer crossed the Atlantic there was a growing tendency for the top American players to ignore the Open. Arnie, typically, denounced his peers' attitude towards the oldest major championship and blazed a trail that literally forced the rest to follow in his footsteps. Keith Mackenzie, then secretary of the Open's governing body, the Royal and Ancient Golf Club of St Andrews, says: 'Without Arnold, the Open would not be the great Championship it is today'.

Still turning on the style on the Seniors Tour

And he still comes. He does so because he loves the occasion, he feeds off the crowds and because he still wants to bend his knee in the general direction of the game that has made his name and his fortune. The joy he shows when he plays well on the over 50's Seniors Tour, which took off when he joined it, is just the same as it was 30 years ago when he first turned professional. Age has not dimmed this grandfather, nor the world's appreciation of his unique talent. Arnie is a one-off. Catch him if you can.

# *CAREER RECORD*

**Victories**

| | |
|---|---|
| 1954 | U.S. Amateur Championship |
| 1955 | Canadian Open |
| 1956 | Insurance City Open, Eastern Open |
| 1957 | Houston Open, Azalea Open, Rubber City Open, San Diego Open |
| 1958 | St Petersburg Open, U.S. Masters, Pepsi Golf |
| 1959 | Thunderbird Invitational, Oklahoma City Open, West Palm Beach Open |
| 1960 | Insurance City Open, U.S. Masters, Palm Springs Classic, Baton Rouge Open, Pensacola Open, U.S. Open, Mobile Sertoma Open, Texas Open |
| 1961 | British Open, San Diego Open, Texas Open, Baton Rouge Open, Phoenix Open, Western Open |
| 1962 | British Open, U.S. Masters, Palm Springs Classic, Classic, Texas Open, Phoenix Open, Tournament of Champions, Colonial National, American Golf Classic |
| 1963 | Thunderbird Classic, Pensacola Open, Phoenix Open, Western Open, Los Angeles Open, Cleveland Open, Philadelphia Open |
| 1964 | Oklahoma City Open, U.S. Masters |
| 1965 | Tournament of Champions |
| 1966 | Los Angeles Open, Tournament of Champions, Houston Champions International, U.S. P.G.A. Team Championship (with Jack Nicklaus) |
| 1967 | Los Angeles Open, Tucson Open, American Golf Classic, Thunderbird Classic |
| 1968 | Bob Hope Desert Classic, Kemper Open |
| 1969 | Heritage Classic, Danny Thomas Classic, Diplomat Open |
| 1970 | Four-ball Championship (with Jack Nicklaus) |
| 1971 | Bob Hope Desert Classic, Citrus Open, Westchester Classic, U.S.P.G.A. National Team Championship (with Jack Nicklaus) |
| 1975 | British P.G.A. Championship, Spanish Open |
| 1980 | U.S. P.G.A. Seniors Championship |
| 1981 | U.S. P.G.A. Seniors Championship |
| 1982 | Marlboro Classic, Denver Post Champions |
| 1983 | Boca Grove Senior Classic |
| 1984 | U.S. P.G.A. Senior Championship, Senior Tournament Players' Championship, Quadel Senior Classic |
| 1985 | Senior Tournament Players' Championship |
| 1988 | Crestar Classic |

The 1961 Open champion

# BEN CRENSHAW

Just when it seemed as if popular Ben Crenshaw might never win a major he found his putting touch on the back nine at Augusta and roared to victory.

Sometime in 1976 a computer boffin decided it would be a useful exercise to try and work out what the ideal height and weight of a professional golfer might be, using the statistics provided by the men who play week in week out on the American circuit. The result suggested that the ideal height was 5ft 9ins, and the perfect weight 12 stones. It was close to but did not exactly fit Jack Nicklaus and it nearly mirrored Tom Watson. In fact, without knowing, a computer had produced the exact (if not vital) statistics of Ben Crenshaw. In some ways it was not much of a surprise. He has always been everyone's idea of a success. Forget his golf. Even standing still he looks good on the course!

Yet Ben Crenshaw is always chasing perfection and gets angry when things go wrong. If you had been standing beside him at the eighteenth green at Royal Lytham while he waited to see if young Seve Ballesteros could beat him to the Open in 1979 – which the Spaniard, of course, duly did – you would have heard enough expletive's spill from 'Gentle Ben's' lips to satisfy a truck full of labourers on their way to work on a cold, rainy, Monday morning. In the 1987 Ryder Cup match at Muirfield Village he was so disgusted with his form that after a few holes he thumped his favourite putter into the ground so hard that the head snapped off and he had to finish his match against Eamon Darcy using his wedge or 3-iron on the greens. As well as losing his temper he lost his match on the last green and crawled away in embarrassment to sit forlornly on the bank watching an American side lose for the first time on American soil.

'Get in there!' – Ben Crenshaw on his way to his 1984 Masters win

But away from the pyrotechnics of the golf course there is no more courteous or gallant sole in the game. It is just that, for Ben, a place in the game's history books is as important as drawing breath itself. Ideally he would love to win an Open at St Andrews! He had come close many times in each of the four majors only to falter towards the end as though drawing back in alarm at the scale of what he was about to accomplish. That is, until the U.S. Masters at Augusta in 1984. Although the British Open, shrouded in its great history, was always the prize Crenshaw craved his next most serious target had always been the Masters. He has never been a consistent player, not even from one hole to the next, but whenever an errant drive or a mis-timed approach shot has threatened his round with terminal damage, his putter has arrived like the Seventh Cavalry to save the day. He is without doubt the best putter of his generation, a positive yet delicate stroker of the ball. He has always been a man who honestly expects to hole, no matter how

far it is from the flag stick, nor how devilish the borrow. With his touch, slick Augusta suits him, if you like, to a tee. Augusta where the Masters is staged annually could be said to be set up for him. With no rough to devour his tee shots and fairways wider than a Los Angeles freeway, Crenshaw has been able to 'go for it' every time he has played in Georgia. Augusta's defences are the frighteningly fast greens, but he has been in his element in the sharply sloping and triple cut areas of perfectly manicured grass on which the event is won and lost each year.

Crenshaw took as naturally to playing golf as some others in the Lone Star State take to drilling for oil. At the University of Texas, a famed breeding ground for future golf stars, he won the North American Collegiate Championship not once but three years in a row before turning professional in 1973. The often difficult problem of gaining a U.S. Tour Players card was easily overcome when he won the Tour school by an astonishing 12 strokes. It meant that when fair-haired Crenshaw finally stepped onto the first tee in his first big time event, the San Antonio Texas Open, his arrival on the professional scene was being heralded almost as if it was the second coming!

It seemed certain that whatever happened next could only be an anti-climax. Yet Crenshaw was not finished. His confidence on supercharge, he more than lived up to all the hype by winning the title. Texas went just a little madder.

A devoted country and western fan, Ben's soft Texan drawl and easy-going manner soon gave him the nickname

In action at the 1988 U.S. Open (top) and celebrating his Masters win at Augusta (above)

Gentle Ben. It is in some respects a perfect description of the man, and yet in other ways it is very far from the truth. There is, you see, underneath that gentle exterior a bubbling volcano of emotion. He may never lose his patience with anyone else, but he is constantly fighting to forgive himself his own errors out on the course. The truth is that he is not just a self-confessed traditionalist golf nut who collects the game's memorabilia and who can talk for hours on the swings and playing records of the 19th and 20th Century heroes, he is also a perfectionist, a man who cannot easily accept his own human frailties.

Crenshaw's love affair with Augusta had been unrequited until 1984 when at last he achieved his goal of winning at least one major title in his career with a 4 under par 68 which gave him victory by two shots over Tom Watson. The tears of relief and joy flowed from Ben's eyes. At least he had his place in history, his name had been woven into a game's fabric. He had earned a locker in the champion's room with Nicklaus, Palmer and the rest. His comment, as he cradled his Green Jacket afterwards, told you everything you needed to know about the man. 'I feel humbled. That's the only way to describe it,' he said. Standing with him was his father, his most loyal supporter on the course, and in the dark days after his marriage break-up and messy divorce.

Twelve months later it was all so different for him as his health deteriorated and his game disintegrated. A year after becoming Masters' champion he tumbled to 149th position on the U.S. money list. It was not so much a fall from grace, it was a nose dive towards oblivion. Rumours were rife. Then late in the year his doctor diagnosed an overactive thyroid. The months of worry were over. The correct medication saw an instant improvement and in 1986 it was just like old times again when he finished in eighth place on the U.S. Tour's money list.

He still wants to add another major to his Masters triumph, and is young enough to do so. Settled happily into his second marriage he is still, at 37, capable of winning any week. His problem is that in the majors he tends to try too hard.

## *CAREER RECORD*

Ben and his hard-earned Green Jacket

**Victories**

| | |
|---|---|
| 1973 | San Antonio – Texas Open |
| 1976 | Bing Crosby National Pro-Am, Hawaiian Open, Ohio Kings Island Open, Carrolls Irish Open |
| 1977 | Colonial National Invitational |
| 1979 | Phoenix Open, Walt Disney World Team Championship (with George Burns) |
| 1980 | Anheuser-Busch Classic |
| 1983 | Byron Nelson Classic |
| 1984 | U.S. Masters |
| 1986 | Buick Open, Vantage Championship |
| 1987 | U.S. F and G Classic |
| 1988 | Doral Ryder Open |

**Did you know...**

1. Ben Crenshaw won his U.S. Tour card in 1973 and promptly won the first tournament in which he played on the circuit – the San Antonio Texas Open.
2. Ben Crenshaw won the N.C.A.A. Championship (the main American College title) three years in a row from 1971 and was named College Golfer of the Year three times as well.
3. Crenshaw slumped out of the top ten money winners to finish 149th in the 1985 season in America. His form slump was caused, he discovered later, by an over-active thyroid.
4. Ben Crenshaw lists a varied number of hobbies – fishing, bird-watching, collecting golf artifacts, country western music and golf course architecture.
5. With Mark McCumber, Ben Crenshaw won the Philip Morris World Cup for America in 1988 at Royal Melbourne in Australia.
6. Ben Crenshaw's only victory on the European circuit was the Irish Open at Portmarnock in 1976.
7. In the 1987 Ryder Cup, Crenshaw broke his putter in the singles match with Eamonn Darcy and had to use a wedge or 3-iron on the greens for most of the round. He lost on the last green.

# *CURTIS STRANGE*

The first man to make a million dollars on the American circuit in one season, Curtis Strange is after more majors and hoping for more rounds like the one at St Andrews in 1987!

Another glorious bunker shot from Curtis Strange

Crowd control that hot June day at The Country Club in Brookline, Massachussets, had been deplorable but the smile on the face of Curtis Strange just before five o'clock was the smile of a man who, at last, had got a monkey off his back. With tears in his eyes as he caught sight of his attractive blonde-haired wife Sarah in the gallery hugging Gill Faldo, wife of Nick Faldo the man he beat, Strange had finally lost the tag no golfer ever wants to be saddled with.

That afternoon Strange won the 1988 U.S. Open. It was his first major. No longer would be referred to in previews for the Masters, the U.S. Open, the U.S.P.G.A. and even the Open here in Britain as the best golfer on the American circuit still to win one of those titles Jack Nicklaus made a habit of collecting. Strange had made the breakthrough to the big time and what a popular winner he was.

The enthusiastic crowd that day and the excited stewards knew exactly what winning meant to Strange and it was far more than realising a dream by winning his country's own national Championship. He had tied on ten under par after 72-holes thanks to a superb bunker shot to within a couple of inches from a trap guarding the front of the left green. Faldo from the back left fringe, had faced a downhill putt with a subtle double borrow for a winning birdie three but got the line fractionally wrong. Next day they

Checking the line at Augusta

Celebration – the 1988 U.S. Open Champion

played off with Faldo, already a major winner (at Muirfield the year before), the favourite over Strange, the man who was finding majors tough to win.

In fact Strange shot 71 and Faldo, never comfortable, took 75. Strange had waited a long time but, at 33, the Virginian with the prematurely grey hair and a flashing smile he did not always have, had made the grade. Afterwards, and still emotional at this success, he said; 'This means I have done what every little boy dreams about when he plays by himself late in the afternoon. He uses four balls and in his mind one belongs to Ben Hogan, another to Arnold Palmer and there is one too for Jack Nicklaus. The fourth ball is his and it is that ball that wins. Ninety-nine per cent of the time that dream does not come true. Today it did and I look on this as the first of many. It might end up being the only one but it is a start.'

It was to prove the highlight of a remarkable year for the golfer who, as a teenager, proudly attended Wake Forest College in North Carolina on an Arnold Palmer scholarship. Arnie was an old boy there as well. By the time the last putt had dropped on the 1988 season – and it happened to be Strange's at the short seventeenth in a winning play-off against the always luckless Tom Kite in the Nabisco Grand Prix at Pebble Beach – Curtis had made history by winning 1,147,644 dollars in a single season and, in the process stretching his career earnings since joining the Tour at his second attempt in 1977 to just over 4.25 millions. Only Jack Nicklaus and Tom Watson are ahead of him and he is closing in on them fast! When you consider that Strange, according to his management team, earns two or three times as much off the course with lucrative corporate contracts as he does on it, you can understand why he is now one of the game's most successful personalities. In 1988 he was voted America's Golfer of the year for the third year running. No one could touch him in 1988.

The kid from Virginia Beach, who had cleaned up on the amateur scene without ever having won the big prize of the U.S. Amateur title, had joined the list of golfing greats 23 years after deciding to quit playing baseball, in which he was even then an above average pitcher and hitter, to devote his time to golf. Baseball's loss has been golf's gain but sadly, as in the case of Jack Nicklaus whose father died early in his professional career, Strange's father was not on hand to see the drama unfold at Brookline. He died when Curtis and his twin brother Allan, older by 60 seconds, were just 14.

If Curtis chose golf it was really hardly surprising. He was, after all, born into a ready-made golfing environment. His father owned a golf course and it was there that young Strange and his brother, who for a time played Tour golf as well before opting instead for the more settled life of a stockbroker, whiled away the summer days. Strange was hitting a fair ball when he was just eight-years-old and when he was 15 he took his first title when he became the Virginian Junior champion. It was all just fun to Curtis but it earned him the Wake Forest scholarship.

Before he turned pro Strange won the prestigious North and South Championship twice, the Western title and the Eastern which, because his father had won it 18 years earlier, was particularly satisfying. He also played Walker Cup and was low amateur at the Masters where he hopes one day to be presented with the winner's Green Jacket. Characteristically he is not certain whether he would want to hang it in the exclusive upstairs Champions' locker room or pop it in a locker downstairs with the rest of the lads. He will do the right thing if and when it happens and he does feel it will one day. After all Strange was the man who opened with an 80 in 1985 at Augusta and with nine holes to play had turned golfing disaster into possible triumph by opening up a four shot lead on the field.

He blew it. He dumped approach shots into the water at the thirteenth and fifteenth, swinging badly at just the wrong time. It was all the encouragement the fast-finishing Bernhard Langer needed. The West German came with a late charge to pip him. Those fans who had not detected a subtle change in Strange's attitude, might have expected to see a show of temper from him on the course and those reporters who were not regulars on the circuit might have expected him to be a 'no-show' in the

'It's there!' – the Ryder Cup in 1987

press room. There was in fact no visible temper. He did have a frustrated look on his face but he did not turn on an unexpecting azalea and decapitate it with his 9-iron or wedge – something that would certainly not have impressed the Masters officials who are sticklers for good old-fashioned manners.

Neither did he shirk his cross-examination by the press although bitterly disappointed. He gave the press corps plenty of his time at the end and in the process won over many of his earlier critics. The old Strange, who had so embarrassingly sounded off at Arnold's Palmer Bay Hill Classic in 1982 and been humiliated publicly for it by the great man, had changed. The golfer who looked so grim and surly in his early years as he tried to cope with the pressure of the Tour, and who had acted so aggressively and abruptly at times as to be almost unapproachable, had mellowed and matured. He had learned more about himself, what made him tick, and as a result had learned to control his temper and keep his emotions in check. He had also learned to smile when things were going right and to stoically accept the kicks of a game that no one has ever claimed was meant to be fair. It was such a transformation that Strange himself called it his big career 'turnaround'.

Winning the Canadian Open later in 1985 helped the rehabilitation process after the Masters disappointment. De-

Curtis looking stylish in shorts

spite the way he had behaved on and off the course just after the Masters had finished and Langer had been welcomed into the Club, Strange had privately been furious with himself for letting the tournament slip through his fingers.

Throughout his career and following the death of his father, it was former World Senior champion Chandler Harper who took Strange under his wing. He is never short of praise for the late Harper and the role he played in the success story but now his guru is Jimmy Ballard who taught him to understand his swing so well that Curtis claims he can now fine-tune it, if necessary, in mid-round.

It was in 1985 too that Strange was involved in controversy surrounding the Open in Britain. He chose to pass it up to play instead at Kingsmill, his home town, the week before as defending champion and in Holland the week after, for substantial appearance money. That latter deal had been struck months before. Royal and Ancient officials kept diplomatically quiet about Strange's non-appearance in what would be Sandy Lyle's Open, but their disappointment was still obvious. Strange got a roasting in the British press because there was just a hint that, unlike the great players of the previous 20 years, Strange may have had little respect for the Open.

In fact he looks forward to them more and more these days. The only reason he down-plays the majors, he told an American golf columnist, is to keep himself from getting too excited about them. Missing the 1985 Open had been just a peculiar set of circumstances. It was well enough known, anyway, that Strange had not stayed away because he had an aversion to seaside golf which tests not only nerve and technique but the ability to manufacture shots in conditions so different from those beautifully manicured fairways and soft, yielding greens encountered week-in, week-out on the U.S. Tour.

On the contrary, he had played in the Walker Cup at St Andews in 1975 and never lost a point, winning three games and halving another over the Old Course. Twelve years later in 1987 he would cause a certain amount of consternation in the Big Room in the R and A Clubhouse when he had the temerity to hole a birdie putt on the historic eighteenth for an Old Course record of 62. Scoring like that was ridiculous! Conditions at the home of golf that day might have been ideal, but 62! It was a score which was marred only by the fact that it was not to help America in the final of the Dunhill Cup but only to help them in their third-place play-off against Scotland. Yet the round remains one of Strange's most treasured scores. Only the fact that it was achieved when there was little or no pressure on him prevents it being his all-time great round.

Strange is not a stay-at-home American like many who, Tony Jacklin asserts, feel uncomfortable if they cannot, at all times see the flashing neon-sign of a Macdonalds or a Kentucky Fried Chicken fast-food outlet. Strange is quite prepared to move around the world playing golf the only way he knows how – with his competitive juices flowing. Whether it be for a million or a few dollars in a practice round with his mates on Tour, Strange always wants to win. He works hard but now can afford to spend more time at home with wife Sarah, a childhood sweetheart he met at a college dance, and his two sons Thomas and David. He loves fishing and will happily relax by spending all night out in a boat in the middle of a river.

Yet he is never away from golf and tournaments too long, as if afraid that the magic he has for low-scoring might somehow, illogically disappear if he allowed himself to get even just a little rusty. Strange is a thrifty fellow, not mean, just careful which is how you might also describe his golf these days. The swing is just a little shorter and, although there is a notable sway of the body, he compensates for it beautifully. Most of all it is his approach to the game that has helped him sweep to the top of the American golfing dollar mountain and genuinely challenge Severiano Ballesteros as best golfer around.

His inspiration has always been and always will be his father. When he finally made it into the elite category and won the U.S. Open he said firmly yet in a voice packed with emotion: 'This was for my dad.' Then, with a lump in his throat he continued: 'I have waited a long time to do this, a long time to thank the people who gave me the advice I needed, the enthusiasm and the knowledge to continue on. Most of all I have to thank my dad. When I was nine I would go to work with him in the morning and come home with him late at night. I learned the basics of my golf swing from him and a lot of other things I probably cannot remember but which I do subconsciously and a couple of things, too, I do and think about nearly every day. Winning the U.S. Open is the greatest thing I have ever done, the greatest feeling I have ever had and it means so much to me. It means that all the work and the time and effort I have put into my golf has paid off. It has got me to a new level.'

It is impossible not to like and admire Curtis Strange, who is yet another in the long line of sportsmen who have been, or are, a tribute to the game. His father would have been proud of him.

## *CAREER RECORD*

### Victories

| | |
|---|---|
| 1979 | Pensacola Open |
| 1980 | Michelob Houston Open, Manufacturers Hanover-Westchester Classic |
| 1983 | Sammy Davies Jun. Greater Hartford Open |
| 1984 | LaJet Classic |
| 1985 | Honda Classic, Panasonic Las Vegas Invitational, Canadian Open |
| 1986 | Houston Open |
| 1987 | Canadian Open, Federal Express St Jude Classic, N.E.C. World Series of Golf |
| 1988 | U.S. Open, Independent Insurance Agent Open, Memorial Tournament, Nabisco Championship |

### Did you know...

1. Curtis Strange became the first golfer to win one million dollars in one American season in 1988 when he won four events plus a Nabisco bonus.
2. Curtis Strange holds the record for the Old course at St Andrews. In the 1987 Dunhill Cup competition he went round in ten under par 62 breaking the old record by three.
3. Hale Irwin, twice a winner of the U.S. Open, considers that Curtis Strange is currently the best player in the world.
4. By the time Curtis Strange was eight years old he was playing golf every day. His father was a golf professional and owned the White Sands Country Club in Virginia Beach, Virginia.

The 1988 U.S. Open Champion

# *TOM WATSON*

It may be that Tom Watson will be the last golfer to so conclusively dominate the American circuit but the magic lasted only so long. Today his trusty putter is cold.

Tom Watson could arguably be the last great superstar in American golf. For eight years from 1977 he dominated the game winning the money list five times. He collected no fewer than five Open Championships in nine years from 1975 and needs just one more to equal Harry Vardon's record.

Now six times P.G.A. Player of the Year Watson is suffering a loss of form caused by a sick putter and burgeoning off-course interests. Winning has suddenly become for him a lot more difficult. In recent years only a Nabisco Grand Prix win at Houston has lightened the gloom of the man with the freckle-face of a latter-day Tom Sawyer, a man who does not have the natural charisma of a Seve Ballesteros, and who even when he was playing at his most devastating still managed somehow to look like your next-door neighbour out for a few holes before dinner. Maybe it was because he never dressed like a superstar. Not for Watson the designer-made, colour-co-ordinated clothes cut to the latest fashion. If they were, they were always incredibly subdued in style and colour. Of course Tom has always been a golfer who has played well within himself and who has controlled his emotions superbly. When he holed his pitch from the rough at the side of the short seventeenth en route to a dramatic victory over everyone's great rival Jack Nicklaus in 1982, it was uncharacteristic for the smiling Watson to dance a jig of delight around the green. Mind you, that shot-in-a-million on the Pacific ocean course comes into that extra special category. Amazingly he had told long-serving caddie Bruce Edwards that he thought he might hole it before he played, despite the fact that, in ice-skating terms, the degree of difficulty surrounding its execution was immense.

Tom Watson on the way to his 5th Open at Royal Birkdale

One man who watched the shot go in with considerable pleasure was another great American golfer and record breaker Byron Nelson, who since 1974 has been Watson's guru, adviser and friend. In return Watson proved a loyal friend to Nelson when his wife died after a long illness a few years ago. There is between the two golfing record-breakers a tremendous bond of respect. In fact Nelson can legitimately take some credit for setting Watson on the right lines after a series of disappointing failures, teaching him how to capitalise on the situation after having played himself into a winning position. It was just this very thing that prompted Nelson to approach Watson at the U.S. Open at Winged Foot in 1974 and suggest

they might work together. Watson had led at half way and finished joint fifth five behind winner Hale Irwin. There was work to be done and both knew it.

Until that meeting at Winged Food, Watson had had the unhappy reputation of being a golfing choker. He was not happy to be dubbed thus by the American golfing media, curiously unwilling to consider any form of praise in Watson's case at that time although they would rally round and applaud him when he became a spectacularly good winner. Form in golf may be a fickle thing but so, too, is the reporting of it. Watson, written off so many times in the early days as just another nice-guy in the pack, quickly became the man to write up as victory after victory made him yet another heir-apparent to the throne Jack Nicklaus had occupied for almost 15 years.

'Choker' is the charmingly cruel American sporting term for a player who, when it comes to the crunch, crumbles. They also call it taking the gas, easing back into the comfort zone. In Britain, for some curious reason, we call it losing one's bottle. Whatever it is called, it adds up to the same thing, a loss of nerve when faced with the final challenge and it is a terrible tag to pick up and an even harder one to lose.

At the 1988 U.S. Open (top) and Watson and Nicklaus in earnest discussions with officials at Turnberry in 1977 (above)

Yet to Watson's eternal credit he not only overcame this early slander with Nelson's help but has shown, beyond all reasonable doubt, that it was a nonsensical slur anyway upon one of the very finest golfers ever to grace the game. The early defeats and setbacks were just part of the painful learning process. He had to learn how to win. Yet until his first victory in the Western Open in 1974 a significant proportion of America's sportswriters had dismissed him as no more than a 'nearly man'. Since turning professional in 1971 he had promised much but delivered little in their eyes.

His problem was that he looked so

good. He looked as if he should be a winner. He could have panicked as the near-misses grew and the whispers began to turn into screams of derision but he did not. There were two reasons for this fortitude of mind and strength of spirit. Watson has always enjoyed that level of self-belief necessary to make the grade in the very top level of golf and as a psychology graduate from prestigious Stanford University in California he understood his psyche better than most men ever do. That first win on the U.S. Tour Watson had been a competitive golfing volcano waiting to erupt. With the Western Open

Firing clear of the rough in the 1983 Open (right) and celebrating another birdie at Augusta (below)

win on the exceptionally tough Butler National course in Chicago Watson 'erupted'. Was it any wonder that Jack Nicklaus, still king of the scene, began to look apprehensively over his shoulder at young Watson?

Over the next decade the constant duel between Nicklaus and Watson became the centre-piece of golf. The respect between the two men was obvious but the competitive spirit buried deep within them both inspired first one and then the other to discover the very sharpest ends of their respective skills. Nowhere did this happen more obviously than during the Open Championship at Turnberry in 1977. After 36-holes the pair were so far ahead of the rest of the field that they may as well have been playing a separate contest. The next 36-holes over the famed west of Scotland links became without doubt the most thrilling exhibition of golf seen in modern times. It was more than merely competitive, it was an epic struggle as each man matched the other stroke for stroke, birdie for birdie before an enthralled gallery watching mouths either open in silent astonishment or roaring their approval at the drama unfolding before their eyes. Coming to the last there was only a shot between them. Watson had the edge. Nicklaus drove off line close to some bushes but played a masterly recovery to 60 feet and holed for a birdie 3. Yet Watson, playing the hole impeccably, holed from 4ft to win. Earlier that same year Watson had triumphed over Nicklaus at the U.S. Masters but the Turnberry duel was something extra-special and, unlike the Masters battle, non-controversial. Watson had mistaken a wave of delight by Nicklaus at Augusta as a personal taunt. His misplaced anger probably drove him on to victory and certainly resulted in some fairly bitter post-match comments. Later Watson would admit his mistake and offer his apology to Nicklaus who, with typical grace, accepted it. Relationships between the two superstars today are fine but they have not become close friends. Perhaps this was inevitable. It is, after all, always difficult for the man who wears the crown to feel deep affection for the man who wants him off his throne.

There is no doubt either that Watson did remove Nicklaus from that throne, did depose him as number one golfer. By the early '80's' the Watson legend was well and truly established and the throne became his for a while as Nicklaus retreated into an elder statesman role. Statistically there can be no doubting Watson's genuine claims to the kingdom of golf. Between 1974 and 1987 he won 32 titles on the U.S. Tour, including two U.S. Masters and the dramatic U.S. Open that finally fell to him in 1982 at Pebble Beach, the magnificent links he used to play when he was a student along the coast at Stanford. He won there because he played one of the greatest shots ever witnessed and because towards the end he had only one man to beat, Jack Nicklaus. When Watson overclubbed at the par three 17th hole to leave his ball in thick, tangled grass behind and above the cup, Nicklaus allowed himself a tight, little smile as he waited by the eighteenth to see if Watson could catch him. It was an impossible shot to even think of holing or at least so improbably that most experts agreed Watson should have been lucky to escape with a one over par 4. Watson holed it for a birdie.

When anyone reviews Watson's career it is his record in the British Open that seals his sporting immortality. He won his first Open at Carnoustie in 1975 after an 18-hole play-off against Australia's gallant Jack Newton. He won again at Turnberry in 1977 and yet again at rainy Muirfield in 1980. He would admit he backed into victory at Royal Troon in 1982 but he won so well at Royal Birkdale in 1983, hitting a majestic two-iron into the heart of the last green to settle it. A prodigious effort by Seve Ballesteros prevented a hat-trick of victories at St Andrews a year later – a hat-trick that would have enabled him to equal that Vardon record. Yet failing to win at St Andrews hit Watson harder than anyone thought at the time. Suddenly the old confidence, the ability to strike a putt five feet past a hole and then make the return, the way Arnold Palmer used to do, deserted him like a man who has had his pocket picked. Having replaced Nicklaus, Watson was now replaced in turn by Ballesteros. The circle continued. Only the names are ever changed. Yet his record in the Open over such a short spell of time and at a period in golfing history when the strength-in-depth of fields has never been more impressive, is an astonishing achievement, possibly the most outstanding of post-war golf. These days Watson is still a force to be reckoned with but no longer the force he once was. His wife Linda, a significant driving force in his career, still urges him on but the old, electrifying response has, for the moment, gone.

When, in years to come, pundits look back on professional golf in the second half of the 20th Century you can be sure there will be legitimate praise for the pro's pro – Thomas Sturges Watson.

## *CAREER RECORD*

### Victories

1974 Western Open
1975 British Open, Byron Nelson Golf Classic, World Series of Golf
1977 British Open, Bing Crosby National Pro-Am, Wickes Andy Williams San Diego Open, U.S. Masters, Western Open
1978 Joe Garagiola Tucson Open, Bing Crosby National Pro-Am, Byron Nelson Golf Classic, Colgate Hall of Fame Classic, Anheuser Busch Classic
1979 Heritage Classic, Tournament of Champions, Byron Nelson Classic, Memorial Tournament, Colgate Hall of Fame Classic
1980 British Open, Andy Williams San Diego Open, Glen Campbell Los Angeles Open, M.O.N.Y. Tournament of Champions, New Orleans Open, Byron Nelson Classic, World Series of Golf, Dunlop Phoenix
1981 U.S. Masters, U.S. F. and G. New Orleans Open, Atlanta Classic
1982 British Open, Glen Campbell Los Angeles Open, Heritage Classic, U.S. Open
1983 British Open
1984 Seiko Tucson Match-play Championship, M.O.N.Y. Tournament of Champions, Western Open
1987 Nabisco Championship of Golf

### Did you know...

1. Jack Nicklaus shot two rounds of 66 in completing the 1977 Open at Turnberry in Scotland but Tom Watson beat him by a shot with rounds of 66 and 65.
2. Tom Watson was the first player to break the half-million mark in earnings in one season in 1980 when he won six tournaments on the U.S. circuit. His year's earnings in America amounted to 530,808 dollars.
3. Tom Watson has won the Open Championship five times matching the performance of J.H. Taylor, James Braid and Peter Thomson. Only Harry Vardon has won more often. He was champion six times.
4. Tom Watson has yet to win the U.S.P.G.A. Championship of golf's four majors. He has won five British Opens, two U.S. Masters and a U.S. Open.
5. Tom Watson topped the American money list four years in a row from 1977 and was American Player of the Year six times between 1977 and 1984.
6. Tom Watson graduated in psychology from Stanford University in California in 1971.
7. The shot Watson is remembered best for is the pitch he played from the rough beside the green at the U.S. Open at Pebble Beach in 1982. In a million-to-one chance he holed it and went on to beat Jack Nicklaus for the title.

The Open Champion – again!

# *LEE TREVINO*

Even lightning could not halt the career of extrovert wise-cracking, hugely talented Lee Trevino who is ready now to make another fortune on the American Senior circuit.

Mention the name Lee Trevino and it is odds on, despite his many achievements, that the conversation will turn quickly to his victory in the Open at Muirfield in July 1972. He retained the title that year but that was not the main point of that week's Championship. It is what he did to Tony Jacklin at the seventeenth hole in the final round that is always the talking point.

Jacklin, winner of the title in 1969 and the U.S. Open the following year, looked to be heading for another triumph. Jack Nicklaus, on a Grand Slam bid, had left his charge just too late on the last day and Jacklin had the edge too on Trevino coming down the seventeenth. They were level but the British golfer had hit two fine shots just short of the green. Trevino bunkered off the tee, was through the back and in the rough in four. If there had been a band up by the eighteenth green they would have been looking out the music for the British National Anthem. Then lady luck took a hand in things. Trevino, casually and with the air of a man who sensed he was going to lose, chipped his ball down and into the hole for a par 5. To the groans of the crowd Jacklin, his concentration ruffled, took four from the edge and carded 6. He never had a chance up the last. Trevino won, Nicklaus even pipped Jacklin for second place and he was, quite frankly, never the same competitor after that.

'Supermex' in action at the 1985 U.S.P.G.A.

Later that year, with Jacklin hardly having recovered from the Muirfield shock, they met again in a World Matchplay tie of such epic proportions that there was nothing quite like it until Sandy Lyle out-birdied Tsuneyuki Nakajima fourteen years later. After the first round of their 36 hole match Trevino led Jacklin by five shots with a 67 – and he needed another 67 to beat Tony on the thirty-sixth after the British golfer had hit him with a 63 including a six under par homeward nine of 32. Trevino that day proved his class as a golfer and as a competitor. Every court needs its jester and Lee 'Buck' Trevino fills that bill perfectly, but it must always be remembered that he is a more polished competitor than a crowd-pleasing ad-libber. His career has been helped by a superb sense of humour and he has often eased the pressure on himself by wise-cracking his way round. Yet in his young days he had little to laugh about.

Home was a shack just outside Dallas. There was no electricity, no running water and just four rooms to house Trevino, his sisters, his mother and his grandfather. He never knew his father, not even who he was, and by the time he was five Trevino was working in the fields

that spread out from the shack and where the family scratched a living by growing some cotton and onions. He was only a little older when he discovered the Country Club just a couple of miles down the road. He learned quickly that golfers would pay him a dollar or even two for the lost balls he would spend hours collecting. He did not know it at the time but golf would turn out to be his salvation. It would transpire that he had a god-given talent for the game.

The Dallas Athletic Club soon became the focal point of young Lee's life, a source of both revenue and enjoyment for the kid with the stocky frame and the smiling Mexican outlook on life. Most of the caddies at the Dallas Club were black and it was while messing around with them behind the caddie shack that Trevino learned the rudiments of a game that was to make him two fortunes – he lost one! More than that the caddies taught him how to hustle. 'These fellows taught

Another fine bunker shot (top) and, at the age of 44, the 1984 U.S.P.G.A. Champion

'How do I get out of here?'

me the killer instinct. When you have a guy on the rack on the course then you have to make damn sure you force him further down', he wrote once.

By the time he was in his teens, Trevino had made a name for himself. He could hit golf balls better with a taped up lemonade bottle than most golfers could manage with their shiny, new clubs. He was street sharp. Everything he did on the course was for a bet. Money was his motivation. He needed it to eat. He needed it to help the family.

Other people older than him liked making money too, however, and one or two of them saw in Lee Trevino the perfect man to ensure their own financial success. His golf was so good by this stage that a couple of 'the guys' started loaning him cash so that he could take part in big money matches, head to head contests with other hot-shot Texan golfers. They always got their cut until Trevino realised what was happening and took decisive avoiding action. He quit the scene!

Trevino was just 17 when he did what a lot of poor kids had done before him and still do. He joined the Marines. During his four years service Trevino rose to the dizzy heights of Lance-Corporal but far more importantly he spent the last 18 months of his army stint doing little else but play golf, teach golf or just talk golf as a member of the Marine's Special Services Unit. By the time he came out, Trevino was more than ready to turn professional.

By 1965, by which time he was almost 26, Trevino had learned more about life than some people twice his age. As he puts it himself 'I had developed a golf game good enough for the tour; I had had two marriages, one divorce and two kids. But one thing was still the same I was broke!'

Trevino was soon to solve his financial problems in spectacular fashion within just a few years. Later in life he had done so well that N.B.C. Television desperate to have him commentate for them, let him write his own lucrative contract!

He actually joined the Tour full-time in 1967, finishing a creditable 45th with 26,472 dollars in winnings. His style of play then, as now, was unorthodox and the way he lunged at the ball, his feet apparently fighting to retain balance,

Sizing up another approach shot at Augusta

Keeping those muscles warm (above), 'I like it' (left) and there goes another good one (below)

fooled some critics into believing that he would not, could not, last the pace. Keener observers noticed, however, that at the crucial point in the swing, that moment when the clubhead makes contact with the ball, Trevino was perfectly in control. His hand-eye co-ordination has always been phenomenal. The swing may have been unorthodox, and not stylish and his technique not one to recommend to anyone, but it worked for him magnificently. Trevino trumpeted his arrival into the higher echelons of American golf in the most stunning way. Like Jack Nicklaus his first victory in the big time saw him land the biggest prize – the U.S. Open. Winning the 1968 Open at Oak Hill, Rochester in upstate New York established Trevino's name and having jumped on the roller-coaster, he has never left it.

He won the U.S. Open again in 1971, this time beating Nicklaus in an 18 hole play-off and took the U.S. P.G.A. Championships in 1974 and incredibly in 1984 at the age of 44 at Shoal Creek, Alabama. Just for good measure this extraordinary man picked up two British Opens in 1971 and 1972. Indeed, in the space of just four weeks in 1971, he won three tournaments in succession – the U.S. Open, the Canadian Open and the British Open at Royal Birkdale. Lee Trevino had not just arrived, it seemed he was determined to challenge even Jack Nicklaus' supremacy on the glittering stages of the world.

But on June 27 1975 his life was torn apart. In truth, his life was almost taken from him when by a million to one fluke he was struck by lightning during the Western Open at Butler National Golf Club in Chicago. Along with his playing partner Jerry Heard, Trevino was lifted bodily into the air, deafened and stunned, and crashed back to earth to lie in a crumpled heap by the side of the thirteenth green. Apart from giving even him, tougher than most, a fright, the bolt from the blue caused permanent damage to his spine. The electrical shock had dissolved most of the lubricant between the discs of his vertebrae in the lower back and Trevino has paid the price ever since. 'Next time' he managed to quip, 'when God wants to play through I'll let him'. He left the course on a stretcher. For a time it seemed his career might be over. A series of operations has kept him going but he has had to adjust to the fact that his body which was once as strong as a mature ox, is now sometimes as weak as a kitten's. These days Trevino has to time his appearances on the Tour carefully and restrict the number of practice balls he hits before an event. He used to be able to hit 1,000 balls a time. Now he hits no more than 50! If the accident has damaged him physically, the lightning has, if anything, strengthened him mentally. His light-hearted, naturally enthusiastic attitude to life, is now even more focused on making sure he can get as much out of each day as he can. Yet at the same time he is a man of contradictions, a human being far more complex than his cabaret act on the course would have you believe. After his own childhood experiences he is well aware of the poverty everywhere and frequently gives money to charity, sometimes to individuals. The only proviso he puts on such gifts is that the recipient does not talk about them. The irony is, you see, that Lee Trevino, extrovert entertainer on the golf course is an intensely private and shy man at heart. He hates large functions and during any tournament he prefers to spend his evenings alone in his hotel room, watching television and dining off the room service menu. He started doing that after an inconsiderate autograph hunter kept annoying him at a private dinner. He is now married again, this time to a woman not much older than his elder son. They first met at a tournament when she tried to get his autograph. She was only a teenager then, several years later they met up again and got to know each other much better. She is his most loyal fan. He remains one of the great crowd pullers, and the gags still spill from his lips in a torrent but the more you get to know him, the more you realise these jokes are a defence against anyone breaking into his private life. He remains now what he was years ago as a poor, Mexican kid in Dallas, a loner. His fame is international, his popularity as strong as ever as he moves into the Senior Tour. He more than justifies his place among the golfing 'greats'.

# *CAREER RECORD*

The 1984 U.S.P.G.A. Trophy

## Victories

| | |
|---|---|
| 1968 | U.S. Open |
| 1969 | Tucson Open |
| 1970 | Tucson Open, National Airlines Open |
| 1971 | British Open, Tallahassee Open, Danny Thomas Memphis Classic, U.S. Open Canadian Open, Sahara Invitational |
| 1972 | British Open, Danny Thomas Memphis Classic, Hartford Open, St Louis Open |
| 1973 | Jackie Gleason Inverary Classic, Doral Eastern Open |
| 1974 | New Orleans Open, U.S. P.G.A. Championship, World Series of Golf |
| 1975 | Florida Citrus Open, Mexican Open |
| 1976 | Colonial National Invitational |
| 1977 | Canadian Open, Moroccan Grand Prix |
| 1978 | Colonial National Invitational, Benson and Hedges (UK), Lancome Trophy |
| 1979 | Canadian Open, Canadian P.G.A. Championship |
| 1980 | Tournament Players' Championship, Danny Thomas Memphis Classic, San Antonio Texas Open |
| 1981 | M.O.N.Y. Tournament of Champions |
| 1983 | Canadian P.G.A. Championship |
| 1984 | U.S. P.G.A. Championship |
| 1985 | Dunhill British Masters |

## Did you know...

1. Lee Trevino was carried off on a stretcher after being hit by lightning at the 1975 Western Open at Butler National, Chicago. Jerry Heard and Bobby Nichols were also hit. 'Next time God wants throught I'll step aside,' quipped Trevino.
2. Lee Trevino won three major titles in the space of four weeks in 1971 – the U.S. Open, the Canadian Open and the British Open.
3. When Lee Trevino scored an average of 69.73 for 82 rounds on the U.S. Tour in 1980 – it was the lowest Tour average since Sam Snead averaged 69.23 in 1950.
4. Lee Trevino was so poor in the early days that he often tells you that he had not seen an indoor toilet until he joined the U.S. Marines.
5. Lee Trevino was involved in one of the great matches in the World Match-play Championship at Wentworth with Tony Jacklin. Trevino won the match on the last green despite the fact that Jacklin completed the second 18 holes in ten under par 63 after going out in 31.

# LARRY NELSON

One of the quiet men of American golf, Larry Nelson, turned out to be a much tougher opponent in the more important Championships than many imagined he would be.

Larry Nelson in the sand at the Masters in 1988

Every professional dreams of winning at least one of golf's majors. A few win two but Larry Nelson, the quiet Georgian who only took up the game on the spur of the moment, is in that rare category. He has won three.

Nelson has won two U.S.P.G.A. Championships and, on both occasions as a result of it, gained a place at the eleventh hour in American Ryder Cup teams. He has also been successful in the U.S. Open, winning at the tough Oakmont Country Club in Pennsylvania in 1983 when Severiano Ballesteros and Tom Watson, then at his best, were the men he slid past so effectively. His closing 36-hole aggregate of 132 – ten under par – beat by four shots the previous Championship record for the last two rounds set up by Gene Sarazen in 1932 at Fresh Meadow. Just to underline how brilliantly he played, he covered the last 32 holes from the fifth in the third round in 11-under par, making a birdie almost every second hole and striking the ball with such precision that he missed only three greens in regulation.

His accuracy off the tee was the key to his success in a year when the United States Golf Association let the rough grow and effectively ruled out the use of the driver off the tee. Yet that June week when the stormy, thundery weather forced the final round to be carried over to the Monday, you had the feeling all along that Larry Nelson, who had proved himself at Atlanta in 1981 by winning the U.S. P.G.A., was going to assume the mantle of greatness with a triumph that would be talked about for years.

He achieved what he set out to do all right. He won – but then he discovered that no-one much cared. That rejection, real or imaginary, would colour his approach to the game for almost five years until, comfortably able to cope in his mind with what had happened immediately after Oakmont, he won another U.S.P.G.A. Championship in the sweltering, unbearable heat of North Palm Beach in 1987 after playing-off with that other Ryder Cup battler Lanny Wadkins. Curiously, you see, his 1983 U.S. Open victory which, you might have thought, would have brought him instant stardom and the in-depth media attention he had not received in 1981, turned out to be an even bigger letdown for the former illustrator at the Lockwood Aircraft factory in Marietta, Georgia. Having achieved that week at Oakmont something he would readily admit he never in his wildest dreams thought he or his game was good enough to do, he expected his victory to catch everyone's imagination. Sadly, as far as he was concerned, the glamour of his success seemed to be lost on the men and women who reported the Championship. Instead of being hailed as a hero, Nelson hardly received any recognition at all. It was almost as if the press, radio and television, despite his earlier major success, still considered him a fluke winner, a one-off seven-day wonder who would again slip back into the pack as quietly as he had emerged never to be heard of again. He did not even take a starring role that year in the official film of the Championship which dealt much more with the failure of Watson and Ballesteros rather than the triumph of the quiet, unassuming, non-charismatic but nevertheless fiercely competitive Nelson. He felt deflated at the reaction to his win when he should have been elated!

A stunned Nelson after just missing a long chip in the Ryder Cup

Talking later to the experienced Tom McCollister, sports writer for the *Atlanta Constitution* who did appreciate the magnitude of what he had done and how he had achieved it, Nelson said: 'When I had worked as hard as I had done to win the U.S. Open I probably expected more, not materially but from the press. Had an ordinary person done something similar in baseball or football it would have been a great story. It did not happen that way at Oakmont. Looking back the disappointment of the way it was perceived had much to do with the way I played from then until I won the 1987 U.S.P.G.A. You see, you are out to achieve things but if someone shares it and enjoys it with you it is more of an accomplishment. My feeling after the success at Oakmont had been played down was that if my triumph was going to be shoved under the rug then I would have much more fun staying home, turning to business and having a lot more fun with the family.'

The fact, too, that he started his own design company by using his talents as a commercial artist, bought a course in Atlanta, and started his own development company seemed to indicate he did mean to retire from the U.S. Tour at 40!

In fact he is still competing as fiercely and as modestly as ever having taken advantage of his so-called re-adjustment period to realise that he still enjoyed and wanted to keep competing. Sitting back quietly and taking stock had made him realise that giving up the Tour would pre-

In action in the Ryder Cup – he taught himself from Ben Hogan's book

vent him from experiencing ever again that very special feeling which only winners who have coped with the toughest pressure down to the line and come through with flying colours ever do. Happily Larry Nelson is not only continuing to play the US Tour with distinction but is talking about what he might achieve in 1997 when he becomes eligible for the Seniors circuit. What helped him cope, too, with what he felt was the lack of recognition of his Oakmont success was his deep relgious beliefs.

Larry Nelson was born in Marietta, Georgia, and had a normal enough upbringing. He studied hard and was good at sports, rather better as a pitcher in baseball than he was on the basketball court where his lack of height – he is five feet nine inches tall – went against him. He had never considered golf until, drafted into the Army and serving as an infantryman in Vietnam, he met and became friendly with a soldier who, to put it mildly, was a golf nut. On his demobilisation injury put paid to any ideas he might have had of becoming a professional baseball player and he turned to illustrating. He was 20 and had never hit a golf shot yet his friend had kindled an interest in him to 'try golf out for size'. He had nothing to lose and one day, with a little time on his hands, he drove into the range which he passed each day on his way to and from work. He did so purely on a whim. That visit changed his life. The very first ball he hit went long and straight. That was encouragement enough. The more he practised the more he liked golf and realised that maybe, if he were to stick in really hard, he could become very good. Every lunchtime he went to the range on Highway 41. He bought Ben Hogan's legendary instructional book *The Modern Fundamentals of Golf* and threw himself into golf with Hogan-like intensity, setting himself stiff targets. His wife bought him a set of clubs and within three months he had shot a nine-hole total of 37, within a year he was good enough to shoot in the 60's and was so determined to carve out a life for himself in golf that he had become a club assistant. After two years of continued improvement he was ready to try his hand at the Florida mini-tours and just three years after hitting that first shot he was good enough to qualify for the US Tour. It was all too easy. Suddenly, he found the razor-sharp competition too tough. It was six years before he won his first event at Inverary, Florida.

He turned out to be a great match-player and scored nine wins out of nine in the 1979 and 1981 Ryder Cup matches, forming a useful partnership with Wadkins. Yet there is a fickleness about golf. Suddenly, and for no apparent reason, he lost his game – especially his putting touch. Coming into the 1983 U.S. Open he was so far down the money list, had such a dismal playing record for the season that no-one gave him a second thought. He figured in no previews for the Championship except in his native Georgia where there was a courtesy paragraph. What nobody knew was that Jack Nicklaus, no less, emphasising the camaraderie of the Tour, had suggested a way he might improve his putting. It was to work wonders for him. When rain forced an abandonment of play on the final day Tom Watson, on the fourteenth, was leading Nelson, on the fifteenth by a shot. When they resumed the next morning Nelson, having hit his tee shot at the short sixteenth to 60 feet coaxed the putt in despite having to negotiate not one but two borrows and having to allow for a break of over a yard. In the end the 35-year-old gentle man from Georgia won by a shot. That gave him as big a thrill as winning the 1981 P.G.A. in his home town.

Concentrating more on business than golf, he slipped down the money list until falling out of the top 60 in 1986. When he arrived at Palm Beach for the 1987 U.S.P.G.A. where, just like at Oakmont, the rough was ludicrously thick just off the fairway, he was not even in the top 100 on the money list – but he played sensibly, conservatively and brilliantly to again win a major. He said he had promised himself he would not quit until he had won one more time. Yet having won again and enjoyed it, he knew that he could never give up competing. The Quiet Man is still going strong.

# *CAREER RECORD*

The 1987 U.S.P.G.A. Champion

## Victories

| | |
|---|---|
| 1979 | Jackie Gleason Inverary Classic, Western Open |
| 1980 | Atlanta Classic, Tokai Japan Classic |
| 1981 | Greater Greensboro Open, U.S. P.G.A. Championship |
| 1982 | U.S. Open, Dunlop International (Japan) |
| 1984 | Walt Disney World Golf Classic |
| 1987 | U.S. P.G.A. Championship, Walt Disney World Oldsmobile Classic |
| 1988 | Georgia-Pacific Atlanta Classic |

## Did you know...

1. Six months after hitting his first golf ball at a driving range near where he worked, 24-year-old Larry Nelson had turned professional. Four years later he was on the U.S. Tour.
2. In the first two Ryder Cup matches Larry Nelson played, he won nine points out of nine.
3. Larry Nelson is one of the stalwarts of the weekly Bible Class sessions held on the U.S. Tour.
4. Rain interrupted play in the last round of the 1983 U.S. Open at Oakmont, Pennsylvania. Nelson holed from 60 feet for a birdie when he returned the next morning to complete the round and went on to win.
5. When winning the U.S. Open that year Nelson shot 132 for the last two rounds – a Championship record.
6. Larry Nelson is a disciple of Ben Hogan. He carried Hogan's prized instructional book around with him all the time in the early stages of his career.

# JOHNNY MILLER

For a time his precision iron-play made Johnny Miller a challenger for Jack Nicklaus' crown but after his British Open in 1976 Miller had climbed all his golfing mountains.

Johnny Miller is one of the shooting stars of golf history. His was a talent that took off like a rocket, charged across the sky then sank, inexplicably, towards some distant sporting horizon, the impetus burned out. Few golfers have risen so high so swiftly. Few have returned to earth with quite as big a bump. Not that this should suggest that Miller must be judged ultimately as a failure. He is certainly not. No man who can boast 23 victories on the U.S. Tour, plus U.S. Open and British Open triumphs, deserves that description.

When you start analysing Miller's career it becomes clear that for a time he not only looked good, he played the game possibly better than it has been played either before or since. His swing has always seemed a gift from the gods but during the mid 70's Miller played like a sporting god himself. He was capable of doing no wrong. His form from 1973 to 1976 was quite breathtaking. Yet the first signs of what wonderful things were to come happened way back in 1966 when the U.S. Open was staged at Miller's home course, The Olympic Club, set high in the hills above San Francisco Bay.

He was 19 at the time and an outstanding amateur. Tall, blond and handsome he attracted attention wherever he played. When the U.S. Open circus hit town, young Miller eagerly added his name to the club list of caddies willing to haul bags round the hilly course just to be part of the Championship. In fact he did not need to caddie, battling his way through the demanding pre-qualifying system and employing a caddie of his own when he stood proudly on the first tee on the opening day of the competition. Miller was even prouder four days later when he stepped off the last green, having finished his first U.S. Open in an astonishing eighth place! Three years later he left Brigham Young University clutching a Physical Education degree and immediately turned professional. It would have been a surprise had he not done so. The agents had been hovering like vultures ever since the 1966 Open.

Johnny Miller at the 1987 U.S. Open

On the way to another birdie

Miller's first win came less than two years later when he took the Southern Open title in Columbus, Georgia. In 1972 he won again, rising to eighteenth in the U.S. money list. Even the great Jack Nicklaus began looking over his shoulder just a little apprehensively! Then, in the 1973 U.S. Open at Oakmont, Miller moved away from the sports sections and on to the front pages of America's newpapers by winning in record-breaking style. Miller powered to victory by recording an amazing last round 63, the lowest ever returned in U.S. Open history that stretched back to 1895. He did it with a brand of flowing, attacking golf that even had the baseball fans tuning in to watch. His round began with four successive birdies and included nine in all.

The following year Miller began the new season like a thoroughbred, trained to perfection, coming out of the stalls in the Derby. He made everyone else on the U.S. Tour look second rate. He won the first three tournaments of the year and went on to take another five titles. Understandably, he finished the year as number one. After each victory he just grinned and drawled: 'I feel I can win every week. All I can do is just keep on trying my very best.' It was clear that 1974 was going to be a hard act to follow. After all, how do you better a hat-trick of wins and eight victories in all?

But to his eternal credit, Miller came up with the answer. This time he won back-to-back events, the Phoenix Open and Tucson Open. More significantly, he won with an aggregate eight-round score of 49 shots under par. It was a blistering performance. No-one has ever won two events with that sort of scoring and possibly no-one ever will again. Miller took another two titles that year to end the season in number two spot just behind Nicklaus who had managed, as ever, to respond to the challenge of a worthy rival. Miller's coach John Gertson was of the view that Miller, who had worked hard to train his muscles for golf, had reached the point where he was not intimidated by his ability.

The following year Miller again kept up the pace, winning twice in America but more importantly taking the British Open after a thrilling duel with the young

1974 was easily his best year with eight victories

Seve Ballesteros over a sun-scorched Royal Birkdale course in Southport. And that really was it. There have been victories since, but Miller has never been quite the same player again. There is no obvious reason for this sudden decline, no injury, no personal problems. The Open victory was his ultimate goal. It was the Championship Tony Lema, another golfer associated with San Francisco's Olympic Club, had won. Miller, inspired by the exploits of that stylist who was so tragically killed in an air crash in 1966, had done what he had set out to do. The Birkdale win was the peak of his golfing Everest.

Perhaps, having achieved so much, it was just impossible for Miller to continue to sustain such a high-level of performance. Maybe his gnawing appetite had been satisfied and the real hunger for success which had driven him on was never to return. Maybe his own intense religious beliefs began to turn him towards what some might regard as a more substantial target. For some years now he has lived with his wife and six children in Salt Lake City. As a Mormon he has always given a significant percentage of his earnings to the church and these days he says that golf comes a distant third after his family and his faith. The man who for a time had been a model golfer, is undoubtedly a model human being. And he is perhaps a man who has got his life into the correct perspective. What is beyond doubt is that he was golfer who had the game of golf more completely under his control for a couple of years than anyone else in recent history. Now, when he talks about those explosive days when his swing flowed out of him like an irresistible tidal wave of talent, Miller himself shakes his head as he contemplates what he did and how he did it. 'When I was really on my game it was as though I did not have to even think about it. In fact when I stood over my ball, my mind just sort of went completely blank. By the time I actually hit the ball I was on another planet. Even I got excited when looked up and saw the sort of shot I hit'.

Johnny Miller, grateful for his glory years, deserves his place in our Hall of Fame.

## *CAREER RECORD*

### Victories

| | |
|---|---|
| 1971 | Southern Open |
| 1972 | Heritage Classic |
| 1973 | U.S. Open, World Cup (team with Jack Nicklaus) |
| 1974 | Bing Crosby Pro-Am, Phoenix Open, Dean Martin Tucson Open, Heritage Classic, Tournament of Champions, Westchester Classic, World Open, Kaiser International, Dunlop Phoenix (Japan) |
| 1975 | Phoenix Open, Dean Martin Tucson Open, Bob Hope Desert Classic, Kaiser International, World Cup (team with Lou Graham) |
| 1976 | British Open, N.B.C. Tucson Open, Bob Hope Desert Classic |
| 1979 | Lancome Trophy |
| 1980 | Jackie Gleason Inverary Classic |
| 1981 | Sun City Million Dollar Challange, Joe Garagiola Tucson Open, Glen Campbell Los Angeles Open |
| 1982 | Wickes Andy Williams San Diego Open |
| 1983 | Honda Inverary Classic, Chrysler Team Championship (with Jack Nicklaus) |
| 1987 | A.T. and T. Pebble Beach Pro-Am |

### Did you know...

1. Johnny Miller won the U.S. Open title in 1963 at Oakmont by shooting a last round 63 which broke the previous record by one.
2. Johnny Miller's early hero was Tony Lema. Both had connections with the Olympic Club in San Francisco. Miller emulated Lema who had won the 1964 British Open when he won that title in 1976.
3. When Miller won the 1975 Phoenix and Tucson Opens in successive weeks, he shot 24-under-par and 25-under-par – a two week burst of scoring that has never been emulated in America.
4. Miller won the World Cup with Jack Nicklaus at Nueva Andalusia in Spain in 1973 and the Chrysler Championship on the U.S. circuit with Nicklaus in 1983.
5. Johnny Miller lists church activities as one of his main hobbies. He is a member of the Church of Latter Day Saints (the Mormons) and gives a tenth of his winnings to the Church.

# RAYMOND FLOYD

He may have lived it up in the early years of his career but now Raymond Floyd is a respected major Championship winner who, on his day, can take on and beat the best.

Today Raymond Floyd graces the game of golf with all the qualities of an elder statesman. He was the logical choice to lead the American Ryder Cup team in 1989 after a career in which he has won two U.S. P.G.A. Championships, a U.S. Masters in record-equalling style, and in 1986 at the age of 43, his first and only U.S. Open. The Floyd portfolio is missing only one essential ingredient that ideally he would have wanted before he retires – a British Open. Sadly that title has eluded him the way the U.S. Open kept slipping away from Sam Snead, and the way the U.S. P.G.A. Championship proved a jinx for Arnold Palmer.

Floyd's talent is such that arguably he should have won even more majors than the four credited to him in the record books. He has been a Tour player for 23 years but the reason why he has not done better – and remember it is all relative because he has done far better than most of his contemporaries – is the high-rolling life-style he had when he first joined the Tour in 1961. Robert Sommers, that shrewd commentator on the American Scene who now works so assiduously for the United States Golf Association, perhaps put it best when he summed up Floyd's early attitude to golf. 'For a time it looked as if Raymond Floyd's career would not last. He was what we used to call a swinger in his early years. At times he seemed to believe that to be absolutely sure of making an early morning starting time, he should not go to bed.' He was quite a lad in those days, wincing now at being reminded of the story that he once had a financial interest in a women's topless band. Whether he did or not, the legend has stuck although today Floyd is one of the most respected golfers on the American circuit. When he won the U.S. Open at Shinnecock in 1986 at the 22nd attempt he was not one of the favourites. In the previous 21 Opens he had only twice finished in the top ten and that was in the far distant past. He had been sixth in 1965 and eighth in 1971. It did not seem to be his Championship until the U.S. G.A. took the event, controversially, to a course with links-like characteristics where Floyd could use his incredible shot-making ability to full effect.

Ray Floyd on his way to victory in the 1986 U.S. Open

He is easily spotted these days walking the fairways with the distinctly snappy stride of a man not quite sure whether he should break into a jog or not, his arms out in front of him, his hands flapping against some unseen insect. The faster he is walking the better he is usually scoring, say fellow professionals about a man whose life was changed when he met

At the age of 43 Floyd celebrates his victory in the U.S. Open

and married Maria Fraietta in 1973. In his playboy years of the late 60's he had carried as much as 20lbs overweight to the start each week but was able to cope so well then with the added strain of a bulging waist-line that he won the 1969 U.S. P.G.A. and three other events despite himself. Gradually his life-style caught up with him, however, and he slumped down the money list, failing even to make the top 70 in 1971 and 1972. The pundits suggested his big-time career was over. He would never win again, they whispered. Then he met his wife, brown haired, slim and very strong-willed. Gradually, with all the added responsibilities, Floyd re-built his career relying on the quirky swing of his that should not really work as well as it does. Somehow he gets away with. Through the green he does not hit the top of the statistics table but, as is so often the case, he has a finely-tuned touch around the greens for a big man – a putting touch that has enabled him to win 21 events on Tour since 1961. Is it little wonder that his distinctive walk has been so often as jaunty as that of a sailor stepping off his ship for a lengthy period of rest and recreation on shore. Raymond Floyd has always had the ability (even if he did not always use it) to carve up any course and outsmart and outstrip any opponent.

Although he now lives in Miami, Floyd grew up in North Carolina. His father was a professional soldier and the young Floyd's learning years were spent in the neat and orderly confines of one of America's bigger garrisons, Fort Bragg. His father, who became a professional himself, was then an enthusiastic amateur but though Floyd was exposed to golf at an early age, the game was pushed into the back of his mind. His first love was baseball.

The Floyd family celebrate – Raymond with Maria and daughter?

On the tee at Augusta

Another perfect approach shot

He admits readily enough that he used to play baseball seriously and golf for fun. The priority changed, however, when he won a national junior golf title in 1960. Suddenly he switched direction when he realised golf offered him the chance of a full-time career. That decision taken, he sharpened his ability to perform under pressure by taking part in a series of matches for money against other young players. He was a sort of 20th Century version of the old wild west gunslinger. Floyd would drive into town, seek out the local hot-shot and away the two of them would go to the golf course. He learned not only how to play a lot of different courses in a lot of different conditions but also how to hole a tricky, downhill putt when the pressure was building overhead like a dark and very ominous cloud. It was an unconventional but remarkably sound training for a professional career. He had to make things work for him. He never did have time to make changes to that swing of his, it remains a blur.

At six foot one and 14 stone, Floyd might have been expected to have a slow, languid swing. Quite the opposite once over his ball he wastes no time getting on with the job. He has always had fast hands, the sort of hands a top class boxer needs. His game revolves round timing more than anything else. When his timing is good, and it usually is, then Floyd is a class act. His last great win, in 1986, was a triumph for his resilience and talent. The New Jersey course at Shinnecock Hills is one of the most difficult in America. But Floyd came from behind on a memorable last day to shoot a six under par 66 and become, at 43, the oldest U.S. Open winner in history. 'Just because a man is over 40 does not mean he is finished. No matter how old you are, you can still dream and if you can do that then those dreams can also come true,' he said later.

With his wife and family by his side, it was Floyd's proudest moment in golf when he stepped off the last green as American Champion. It was the ultimate for him, the proof, if any was needed, that he was different from most of the others. That day he was ice cool but he has a temper and a pair of eyes that can turn colder than the barrel of a gun yet he rarely lashes out verbally. Over the years he has established an enviable reputation as a man who realises he is in a position of some influence and who is determined not to abuse it. So it was to Floyd that the P.G.A. of America turned in 1987 when they asked him to skipper the 1989 American Ryder Cup side. After nearly three decades of dominance in the Cup, American had lost to Europe in 1985 and 1987 and the officials, the players, the public did not like it. The time had come for a tougher sort to take control, a man who could be relied upon to command total respect. Raymond Floyd fits the bill perfectly.

Ryder Cup captain Floyd blasts this one close

# *CAREER RECORD*

## Victories

| | |
|---|---|
| 1963 | St Petersburg Open |
| 1965 | St Paul Open |
| 1969 | Jacksonville Open, American Golf Classic, U.S. P.G.A. Championship |
| 1975 | Kemper Open |
| 1976 | U.S. Masters World Open |
| 1977 | Byron Nelson Classic, Pleasant Valley Classic |
| 1979 | Greensboro Open |
| 1980 | Doral-Eastern Open |
| 1981 | Doral-Eastern Open, Tournament Players' Championship, Manufacturers Hanover-Westchester Classic |
| 1982 | Memorial Tournament, Danny Thomas Memphis Classic, U.S. P.G.A. Championship |
| 1985 | Houston Open |
| 1986 | U.S. Open, Walt Disney Oldsmobile Classic |

## Did you know...

1. Raymond Floyd achieved one of his major career goals when he took the 1986 U.S. Open at Shinnecock Hills on Long Island. He closed with a 66 to become the oldest winner of the title at 43.
2. Raymond Floyd tied Jack Nicklaus record aggregate of 271 when the won the U.S. Masters in 1976.
3. One of Floyd's most impressive victories was in the 1982 U.S.P.G.A. Championship in the sweltering heat of Tulsa, Oklahoma. He set Championship records with his 132 half way total and his total of 200 for three rounds. He missed the 72 hole record by just one after dropping two shots at the last.
4. Raymond Floyd received what he described as a great honour when selected to captain the American Ryder Cup at The Belfry in 1989. He played in the match in 1969, 1975, 1977, 1981, 1983 and 1985.

The 1986 U.S. Open Champion

# HALE IRWIN

Studious-looking Hale Irwin won two American Opens but a missed putt of little more than two inches may have cost him a British Championship title.

Hale Irwin in 1986 at the Masters

Hale Irwin's 1974 U.S. Open victory came two weeks after he had dreamed of doing so. A rare glimpse of the future, or a triumph for positive thinking? Possibly both, although analysts of such phenomena could claim it as a huge desire for recognition.

Despite establishing himself as one of the most successful players on the U.S. Tour over the previous four years, Irwin was charged with being colourless, his game unenthralling. 'Maybe I'll come out tomorrow on a pogo stick. Maybe then they'll notice me,' Irwin said somewhat sourly of the fans in 1974. But his resolve to gain recognition soon manifested itself, first in his dream and then in victory itself at the difficult Winged Foot course in New York. Winning the national title was guaranteed to give Irwin the recognition he craved – winning at Winged Foot added a touch of greatness to the achievement – and earned him an automatic invitation to the World Match-play championship. He took the title in 1974 and 1975. He seemed to be heading for a hat-trick when he led David Graham of Australia going into the final stretch of the 1976 final. Time and again Irwin seemed to have Graham at his mercy only for the Australian's putter to prove not so much hot as molten, his most audacious thrust coming at their 33rd hole when he rolled the ball into the cup from a monstrous 60 feet, Irwin, two up with four to play, eventually lost the sudden death play-off at the second extra hole. Dynamism had once again overshadowed dependability and the frustrated Irwin is alleged to have kicked his golf bag around the Wentworth locker room after his ordeal.

But Irwin's consistency has not gone unrewarded, and he finished in the prize money in 86 consecutive tournaments from the 1975 Tucson Open to the 1979 Bing Crosby Pro-Am, before missing a 36-hole cut. Only two of the game's greatest, Byron Nelson (113 in the 1940's) and Jack Nicklaus (105 in the early 1970's) can claim longer runs on the U.S. Tour.

During his second U.S. Open triumph, at the Inverness Club in Toledo, Ohio, in 1979, Irwin added to that chapter of golfing folklore concerned with tales of outstanding shots which helped mould the destiny of major championships.

At Royal Lytham St Annes a month later he threatened to make another indelible mark in the history books by becoming only the fifth player to win the British and U.S. Open titles in the same year but Ballesteros received the title, the famous claret jug and was dubbed by Irwin 'The Parking Lot champion'.

Four years later Irwin was to get within touching distance, two inches in fact, of an 18-hole play-off for the Open championship with fellow American Tom Watson at Royal Birkdale. Having missed the cup by just two inches with his birdie attempt at the 198-yard 14th, Irwin, holding the putter in both hands, attempted to hit the ball in left handed – and missed it altogether. Irwin's fine individual record is complemented by his appearance in four straight Ryder Cup matches, between 1975 and 1981, and his victory with John Mahaffey in the 1979 World Cup, when he also won the individual title – but he will forever regret that the fates conspired twice to prevent him winning an Open in Britain – a win which would have crowned his illustrious career.

# *CAREER RECORD*

## Victories

| | |
|---|---|
| 1971 | Heritage classic |
| 1973 | Heritage Classic |
| 1974 | World Cup, U.S. Open, Piccadilly World Match-play Championship |
| 1975 | Western Open, Atlanta Classic, Piccadilly World Match-play Championship |
| 1976 | Glen Campbell Los Angeles Open, Florida Citrus Open |
| 1977 | Atlanta Classic, Hall of Fame Classic, San Antonio-Texas Open |
| 1978 | Australian P.G.A. Championship |
| 1979 | South African P.G.A. Championship, World Cup, U.S. Open |
| 1981 | Hawaiian Open, Buick Open, Bridgestone Classic (Japan) |
| 1982 | Honda Inverary Classic, Brazilian Open |
| 1983 | Memorial Tournament |
| 1984 | Bing Crosby Pro-Am |
| 1985 | Memorial Tournament |
| 1986 | Bahamas Classic |
| 1987 | Fila Classic |

## Did you know...

1. Hale Irwin was a successful American football player before he turned to professional golf.
2. Hale Irwin went 86 consecutive events on the U.S. circuit between 1975 and 1979 without missing a half-way cut – a measure of the consistency of his play.
3. Hale Irwin has earned the reputation for winning tournaments on the tougher courses. He won his two U.S. Opens at Winged Foot, noted for its small greens, and at the Inverness Club, Toledo, Ohio which is also noted for its tightness. He has also won at Butler National, Riviera in Los Angeles, Pinehurst No 2, Muirfield Village and Pebble Beach – courses also known for their toughness.
4. Hale Irwin missed a two inch putt in the 1983 Open in Britain and missed a play-off with Tom Watson by a shot.
5. Only David Graham's incredible putting prevented Hale Irwin from scoring a record three in a row World Match-play Championships in 1976. Irwin lost at the thirty-eighth.

# 'FUZZY' ZOELLER

**He wisecracks his way round like Lee Trevino but two play-off wins in major championships indicate that 'Fuzzy' Zoeller's golf game is as razor-sharp as is his sense of humour.**

Fuzzy Zoeller plays golf the way he lives his life. Any more laid back and he would be horizontal, while being sociable comes naturally to him. Grinning always seems a better alternative to the scowl. His is in many ways the walking, talking antidote to the blandness that increasingly affects the images of players on the mighty U.S. Tour who chase record prize money each year.

Every other golfer in the States seems to have been formed in the same Californian image – tall, slim, blond young men who approach the game with all the natural enjoyment of a factory worker joining the Monday morning shift. But Fuzzy sweeps in and out of town like a welcome breeze of fresh air. He prefers it when he wins but he never has been the sort of fellow who wants to kick the cat just because a couple of putts have not dropped. Life, he says, is too short to hang around hoping for it to get better. You have to go out there, grab life by the throat and shake it hard so the apples start to fall your way. Zoeller radiates the sort of unsophisticated Mid-West charm that helps convince you that mom's apple pie really is the best in the world. To suggest, however, that, just because he relishes the simple things in life, he is a simple sort of man would be a travesty of justice. Beneath that earthy, open exterior there is a keen brain and a large heart.

'Fuzzy' – always a big favourite with the fans

Whether playing in the United States or Europe, Japan or Australia, Fuzzy always attracts a gallery. It is not just that his golf is worth watching – which it is – but more that the fans know he knows he is out there to give a show. His nature dictates that if you walk with him often enough then sooner or later you will find yourself talking to him too. 'Heck, the only guy I know who can concentrate properly right through 18 holes is Jack Nicklaus. I can't. No way. Chatting to the fans, relating to them helps me relax out there. It relieves the pressure and clears the mind so that when it's time to go to work again I'm ready for the next shot,' is his explanation. At five foot ten inches tall and round 13 stone, Zoeller is close to the perfect height and weight for golf. Big enough to clout the ball prodigious distances his centre of gravity is low enough to help him maintain perfect balance even when conditions are bad enough to blow most player's swings out of kilter. Yet suc-

In the sand at Augusta (left) and lining up for another birdie attempt (below)

cess did not come that easily to the man who grew up alongside the fairway at Valley View Country Club, who swung his first club at three years of age and who entered his first competition just two years after that!

After turning professional in 1973 he finally made the U.S. Tour in '75 and showed a trading loss on his first 12 months work when he ended up in 146th position with a meagre 7,318 dollars to his credit, scarcely enough to cover travelling expenses. He had to get better quickly and he did, grafting away throughout the off-season, relentessly hitting thousands of balls on the practice ground near his home. It was work that paid off because 12 months later Zoeller was able to wipe out his debts when he moved up to 56th position on the U.S. money lists with 52,500 dollars.

It was good progress, but hardly the stuff that dreams are made of, and though Fuzzy continued to improve steadily he always seemed to fall apart whenever he had the chance to win. Maybe concentration was his problem or maybe, some people suggested, this nice man just lacked the killer instinct. Whatever the reason for his reluctance to step on to the winner's rostrum, he overcame any problems brilliantly in 1979. First he won the San Diego Open to get the monkey off his back and then he took the U.S. Masters title when he cashed in on Ed Sneed's nightmare triple bogey finish. He had to play-off against Sneed and Tom Watson and won at the second extra hole. Once established as a star, Fuzzy clung on to the status, turning himself into a steady performer and a man who, when he was hot, could burn the opposition off the track. His finest moment came in 1984 during the United States Open at Winged Foot, a course built in the shadow of New York. He went into the Championship a respected and much-liked golfer – he came out of it a hero. This was not so much because of the modest way he accepted victory but more the sporting way he accepted what would have been a numbing defeat. The chance for his personality to bubble to the surface came at the last hole on the last day when Zoeller stood waiting to play his approach shot into the eighteenth while Greg Norman prepared to strike a 60ft putt up ahead. Incredibly Norman holed what Zoeller thought was for a birdie. Fuzzy's response was instinctive and heart-warming. He pulled a white towel out of his bag and waved it over his head as Norman danced his way around the green. In fact Norman had missed the green badly in two and the putt was for par. When Zoeller calmly made a final par he and Norman had tied and faced an 18-hole play-off the following day.

The play-off was an anti-climax – unless, of course you were a Fuzzy Zoeller fan! The American trounced the Australian by eight shots, 67 to 75, and Norman proved himself to be equally sporting when he commented afterwards that is was probably the right result, given the audacity of his final putt the evening before. More than anything else he had done on the golf course before or since, Zoeller's wit and sportsmanship on that Sunday and Monday in New York State propelled him into the very soul of American sporting consciousness. Against a backdrop of declining standards right across the sporting spectrum his behaviour stood out like a rare beacon of hope.

In that respect it was particularly cruel when just two months later Zoeller had to pull out of the U.S.P.G.A. Championship in Birmingham, Alabama, with the recurring golfer's affliction... back trouble. Instead of crashing his ball off the first tee, Zoeller was admitted to hospital. His season was over, and in fact his career was almost over. He needed surgery in New York for ruptured discs. Behind the smiles he had played in pain for weeks. Typically, and against the odds, he has fought back from this traumatic experience. He has even won again on the U.S. Tour but, increasingly, his attention is drawn to his wife, the daughter of an oil magnate, and his three daughters. When the pain gives him a break he is still capable of playing like a dream and even though the truly great days may be over for Fuzzy, he is still a delight to watch on the course and a pleasure to chat with in the clubhouse afterwards.

## *CAREER RECORD*

### Victories

1979 Wickes Andy Williams San Diego Open, U.S. Masters
1981 Colonial National Invitational
1983 Sea Pines Heritage Classic, Las Vegas Pro-Celebrity Classic
1984 U.S. Open
1985 Hertz Bay Hill Classic
1986 A.T. and T. Pebble Beach National Pro-Am, Sea Pines Heritage Classic, Anheuser Busch Golf Classic

### Did you know...

1. Fuzzy Zoeller is one of a select group who won the U.S. Masters at their first attempt. Usually it takes a year at least to get to know the course but he beat Tom Watson and Ed Sneed in a play-off for the title in 1979.
2. Fuzzy Zoeller has had back trouble throughout his professional career – the result of a painful accident he incurred while playing basketball in High School.
3. In 1985 Zoeller won the Bobby Jones award presented annually for "distinguished sportsmanship".
4. Fuzzy Zoeller has never been American's top money-earner but he was No 2 to Hal Sutton in 1983 when he won 417,597 dollars.

# NANCY LOPEZ

She comes from Roswell in New Mexico but Nancy Lopez, whose personality is as bright as her golf is brilliant, has played herself into the international record books.

Loosening up before teeing off (left) and Nancy in action at Mission Hills (below)

She smiles a lot. She bubbles with personality and she makes barrow-loads of birdies and eagles every year.

The effervescent Nancy Lopez has done for the women's tour in America what Arnold Palmer did 15 years earlier for the men's tour and what Severiano Ballesteros has done more recently for European golf.

Nancy Lopez is a 'one off' superstar who, it has been claimed, would rather come in fifth than attempt to win by playing safe! Just 5 foot 4 inches tall but with a superbly rhythmical swing and an ability to carry the ball a long way through the air, Nancy in the early days was a superb putter. Faced now with the prospect of bringing up a family as well as playing the circuit, it is maybe not surprising that that putting touch is less deadly that it once was. Yet it remains more effective than that of most of her friends on the U.S. Tour.

The girl with shining brown hair and sparkling brown eyes was encouraged by her father Domingo to take up golf at the tender age of eight. At nine she had won her first tournament by 110 strokes. No, that is not a misprint! Within four years she stunned the golfing world with her first major win. Not yet a teenager, Nancy won the New Mexico Women's Amateur Championship. It was an incredible success...and she has simply continued being successful ever since.

In a brilliant amateur career she won the U.S. girls' title in 1972 and 1974 and the

As stylish as ever, on her way to two more victories

Western Junior three years in a row from 1972. In 1975 she won the Mexican Women's Amateur event on a foray across the border from the new family home in Roswell. She was joint runner-up that same year in the U.S. Women's Amateur and before turning professional had been named as most valuable player and female athlete of the year twice at the University of Tulsa, where she was an all round sportswoman. After playing in the Curtis Cup and World Cup everyone predicted a bright future when she decided to turn professional. Everyone's prediction came dramatically true. She took the pro world by storm, breaking all sorts of records while having fun!

Before qualifying for the U.S. Tour and playing for money, Nancy finished second again in the U.S. Open, this time the 1977 version behind Hollis Stacey. To date she has still not won this most prized crown, and it is the only flaw in her otherwise staggeringly brilliant curriculum vitae.

When she had earned her card she could hardly have made a more dramatic start to her professional career. She won nine times in her first full season, including a record five times in a row, and made a record 189,813 dollars in prize-money. She was Golfer of the Year and set new standards for a rookie on Tour. The following year she won eight times and her stroke average of 71.20 stood as the Tour record until 1985 when she herself broke it with a staggering 70.73 average. In 1979 she also married, but was divorced from sportscaster Tim Melton four years later. Now happily married to star footballer Ray Knight, she dismisses her earlier marriage upset simply as 'her practice round'.

In her record breaking 1985 season she played 25 events, posted 21 top-ten finishes and won five times. She was never out of the top five in 12 consecutive events and became the first player to break the 400,000 dollar barrier in earnings. She laughed and danced all the way to the bank. With end-of-year bonuses she stretched her income in American prize-money alone to 541,472 dollars in 1985 – just a few dollars short of what Curtis Strange earned for finishing No. 1 on the men's circuit. It had been a great year for her, highlighted by her 20-under-

Lining up a putt at Mission Hills

par win in the Hedredon Classic in which she made no fewer than 25 birdies in rounds of 66, 67, 69 and 66.

Yet 1987 was an even more significant year for the golfing mum. She knew she needed 35 tournaments wins to make the golfing Hall of Fame and hit that number when she took the title in Sarasota, Florida. She was the Hall's eleventh member, the one who made it quickest and the youngest. At the end of the 1988 season Nancy had won 39 events and passed through the two million dollar barrier in earnings – only the third golfer to do so. The others are Pat Bradley and Joanne Carner whose 'go-for-it' style of play Nancy admits she has always liked to copy.

She admits she wants it all ways. She told a golf magazine reporter not so very long ago that she wanted to be a great golfer, a great wife and a great mother all at the same time. It is just the kind of challenge Nancy loves to take on and, of course, win. Husband Ray is determined she should not give up her main-line career. He does not want her in a few years time to look back on her performances as a pro wondering whether she could have been the greatest woman golfer of all time. She is already a millionaire twice over and her contracts bring in another sizeable whack of the green-backed paper money that make bank managers so pleased. Husband Ray is in the dollar milionaire bracket, too, so the family is very well off but live quietly and carefully. That is their style. After all the young Nancy once used the same golf glove for eight years. She remembers the days when things were not so affluent for her and her highly supportive family.

These says she seldom plays 'away'. In the late 70's when David Foster was in charge of the massive Colgate company which sponsored the European Women's Open at Sunningdale for five years, Nancy was always there and twice she won it. Now her visits to Britain are few and far – too far – between.

Hopefully she will not lose her competitive edge, her keen desire to win or her enjoyment at playing the game for a long time. Nancy Lopez is, after all, one of those rare people whose natural charm, energy and massive ability have helped convince many people to try the game. And she is only 32. The world of women's golf will be a less lively place when she does decide to call it a day.

## *CAREER RECORD*

### Victories

| | |
|---|---|
| 1978 | Bent Tree Ladies Classic, Sunstar Classic, Greater Baltimore Classic, Coca Cola Classic, Golden Lights Championship, L.P.G.A. Championship, Bankers Trust Classic, Colgate European Open, Colgate Far East Open |
| 1979 | Sunstar Classic, Sahara National Pro-Am, Woman's International, Coca Cola Classic, Golden Lights, Lady Keystone Open, Colgate European Open, Mary Kay Classic |
| 1980 | Women's Kemper Open, Sarah Coventry Tournament, Rail Charity Classic |
| 1981 | Arizona Copper Classic, Colgate Dinah Shore Tournament, Sarah Coventry Tournament |
| 1982 | J. and B. Scotch Pro-Am, Mazda Japan Classic |
| 1983 | Elizabeth Arden Classic, J. and B. Scotch Pro-Am |
| 1984 | Uniden L.P.G.A. Invitational, Chevrolet World Championship of Golf |
| 1985 | Chrysler-Plymouth Charity Classic, U.S. L.P.G.A. Championship, Mazda Hall of Fame Championship, Henredon Classic, Portland Piong Championship |
| 1987 | Sarasota Classic, Cellular One Ping Championship |

The 1979 European Women's Open Champion

# BILLY CASPER

To his long lasting regret he never won an Open in Britain but burly Billy Casper made a valuable contribution to the game and on one notable occasion upstaged Arnold Palmer.

Billy Casper often put God before golf – and his dedication to his religion is something I remember talking at length with him about in Morocco a few years ago. The big, burly Casper, who at that time was in to eating moose steaks as part of his diet, was playing in an invitational event because he had taught King Hassan, who sponsored the tournament, how to play the game.

Billy, twice a U.S. Open winner and once triumphant at Augusta in the Masters, and I somehow got detached at a function and found ourselves sharing an alcove in one of the Royal Palaces. Curiously we did not speak about golf, nor did we speak about King Hassan and his palaces. The subject of our discussion over a period of almost an hour was the Church of the Latter Day Saints – the Mormon Church of which Billy has been and still is a loyal, fully paid-up supporter. These days the exploits of the so-called Bible Class brigade on the U.S. Tour are well chronicled – Larry Nelson heads the team which includes Scott Simpson, Larry Mize and a host of other big names. But Casper was ahead of them all in putting Church before golf and in giving the Church ten per cent of all his winnings.

Augusta 1987 – scene of his 1970 Masters triumph

People first realised Casper's religious connections when, just days after he had won his now famous play-off with Arnold Palmer in the 1966 U.S. Open at the Olympic Club in San Francisco, he politely turned down the opportunity to play in the British Open at Muirfield the following month because of a prior engagement. He had committed to competing, for absolutely nothing, in a Mormon Church invitational tournament at Salt Lake City. When you pass up playing in the oldest and most revered Championship in the world to tee up in a modest little church tournament then clearly religion is very important in your lift. It has been for Casper, his wife Shirley and their family of eleven, five of them adopted!

Billy has been a pro for 35 years, joining the U.S. Tour in 1955 after having attended the famous University of Notre Dame in his days before he converted to Mormonism. He scored his first Tour win a year later and won at least once each season until 1972. In fact his consistency in the 60's was remarkable. His average score for 900 official rounds played in the 60's was 70.43 and that was better than

Time for another moose-steak diet?

Golfer of the Decade Arnold Palmer who averaged 70.48 for 777 rounds. Casper won the Vardon Trophy for the low scoring season average in the 60's five times to Arnie's four, but Palmer was always the fans' favourite, the golfing king, constantly capturing the headlines wherever he played until Jack Nicklaus came along. It was just Casper's bad luck that his best period coincided with Palmer's and that on most occasions he had to be content playing second-fiddle to a man he admires tremendously.

There was, however, one occasion when Casper snatched all the headlines – that week in 1966 when he caught Palmer on the final day and then beat him in the Monday play-off to win his second U.S. Open title in eight years. Casper had been successful in the Championship in 1959 when beating Bob Rosburg, now well-known as an on-course commentator in the States, but the drama of that win could not compare with what happened in San Francisco seven years later. With nine holes to play Casper, playing with Palm-

Sporting his favoured plus fours at Augusta

Showing his style of old in 1985

er, was seven off the lead. Palmer was strolling to success. An outward 32 had effectively coped with all opposition. The back nine was, so everyone thought, going to be a dawdle. In fact Casper was concerned, not about winning, but about holding second place ahead of the ever menacing threat of Golden Bear Jack Nicklaus.

Palmer dropped a shot at the tenth but both parred the next two holes. Then Arnie slipped up again at the par 3 thirteenth but he still had a comfortable five-shot lead with five to play. Casper was looking for a miracle but refused to give in and was sustained, he said later, by his faith. He prayed quietly to himself initially to stay second on his own. Winning was not really in his mind after both parred the long fourteenth. He was, after all, five down with just four holes to play. Then suddenly there was a two shot swing at the short fifteenth. Palmer, knowing no other way than to attack, went for the pin instead of the heart of the green and ended in a bunker. He came out long and two putted for a 4. Casper, always regarded as one of the game's greatest putters, stroked in a 35 foot putt for a birdie. Two of Palmer's lead had gone and what had been a three-stroke cushion was reduced to just one at the sixteenth which is over 600 yards long. Arnie hooked into the rough, was bunkered by the green and took 6 to Casper's perfectly executed birdie 4. Suddenly Arnie's famous army was restless and fearing an upset. When Palmer dropped a shot at the seventeenth the pair were level playing the last and the rest is history. They tied and in the play-off Casper shot 69 to win by four. It was probably Casper's greatest triumph.

If anything upsets him a little it is the suggestion that the 1966 U.S. Open is remembered not as the one he won but as the Championship Palmer let slip. Arnie did, of course, but Casper points out that Palmer was still round in a highly creditable 71 on the final day having been to the turn in 32. Casper was home in 32 for a 68. It was as much for his performances in the U.S. Open as in any other event that Casper became renowned as a putter with an extra special touch and eye on the greens. In 1959 at Winged Foot he had required only 114 putts in 72 holes, three putting on just one occasion. At Olympic he did not three putt once in the four rounds of the Championship and needed just 117 putts in all. By any stretch of the imagination that is good putting under pressure but the rest of his game was good too! Casper's other major win was at Augusta against Gene Littler after both had tied on 279 in 1970. He won the extra 18 holes by five shots. In all he won 51 events on the main American circuit but must regret never having won an Open in Britain to underline just how good a player and competitor he was in his heyday and still is on the Seniors Tour today. Adding to the poignancy of that disappointment is the fact that Johnny Miller, another Mormon golfer who learned much from Casper's knowledge and expertise, did win the Open at Lytham in 1976.

Casper always has had a weight problem. Diets helped him shed pounds but just as quickly, when giving up the regime, he put on weight again. Now he is as rotund as they come with his great girth emphasised by the baggy plus fours he now wears as his standard golfing attire. Once a fruit farmer in Utah until the crops failed one year and cost him a fortune, Casper has been more than grateful to the Seniors Circuit. In his first year he likened himself to a child being given the freedom of the sweet shop. There was so much money to be picked up, he said, that the sponsors might just as well have spread it over the fairways and greens.

Yet if his golf career was notable without being spectacular, burly Bill Casper should be remembered for all the generous charity work he and his family have been involved in over the years, usually, and deliberately quietly and without fuss. Not that he could keep quiet his trip to entertain the troops in Vietnam during the years of hostility there. He comforted the wounded and went on missions with the able-bodied spurning the offer of additional protective gear to that worn by the regular soldiers dodging bullets every day. Truly Bill Casper is a world star who has never gained the respect his golf and charity work deserved.

## *CAREER RECORD*

### Victories

| | |
|---|---|
| 1956 | Labatt Open |
| 1957 | Phoenix Open, Kentucky Derby Open |
| 1958 | Bing Crosby Pro-Am, New Orleans Open, Buick Open, Havana Open |
| 1959 | U.S. Open, Portland Open, Lafayette Open, Mobile Open, Brazilian Open |
| 1960 | Portland Open, Hesperia Open, Orange County Open, Bakersfield Open, Brazilian Open |
| 1961 | Portland Open |
| 1962 | Doral Open, '500' Festival |
| 1963 | Bing Crosby Invitational Pro-Am, Insurance City Open |
| 1964 | Doral Open, Colonial Invitational, Seattle Open, Alamaden Open |
| 1965 | Bob Hope Desert Classic, Insurance City Open, Western Open, Sahara Invitational |
| 1966 | U.S. Open, San Diego '500' Festival, Hartford Open, Lucky Open |
| 1969 | Bob Hope Desert Classic, Western Open, Alcan Open |
| 1970 | Los Angeles Open, U.S. Masters, 1V-B Philadelphia Open, Avco Open |
| 1971 | Kaiser Open |
| 1973 | Western Open, Sammy Davis Jnr. Greater Hartford Open |
| 1974 | Lancombe Trophy |
| 1975 | New Orleans Open, Italian Open |
| 1977 | Mexican Open |
| 1982 | Shoot Out at Jeremy Ranch, Merrill Lynch Golf Digest Commemorative Pro-Am |
| 1983 | U.S. P.G.A. Senior Open |
| 1984 | Senior P.G.A. Tour Round Up, Legends of Golf (with Gay Brewer) |
| 1985 | Union Mutual Seniors Championship , Doug Sanders Invitational |
| 1987 | Del E. Webb Arizona Classic, Greater Grand Rapids Open |

### Did you know...

1. Billy Casper served on eight successive American Ryder Cup teams and captained the side that beat the first European team in 1979 at White Sulphur Springs.
2. Casper came from seven behind with nine to play to beat Arnold Palmer in the 1966 U.S. Open. He tied Palmer and beat him in the play-off.
3. Billy Casper was the second man after Arnold Palmer to reach a million dollars in official Tour earnings. He did so in January 1970 when he won the Los Angeles Open. That was his 43rd of (to date) 51 victories he has scored on the U.S. circuit.

# *JACK NICKLAUS*

Voted the American golfer of the last 100 years, Jack Nicklaus has won more majors than anyone else but believes that one day his records will be broken. No one else agrees.

When American golf celebrated its 100th anniversary in 1988, Jack Nicklaus was crowned Golfer of the Century at a glittering evening at the Waldorf Astoria Hotel in New York. The competition he had faced had been fierce – Bobby Jones, the greatest amateur of them all, Arnold Palmer, the man who started the modern boom and still probably the most loved golfer of all time, the iron-willed Ben Hogan, whose influence in golfing teaching and whose performance in adversity are legendary, and the big-hitting backwoodsman Sam Snead.

All had their supporters but when the vote was announced there was a clear winner – the Golden Bear, the man with a record 18 major professional titles under his belt and two U.S. Amateur Championships as well; the golfer who has made over five million dollars in prize-money on the American circuit alone and taken 89 first prize cheques around the world in an amazingly successful career. In the end no-one at the Waldorf Astoria that June evening in New York was really surprised.

Jack Nicklaus on his way to his second Open victory at St Andrews

Jack Nicklaus has been re-writing the golfing record books for thirty years. Few superstars – and in his case that cliched word is certainly apt – have remained at the top of their sport longer than Nicklaus, who shot 51 in the very first nine holes he ever played as a ten-year-old. Twenty-five years separate the winning of his first major pro event – the U.S. Open at Oakmont, Pennsylvania – and, to date, his last – his sixth U.S. Masters triumph at Augusta in 1986. As a professional competing in 108 of the so-called majors – the U.S. Masters, U.S. Open, the Open in Britain and the U.S. P.G.A. Nicklaus has won 18, been second or tied second 18 times and been third or tied third nine times. In all he has had 68 Top Ten finishes in the majors – the most important tournaments in world golf and, in that time, has missed the half-way cut only seven times and had to withdraw through injury just once.

At the end of 1988 his record in those Championships which traditionally provide the toughest opposition, was frankly staggering. He has never been outside the top 30 as a professional in the U.S. Masters, has only three times failed to make top 30 in the U.S. Open, only twice been worse than thirtieth in the U.S. P.G.A. and in the Open in Britain three of his five finishes which were worse than 29th were in the past five years. Not only has he won golf's modern Grand Slam – victory in all four majors at least once – he has done it an incredible three times. He has a record six U.S. Masters Green Jackets in his locker at Augusta, he has won the U.S. P.G.A. Championship a record five times

(Walter Hagen won it five times when it was a match-play event), he has won a record-equalling four U.S. Opens along with exiled Scot Willie Anderson at the turn of the century, Bobby Jones and Ben Hogan and has three times won the Open, twice at St Andrews, the home of golf. He says he thinks his record will be broken in time. Few would agree with him. The growth of the professional game and the strength in depth today of the competition make it highly unlikely that any one golfer could ever come close to matching what Jack Nicklaus has done. His average score in the 480 tournaments he has played on the U.S. circuit over the past 26 years (1962-1988) is 70.78. Just let that statistic soak in. He has not even averaged 71 for the 1500 or so rounds he has played in America allowing, of course, for the fact that even the Golden Bear has, from time to time, gone home before the weekend rounds victim of the two-round cut!

For 16 seasons in a row he made more than 100,000 dollars although he is quick to point out that those monetary statistics must be kept in perspective. The value of the dollar and the size of the prize-funds over the years has a distorting effect. So what! When Nicklaus played on Tour for the first time in 1962 and collected his first cheque of 33 dollars 33 cents in the Los Angeles Open, the total prize fund was less than two millions. Today it is 40 millions. He took nine seasons to make his first prize-money million in the States. Three years later, in 1970, he had made his second million. He broke the three million barrier in 1977, completed his fourth million in 1983 and pipped Tom Watson to five million in 1988. All that in America alone!

Yet to assess Nicklaus on the monetary statistics of his career would be to do

Jack in trouble at Augusta (above) and celebrating on the same course (left) on his way to the 1986 Masters

him a grave injustice. The financial details of his golf are fascinating but what makes him a legend in his own lifetime, whether he likes it or not, is the manner in which he has played the game over the years. In an age when the tennis tantrum has become fashionable and the professional foul in football accepted as quite legitimate in certain circumstances, Nicklaus has jealously guarded the reputation of golf for sportsmanship. He has been magnanimous in victory and gracious in defeat. Apart from one sad incident (which I am sure he now regrets) in the World Match-play Championship at Wentworth

Punching clear of the Augusta sand

in which he argued with the referee about getting relief in the rough because of an advertisement hoarding in the far distance, he has accepted that golf was never meant to be, as he himself would say, a fair game. Nicklaus' attitude may result from the fact that the long-time hero of a golfer who has himself been an inspiration and example to millions of golfers around the world, was Bobby Jones – a man always noted for his sportsmanship.

Son of Columbus pharmacist Charlie Nicklaus, Jack learned his early golf under the tutelage of Jack Grout (still his mentor) at the Scioto Country Club not far from the Muirfield Village complex in Ohio where, each year, he now holds his Memorial Tournament. From early on he was aware of Jones, who had won the 1926 U.S. Open at Scioto. Later he would come to admire Jones even more for his attitude to the game, his scrupulous behaviour on the course and his fierce belief in and defence of the honesty and integrity of golf. Yet Jack's interest in the game began almost by chance. His father injured an ankle in a basketball game and, as part of the recuperation process, was told to walk three or four miles a day. It was as a result of the accident that Jack's late father turned to golf and suggested his ten-year-old son caddie for him whenever he could. Jack did, caught the golfing bug, and within three years had won the Ohio Junior Championship. His progress was so meteoric that he qualified for and played in the U.S. Amateur at the age of 15 (losing in the first round) and at 17 had earned the right to play in the U.S. Open, missing the half-way cut when making his debut at the Inverness Club at Toledo not far from his home. He played in his first P.G.A. Tour event as an amateur when he was 18, was one shot off the half way lead and finally finished 12th. His huge talent was obvious and with two U.S. Amateur titles already won – he beat Charlie Coe one up in 1959 at Broadmoor, Colorado, and Dudley Wyson 8 and 6 in 1961 at Pebble Beach where he would later win a U.S. Open – he had already begun to make his mark on the pro scene. While still an amateur he finished fourth in the 1961 U.S. Open at Oakland Hills, Michigan. Only Gene Littler, Bob Goalby, Doug Sanders and Mike Souchak finished ahead of him. He was ready to burst on the professional scene.

Jack had married schoolgirl sweetheart Barbara Bash in 1960 when he was just 20 and she was an inspired choice. Mother of his five children – Jack Jun., Steven, Nancy Jean, Gary and Michael – Barbara has played a vital part in the success story of her husband. The wife of any professional golfer must have special qualities – the strength and independence to run the home and bring up the family single-handedly, the ability to act as in-house psychologist, adviser, comforter and above all supporter – not least on the fairways around the world. Barbara Nicklaus has filled the multi-purpose role as admirably as her husband has played golf. She has walked hundreds of miles supporting Jack and enjoyed with him his many successes. When he started with a record-equalling 63 in the 1980 U.S. Open that he won at Baltusrol, New Jersey, she admitted with a smile, that having watched the 63, she went to their rented home that night and prepared the same meal she had prepared for Jack the night before in a bid to keep the magic going. I seem to recall it was nothing more exciting than spaghetti! The golf was much more interesting with Jack holding off the stout Far East challenge of Isao Aoki on the Sunday afternoon. That was major pro win number 16! On that occasion he was cheered off the course. He spent two hours answering questions in the press-room but when he won his first major as a professional in his rookie year it was very different.

When Nicklaus joined the U.S. Tour, Arnold Palmer was king. Arnie looked the part. He had tremendous presence. He played golf with a flourish. He was as exciting to watch then as Severiano Ballesteros is today. Arnie, son of a professional at a club in the Pennsylvanian mountains, was everybody's hero. He was the general of an army of fans, a warm, appealing troubador. Jack, on the other hand, was overweight. A crew-cut only emphasised the roundness of his face. He was nothing like the sleek Nicklaus we know today. In 1962 he was known as 'Ohio Fats' and, if there was a derogatory hint in that, it was understandable because he had the temerity not only to challenge Palmer but to eclipse him as far as performance was concerned. Palmer was loved (and still is). Nicklaus has never generated the warmth of Arnie at any time in his career although initial crowd hostility to him has given way to total admiration for what he has achieved. Nicklaus realised, early on, that he could never hope to command Palmer's warm rapport with the fans but he knew he could win their respect and has done so in many ways. Nicklaus has always been less outgoing than Palmer. The Bear's style has been far more reserved than that of Arnie over the years although he is mellowing as he approaches 50 and prepares for the opportunity to play the Seniors circuit. Back in 1962 he had to face up to Palmer fans actually shouting out 'miss it' when he stepped up to putt. It is a tribute to his strength of character that he understood the situation and it is a measure of the man that he could cope with that and win the fans over in time. What helped him cope, of course, was his great love of the game and the thrill he gets of handling, better than anyone else, the pressure on the final day. It is his ability to keep cool, to keep swinging slowly and to maintain a strict routine under pressure that separates him from the others. When Nicklaus feels that either because of his continual back problems or simply because of his inability to practice regularly he can not play himself into a winning position over the final nine holes and win, then that will be the time for him to retire from competitive golf and concentrate totally on the multi-million pound golf course designing and building empire he runs.

These days he gets almost the same enjoyment out of seeing a course develop from an embryonic idea through the drawing board to reality, and relishes the opportunity to leave a legacy behind that will more than augment what he did as a player. Because there are Nicklaus courses being built all over the world he travels the world in his own company jet. His 'Air Bear' jet with six beds is a luxury which, he says, pays for itself!

Yet back in 1962 he could only dream of what he might achieve as a professional golfer. His decision to quit amateur golf and to abandon his training as a pharmacist was one of the best he ever made. In his first full season he won the U.S. Open where he turned the tables on Palmer who had beaten him into second place at Cherry Hills in Denver in 1960 when Jack was still an amateur. Jack needed 18 extra holes to get the better of Arnie but did so with a 71 to Palmer's 74 on a week when he three-putted just once on greens traditionally very fast. That week underlined the end of the Palmer era and the start of

Back in the UK again – the 1988 Open

the Nicklaus reign.

Within a year Nicklaus had won the U.S. Masters and U.S. P.G.A Championship. When he won the Masters again in 1965 he had a nine stroke cushion with a record 17-under par 271 total over the two other members of golf's Big Three of the day – Palmer and South African Gary Player. He had to play-off with Tommy Jacobs and Gay Brewer to win in 1966 when he became the first and, to date, only golfer to win back-to-back at Augusta and it was that year, too, that he came to Muirfield and won his first Open in Britain after a desperate battle with Dave Thomas, the towering Welshman, and Doug Sanders whom he would beat again for the title in a play-off in 1970 at St Andrews. That year he also won the World Match-play at Wentworth. Between his two British Open wins he scored his first U.S. Open triumph at Baltusrol, this time beating Palmer by four shots and by winning the U.S. P.G.A. again in 1971 he had completed a record double 'Grand Slam'. Indeed he was unlucky not to win the U.S. Open that same summer, when Lee Trevino pipped him in a play-off, and the U.S. Masters where Charles Coody, the tall Texan, beat him and Johnny Miller by two shots. In 1972 victory again at the U.S. Masters plus another U.S. Open win, this time by three shots from Bruce Crampton at Pebble Beach, meant that he needed just one more major title to beat his hero Bobby Jones' tally of thirteen. He came third at Augusta, fourth in the U.S. and British Opens but finally broke the record at Canterbury, again beating Australian Crampton but this time in the U.S. P.G.A. Nicklaus was at his best in 1975 when he won a fourth U.S. P.G.A. and a fifth Masters at Augusta where he pipped the hot Johnny Miller and the luckless Tom Weiskopf, like Nicklaus a former Ohio State golfer who always played in the shadow of the Bear. Both Weiskopf and Miller had chances to catch Nicklaus but could not birdie the last. Weiskopf, finishing second for a fourth time, was virtually speechless at the end. 'I just cannot play any better than I did this week,' he told reporters. 'I gave my all and it was still not good enough'. Weiskopf would never win the Masters and neither would Miller, who remained more resolute that night in the Augusta press room.

After losing a remarkable shoot out with Tom Watson for the Open at Turnberry in 1977, when he shot a closing two rounds total of 132 and lost by one yet finished ten ahead of third-placed Hubert Green, he came back to win another Open at St Andrews a year later after a last-day battle with New Zealander Simon Owen, who led with three holes to play, Ben Crenshaw, Tom Kite, Raymond Floyd and Britain's Peter Oosterhuis. Two years later in 1980 came his second Baltusrol triumph in the U.S. Open and another U.S. P.G.A. success when he won by a record seven shots from Andy Bean at Oak Hill, New York. That, everyone thought, was that. Constant back problems and his desire to switch more to designing courses than playing them would combine, it was felt, to end his avid collection of major titles although he had promised himself a minimum of 20 if you added in his two U.S. Amateur titles. We should have known better than retire him early. He had won only 19 majors after all! There was still one great major victory to come and, although five seasons would pass before he reached his target, it was, appropriately enough, to happen for him at Augusta. For him April 13, 1986 was far from unlucky. At the age of 46, and with his son Jack Junior acting as his caddie, he strode the Augusta course like the true champion he is. The atmosphere was

The Golden Bear in typical pose

electric, the noise echoing through the trees fantastic as Jack Nicklaus, golfer supreme, shot the score he had predicted he would need to shoot in the last round to win – a 65 that helped him to a dramatic, pulsating and deserved one shot victory over Greg Norman.

If his 1975 Masters victory over Miller and Weiskopf had been nerve-jangling it could hardly compare with what happened in 1986. Arguably, at the age of 46, Nicklaus, with a bad back, eye-sight problems and a few other aches and pains, should have had no chance but, giant that he is, he made one last dramatic flourish. After eight holes on the final day he trailed playing partner Sandy Lyle by one but a birdie at the ninth set him up for an inward 30 on greens just the way he likes them – slick as marble table tops. That afternoon he proved he had not lost his putting nerve. His hands were rock steady on the club and, with son Jack consulting with him on the lines of putts, Nicklaus strode, like a colossus, to some might say his greatest success – helped by a majestic eagle from 12 feet at the fifteenth, where water guards the green and an improbable, impossible, unbelievable 5-iron tee-shot to a foot at the short sixteenth where getting the ball near the hole on the sloping glassy green seemed beyond human capability. When he sank a ten footer for a third birdie in a row at the seventeenth, even the late charging Norman could not catch him. Nicklaus' draw partner for the day, Lyle, just watched in amazement as the golfer who 25 years earlier had been barracked by the fans for daring to upstage Arnie Palmer, was cheered on to victory by them. It was one of golf's most memorable moments and maybe Nicklaus' finest triumph. When it was all over he hugged his son. It had been, truly, a family affair for a man with strong family loyalties, a man who made the promise to wife Barbara when they got married that he would never stay away more than three weeks in a row and has broken that promise only once.

That week in Augusta he used a new Jumbo-headed putter which he called the Response. His victory ensured gross sales of the club of over five million dollars in the following year. The factory could not make enough of them. Today Nicklaus heads his own golfing empire – Golden Bear Inc. with a dollar turnover of 150 millions a year. This branch of his activities covers his golf course design work, his golf club administration business – Nicklaus will design, build and then run your golf club for you if you wish – and all the other commercial ancillaries surrounding the Golden Bear – a nickname he was given on a visit to Australia by local journalist Don Lawrence and which happily stuck. Nicklaus will be forever remembered for what he achieved in golf but also what he has contributed towards the well-being of the game. For someone who has been in the public eye for so long, Nicklaus is remarkably normal. He skis in Vail, plays tennis in Florida, fishes wherever he can (he once caught a record 600 lbs marlin off the Queensland coast) and is an ardent follower of his children whenever they are competing. His family means so much to him and they are such a team that he was delighted when, a few years ago, they were selected as America's top sporting family. Despite his success Nicklaus is approachable at all times, even if jealously protected by a team of assistants led by a shrewd old Canadian journalist who knows the ropes like noone else. Nicklaus can at times be rather sharp even with journalists he knows –

'How did it stay out?'

especially with journalists he knows – in press interviews when in his waspish mood, but on most occasions he is the perfect ambassador for the game, a man, rare these days, never to have been involved in any kind of scandal.

Perhaps the key to his success over the years, apart from the fact that he is supremely talented, stems from the fact that golf is far more than a job for him. He loves the game and incredibly remains as competitively sharp and enthusiastic today, especially when it comes to the majors, as he was 25 years ago. He has always loved a challenge and has always had the great advantage over so many others on the Tour that he can concentrate perhaps better than anyone on the course. He has always prepared meticulously and has stood seemingly longer than anyone else over putts and holed more than his fair share. Although he did not introduce yardage chart golf to the world, he embraced it and popularised it. Today, no self-respecting professional would venture out without a yardage chart! Bobby Jones said after watching Nicklaus in action: 'That man plays a form of golf with which I am not accustomed.'

The contribution he has made to the game in general and in specific terms to events such as the Ryder Cup has been enormous. Ironically, having supported the idea of bringing in the Continentals and changing the British and Irish side to a European one he became the first American captain to lose the Cup match on home soil at his own club Muirfield Village in 1987. It was close and, despite his disappointment, he was, as always the perfect loser. To do justice to the career of Jack Nicklaus, to highlight where, when and how he has influenced the game would take several volumes. Here I have but touched on some of his triumphs. In conclusion I would go as far as to say there never will be the likes of him again. Those of us who have grown up with him and been privileged to share in his great victories around the world by simply being there have indeed been fortunate. Jack Nicklaus is in a class of his own. The game has been good to him but he, in turn, has been magnificent for the game.

## *CAREER RECORD*

The 1978 Open Champion

### Victories

| | |
|---|---|
| 1959 | U.S. Amateur Championship |
| 1961 | U.S. Amateur Championship |
| 1962 | U.S. Open, World's Fair Tournament, Portland Open, World Series of Golf |
| 1963 | Palm Springs Open, U.S. Masters, Tournament of Champions, U.S. P.G.A., Sahara Invitational, World Cup (team with Arnold Palmer), World Series of Golf |
| 1964 | Portland Open, Tournament of Champions, Phoenix Open, Whitemarsh Open, Australian Open, World Cup |
| 1965 | Portland Open, U.S. Masters, Memphis Open, Thunderbird Classic, Philadelphia Open |
| 1966 | British Open, U.S. Masters, Sahara Invitational, National Team Championships (with Arnold Palmer), World Cup |
| 1967 | U.S. Open, Sahara Invitational, Bing Crosby Pro-Am, Western Open, Westchester Open, World Cup, World Series of Golf |
| 1968 | Western Open, American Golf Classic, Australian Open |
| 1969 | Sahara Invitational, Kaiser International, San Diego Open |
| 1970 | Open Championship, Byron Nelson Classic, National Four Ball (with Arnold Palmer), Piccadilly World Match-play, World Series of Golf |
| 1971 | U.S. P.G.A., Tournament of Champions, Byron Nelson Classic, National Team Championship (with Arnold Palmer), Disney World Open, Australian Open, World Cup |
| 1972 | Bing Crosby Pro-Am, Doral-Eastern Open, U.S. Masters, U.S. Open, Westchester Classic, Match-play Championship, Disney World Open |
| 1973 | Bing Crosby Pro-Am, New Orleans Open, Tournament of Champions, Atlantic Classic, U.S. P.G.A. Championship, Ohio Kings Island, Walt Disney Classic, World Cup |
| 1974 | Hawaiian Open, Tournament Players' Championship |
| 1975 | Doral Eastern Open, Heritage Classic, U.S. Masters, U.S. P.G.A., World Open, Australian Open |
| 1976 | Tournament Players' Championship, World Series of Golf, Australian Open |
| 1977 | Gleason Inverary Classic, Tournament of Champions, Memorial Tournament |
| 1978 | Open Championship, Gleason Inverary Classic, Tournament Players' Championship, IV-B Philadelphia Classic, Australian Open |
| 1980 | U.S. Open Championship, U.S. P.G.A. |
| 1982 | Colonial National Invitational |
| 1984 | Memorial Tournament |
| 1986 | U.S. Masters |

# *IAN WOOSNAM*

Welshman Ian Woosnam made history when he became the first British golfer to win £1 million in one year but he will be judged, eventually, by the number of majors he can win.

Ian Woosnam – how many majors will he win?

Welshman Ian Woosnam relishes a challenge. As a youngster at school before he caught the golfing bug he would take on bigger, stronger, older lads from classes above him and beat them in the boxing ring. He loved it and enjoys himself just as much today when he can outgolf rather than outpunch Severiano Ballesteros, Sandy Lyle and Nick Faldo in important golf tournaments.

To date he has not managed to tuck a major title under his belt but he has the game and the desire to win an Open. Whether he will achieve that level of greatness reserved for major winners we shall just have to wait and see, but you can be sure Woosnam will be trying as hard as he can to do so. He knows no other way to operate. Coming second is just not good enough for Ian. Taking part may be important but for the terrier-like Woosnam, built in the same mould as two other great Welshmen Dai Rees and Brian Huggett, winning is the great motivator. He may have a swing which Severiano Ballesteros describes as the best in Europe but he has that other very necessary ingredient which goes to make a special champion – determination. Sometimes he may run out of patience but there is plenty of time for him to achieve whatever he wants to even if it is not necessarily the worldwide rewards that the jet-set lifestyle of Sandy Lyle produces. Woosnam enjoys life at home with his wife Glendryth and two children too much to spend all the time on the road.

Woosnam shot rapidly to stardom and is learning – sometimes the hard way – that international golfing success brings its pressures and responsibilities. Everyone has to learn how to handle it. Woosnam has had his problems in the last two years but has always come bouncing back. Maybe at times he has said too much on certain issues, and at other times not been open enough, but he has had to

In action in the Ryder Cup (right) and acknowledging the Wentworth crowd (below)

appreciate that people are interested in him and his golf. What he does and says, how he reacts and performs is news. Gone are the days when he could operate almost anonymously on the Tour as one of the pack.

Yet he is only too well aware that getting to the top is rather easier than staying there. Take the 1987 season for instance. That year he reached heights previously unscaled when he became Europe's first 'million pound man'. It was a phenomenal year for the gritty Welshman who began his triumphant march in far-off Hong Kong where he became the first British player to win the title and set a tournament record in the process. He ended his record-breaking season in equally far flung places – Sun City in Southern Africa, where he won the One Million Dollar Challenge, and Hawaii, where he won the World Cup with David Llewellyn and took the individual award too. That was a magic moment for Wales.

In between he scorched his way through Europe with wins in Jersey, Madrid, the Scottish Open, Lancome Trophy and Suntory World Matchplay, compiling a stroke average of 69.81. But then, at the beginning of 1988, things began to turn sour. He had a bad time in America, he changed his clubs and lost his form. To answer the doubters, however, Ian won three of Europe's most prestigious titles, the Volvo P.G.A. Championship, the Carrolls Irish Open and the Panasonic European Open to finish fourth among the European money winners.

One of the most astonishing things about Ian Woosnam is the length he hits the ball. For a man so small in stature – he stands only five feet four inches – he can outhit far more powerful men. The frame may be small but it is solid and strong, like his mental approach. When he is playing well he oozes confidence, he knows he can win against the best in the world and although he has not yet won a major we should not have too long to wait.

The son of a Shropshire farmer, Ian was born in the town of Oswestry, where he still lives, on the England-Wales border. His allegiance, however, lies firmly with Wales and he says: 'I'm a Taff to the core'. His local golf club, Llanymynech, has 15 holes in Wales and three in England. He turned professional in 1976, having once lost the Shropshire and Herefordshire Boys Championship to none other than Sandy Lyle. But there were a lot of lean years before he eventually made the breakthrough in 1982 by winning the Swiss Open. He had struggled to make a living around Europe as a Monday pre-qualifier unable to make it into the exempt class. Then, in 1982, his game took off, catapulting him through the ranks to number eight among the money winners. There was no going back. He finished ninth the following year and from then on it has been sixth, fourth, fourth, first and fourth.

Ironically his success story in 1987 was sparked by accident. A friend wanted a photograph of Ian driving and on examination of the picture he discovered several technical faults. He worked hard on his game before the start of the season and then reaped rich rewards.

Woosnam's natural resilience shows why he was a major part of Tony Jacklin's plans when Europe beat the Americans in the Ryder Cup matches of 1985 and 1987. At Muirfield Village in 1987 he teamed up with Nick Faldo for foursomes and fourballs in an undefeated partnership which produced three and a half points out of a possible four, a major contribution to an historic victory.

Yet, strangely, he has not enjoyed playing in the United States, mainly because of the steamy heat of summer. He has never played well there and has had problems with the Bermuda grass collars around the greens. It requires a special technique to play out of this particular grass so close to the green and Woosnam is taking time to learn the art of handling it. More recently, however, he has been more comfortable when playing there, the result, no doubt of improved confidence but he does not see himself making America a full-time base. He believes that there is no real need to go to America to prove himself as many of the best players in the world are on the European Tour. He will obviously continue to play in the U.S. Masters and the U.S. Open but is not interested in trying for a U.S. players' card.

Woosnam has been to the top and enjoyed banner headlines but has also suffered the jibes in a difficult and frustrating period in his life especially when he gave up his Dunlop clubs at the end of his successful 1987 season to sign a new contract with Maruman. He thought at the time he would be able to play with anything if the clubs were manufactured to the same specifications as the old ones with which he won his million but he learned differently. It took almost a full season to get his new clubs right. He weathered the storm of criticism. He is content to do his own thing, safe in the knowledge that the world will continue to admire Ian Woosnam and his golf for a long time yet.

## *CAREER RECORD*

### Victories

| | |
|---|---|
| 1979 | News of The World Under-23 Match-play Championship |
| 1982 | Cacherel Under-25 World Championship, Swiss Open |
| 1983 | Silk Cut Masters |
| 1984 | Scandinavian Enterprise Open |
| 1985 | Zambian Open |
| 1986 | Lawrence Batley Tournament Players' Championship, 555 Kenya Open |
| 1987 | Hong Kong Open, World Cup (individual and team with David Llewellyn), Sun City Million Dollar Challenge |
| 1988 | Carrolls Irish Open, Volvo P.G.A. Championship, Panasonic European Open |

### Did you know...

1. Ian Woosnam became the first British player to win the World Match-play title in 1987 – the 24th year of the popular tournament held at Wentworth each autumn.
2. Ian Woosnam and Nick Faldo made a devastating partnership in the 1987 Ryder Cup match at Muirfield Village in America. They won three and a half points out of four as Europe roared to a first ever victory over the Americans on U.S. soil.
3. Ian Woosnam became the first European golfer to make £1 million in one calendar year in 1987. That year he won in Jersey, Madrid, Paris, Wentworth, Hong Kong, Kapalua (Hawaii) and Sun City, Bophuthatswana.
4. Welshman Ian Woosnam partnered David Llewellyn to victory in the rain of Hawaii in the World Cup in 1987. They became the first home country to win the title since Christy O'Connor Sen. and Harry Bradshaw won for Ireland in 1958 in Mexico.

The 1988 P.G.A. Trophy

# TONY JACKLIN

He won the Open Championship in 1969 and the American Open less than a year later and now Tony Jacklin is proving to be an inspired Ryder Cup captain.

Few people would argue that Tony Jacklin, son of a Scunthorpe lorry driver, changed the face of British professional golf. His victory in the 1969 Open championship at Royal Lytham and St Annes and his success 49 weeks later in the 1970 United States Open, made people sit up and take notice of what was happening in golf on the British side of the Atlantic.

Jacklin, a boy prodigy but little-heralded outside his native county of Lincolnshire, knew what he wanted almost from the day he first picked up a golf club at the age of nine and it was no surprise when he told a golf magazine soon after turning professional: 'I want to be the best golfer in the world.' He achieved that ambition in sensational fashion, made a fortune from the game and then went on to equally great heights as captain of Europe's Ryder Cup team which plays the Americans every two years.

Those who were at school in Scunthorpe with this small but always sturdy boy had no inkling that one day he would be a champion golfer and be given an American-style ticker-tape reception in his home town as he rode through the streets like a film star in an open car after his tremendous victory at Royal Lytham. Just ten years earlier, he was in his last term at school and pondering his future. Having already won everything in sight in Lincolnshire, including the county Open championship at Elsham, he only wanted to be a professional golfer. But his parents steered him towards safer prospects and, like most school leavers in Scunthorpe, his first job was in the local steelworks as an apprentice fitter.

Celebrating the 1987 Ryder Cup victory with Seve

He hated the job and so intense was his passion for golf that he cycled the three miles from work every day to hit practice shots for a mere 15 minutes at Holme Hall Golf Club in his lunch hour. And when work was finished, he cycled back to the club and practised until it was dark. Such was his dedication that a Holme Hall member, Scunthorpe solicitor Eric Kemp, gave him a job which paid just £6 a week but allowed him every afternoon off to play golf.

'But it wasn't what I wanted,' recalled Jacklin some years later in a book called *The Price of Success*. 'I didn't want to stay close to home and do what was expected of me. I wanted to be a professional golfer.' Without telling his parents, Jacklin applied for several jobs as an assistant professional and was invited to Potter's Bar by Bill Shankland, a tough Australian, who had turned to professional golf after a glittering career as a Rugby League player. 'I hadn't told Dad I'd written for the job but I asked him to come down with me to the interview and said I would only take the job if he

thought it was all right,' said Jacklin.

Jacklin became the assistant to Shankland at Potter's Bar and although it was a stormy relationship he learned a lot from the no-nonsense Australian. A Potter's Bar member, Johnny Reubens, eventually backed Jacklin financially and that was the start of his brilliant playing career. Since then he has won all over the world and his great golfing deeds have spurred others to strive for fame and golfing fortune.

In the sand at the 1988 Open and (left) the celebrations continue at Muirfield Village in 1987

Jacklin, always a confident young man, had decided early in his career that to get on he needed to make the grade in America. Although he was later to tire of the junk food and motel life that is part of the American circuit, Jacklin initially revelled in the American way of life and proved his class and determination by winning tournaments – something that shocked Americans unused to foreigners picking up first prize cheques. What he learned in the States stood him in good stead when he went to Lytham in 1969. He had won an event there a year earlier and while it was not one of his favourite courses, he had respect for it. That week was undoubtedly his week. He won, in the end, from Bob Charles, the left-hander who had taken the title at Lytham in 1963 and how Britain celebrated. Tony after all was the first British winner since Max Faulkner in 1951, and the first home winner in 18 years. Jacklin celebrated by taking Pan-Am's new-fangled jumbo jet to America and four days after his historic win he was teeing up again as just one of the boys in another U.S. event.

He certainly was not just one of the boys in the 1970 U.S. Open at Chaska where his putter worked like magic to give him a U.S. Open title. For just under four weeks he held the titles of both

A tense moment for the captain

Jacklin in 1967 – before his famous Open victories

Britain and America simultaneously and might have completed a Trans-Atlantic title double but for a severe thunderstorm which hit the Old Course at St Andrews in the Open a few weeks later. Jacklin, who had gone out in 29, had hit into a bush at the fourteenth when a peal of thunder put him off at the top of the back swing. That one crucial bit of first round bad luck probably cost him a second win. He was in contention again in 1971 and held a one shot lead with two holes to play in the 1972 Open.

What happened at Muirfield on that summer's day almost certainly ended his career as a world class player. He had already realised that his dream of being world number one was always going to be thwarted by a man just a few years older – Jack Nicklaus. He had rationalised that in his own mind but he took months to recover from the blow he suffered at the hands of Trevino. The American, apparently out of it and, trailing Tony by a shot, holed a pitch from the rough at the back of the green for a par 5. Jacklin, stunned, took four from the edge for a 6 as he momentarily let his concentration slip. From being level he was suddenly one behind with just one hole to play. Trevino never faltered and Jacklin was even overhauled by Nicklaus in the run-in.

He never again challenged for a major title, although ten years later he did beat West German Bernhard Langer in a sudden death play-off for the British PGA championship at Hillside, Southport. Later, when he had cut back on his playing programme he became a natural choice, in 1983, to lead Europe's Ryder Cup team into battle against the Americans in Florida and he came within a whisker of pulling off an amazing victory.

Jacklin had been controversially left out of the 1981 side when the selection panel had decided he was too old to play at 37 – a verdict that hurt him badly. He had vowed he would never have anything else to do with the Ryder Cup again, but time proved a great healer. He realised the match was more important than the pride of any one individual and when asked to captain the team he agreed – as long as things were done his way, the first class way. He also persuaded Severiano Ballesteros, another 1981 reject, to bury the Ryder Cup hatchet and join him. Together they have provided an inspirational lead. After losing by a slender point at West Palm Beach the first year he was in charge, the match was scheduled two years later for The Belfry. The nucleus of the side was the same and Jacklin and his team became heroes. Spurred on by an unashamedly partisan crowd they beat America for the first time since Dai Rees' side had been successful in 1957. It was an emotional occasion and the pilot of the British Airways supersonic Concorde, en route to Birmingham to pick up the American players, heard the news from ground control and did an enthralling victory roll over The Belfry course.

Two years later Jacklin was again named as Ryder Cup captain, this time against Jack Nicklaus at Muirfield Village, Ohio, and once again the Europeans came out on top. Jacklin was so overcome by emotion he could hardly speak. He himself had never played on a winning Ryder Cup team although he had achieved the next best thing – a tied match at Royal Birkdale in 1969, just a few months after winning the Open. The Royal Birkdale script could not have been written better. Jacklin was paired against Nicklaus in the final singles match on the final afternoon and the entire outcome rested on their result. Jacklin holed a 35 foot putt for an eagle three on the seventeenth green to square his match against Nicklaus and both players hit the eighteenth green in two shots. Jacklin putted first and left the ball a good two feet short of the hole; Nicklaus, with a long birdie chance for victory, gave his putt a good rap and knocked the ball four feet past the hole.

The Golden Bear, as Nicklaus is universally known, sank the return and then magnanimously picked up Jacklin's ball marker to concede the half and, more importantly in the great man's mind, avoid either side winning or losing on the outcome of such a short putt. Such actions are the way of golf. Jacklin has followed such a code all his life and will go down in history as one of Britain's greatest golfers.

Yet his life has not been without its sadness. In 1988 his wife Vivien died suddenly at the wheel of her car as she was returning to their home in Sotogrande, close by Gibraltar and near to where Jacklin is building the impressive San Roque course. Her death devastated the golfing world. She had shared the agony and ecstasy of Tony's rise to the top. She was as much a part of the winning Ryder Cup side as Tony himself. Fortunately he had his three children to help him cope – Bradley, Warren and Tina. Now remarried, Jacklin is rebuilding his life in Spain.

## *CAREER RECORD*

### Victories

| | |
|---|---|
| 1965 | Gor-Ray Assistants' Championship |
| 1966 | Kimberley Tournament (South Africa) |
| 1967 | Forrest Products (New Zealand), New Zealand P.G.A. Championship, Pringle Tournament, Dunlop Masters |
| 1968 | Jacksonville Open |
| 1969 | British Open Championship |
| 1970 | U.S. Open Championship, W.D. and H.O. Wills Tournament, Lancome Tournament |
| 1971 | Benson and Hedges Festival |
| 1972 | Jacksonville Open, Viyella P.G.A. Championship, Dunlop International (Australia) |
| 1973 | Bogota Open, Italian Open, Dunlop Masters |
| 1974 | Los Lagartos Open, Scandinavian Enterprise Open |
| 1976 | Kerrygold International Classic |
| 1979 | German Open, Venezuela Open |
| 1981 | Billy Butlin Jersey Open |
| 1982 | Sun Alliance P.G.A. Championship |

### Did you know...

1. Tony Jacklin was the first British golfer to win the Open in Britain for 18 years when he won the title at Lytham in 1969. The previous home winner had been Max Faulkner in 1951.
2. On one occasion Tony Jacklin hit balls off the roof of the Shell building into the River Thames as a publicity stunt.
3. At the height of Tony Jacklin's playing career he made his own record singing songs show-business describe as 'standards'. It was good but he did not make the charts.
4. Tony Jacklin was always a streak putter as a player. He produced one of his hottest putting performances when he won the U.S. Open by seven strokes. He led every round and was the only player to finish under par on 281 at Hazeltine.
5. Tony Jacklin won only one Open in Britain but with just a little bit of luck might have won at least two more. He won in 1969 but was third in 1971 and 1972 and fifth in 1970.
6. Tony Jacklin led his European team to a first win on American soil in the 1987 Ryder Cup match at Muirfield Village in Ohio. They had come within a point of winning in America in 1983 at Palm Beach Gardens.

The Ryder Cup

# SANDY LYLE

He was hitting balls at the age of three so, not surprisingly, golf comes easily to Scotland's Sandy Lyle, son of a golf professional and with two majors already behind him.

The tension had been building all afternoon at Augusta that April Sunday in 1988. Sandy Lyle, who had been the first British winner of the Open in 16 years when he had triumphed at Royal St George's three years earlier, had been the pace-setter for three rounds but suddenly it looked as if he was letting the chance of a U.S. Masters victory slip away. When his ball, caught by a swirling gust of wind, dropped short of the green at the short twelfth and rolled back into the water there was despair on the likeable, big Scot's face. It is tough to lead any tournament from start to finish, far less a Masters, but was there to be disappointment after all for the then 30-year-old son of a golf professional who was never ever going to be anything other than a golf professional himself!

The fact that Sandy Lyle now has a corner all to himself in the upstairs Champions' Locker room in the Colonial-style clubhouse at Augusta is the proof that despite what happened at the twelfth on Augusta's famous and fearsome Amen Corner it all worked out well for him in the end. But only after one of the most dramatic finishes in the 55 years history of the tournament, traditionally the first major of the year. Not many players ever birdie the last to win at Augusta but Lyle did so brilliantly. The broad-shouldered American Mark Calcavecchia was in the clubhouse on six-under-par 282. Lyle, playing with Ben Crenshaw, a former Masters' winner, was six-under when he stepped on to the last tee. The hole, stretching up a far steeper hill than it ever looks on television to a green in front of the clubhouse, bends away to the right at about the spot that most players' tee-shots would hit the ground. Two bunkers guard the outside corner of the dog-leg. The safe line is just left of the centre of the fairway to open up the green. Lyle knew he needed to put one last good swing on his drive. One of the longest hitters in world golf, Lyle selected his one-iron, a club which he knew he could hit as far as his three-wood and probably straighter. Pinpoint accuracy was important. Sandy, handling the pressure beautifully, knew the priority was to hit the fairway at all costs and give himself the chance to get near enough to the stick on the slick last green with his second to snatch victory from Calcavecchia and prevent Crenshaw, who was a stroke worse than the other two with one to play, from nipping in.

The television cameras showed the disappointment and anguish on the Scot's face when he pulled the tee-shot into one of the bunkers. The 250 yards he had to walk up the hill from the last tee with faithful caddie and friend Dave Musgrove

Sandy celebrates another birdie putt

was lonely and seemingly endless. He had blundered but, such is his knowledge of the game, he knew he could still make the green if he was lucky. The crucial factor was how the ball was lying in the sand. If it had plugged or ended up close by the lip of the trap his chance of victory would depend on his making par and winning a play-off but he was lucky. The ball was lying far enough back in the bunker and well enough up in the sand for him to get a seven-iron to the green but only if he swung slowly, deliberately and with the precision of a surgeon using a scalpel. He stepped into the trap, the white sand throwing up a bright glare on his boyish face. This then was the moment he needed to prove his class. Up the hill 150 yards away by the green his father and mother could hardly bear to look but Sandy was equal to the occasion. He picked the ball out of the bunker cleanly and it sailed high into the evening sky and on to the green, landing on the edge of the upper shelf right behind the stick which was, however, on the lower level. For a second or two the ball wavered as if uncertain whether or not to roll down the hill towards the hole on a green as smooth as

A 'sandy' shot at Augusta (top) and on the 18th tee in the 1988 Masters

Sandy on the way to his historic Masters victory

In action in the U.S.A. again – this time in the Open

glass. Everyone around the green (especially Calcavecchia), and millions watching the telecast live around the world, held their breath as the ball began to move, slowly at first, then quickly gathering speed until it lay just ten feet from the hole. Severiano Ballesteros (twice) and Bernhard Langer had won for Europe in the 80's but no Briton had ever landed the title. Lyle's putt would not have been an easy one in a pre-tournament practice round at five dollars a corner. It was mind-numbing to have to hole to win a second major. The crowds who had cheered themselves hoarse throughout the afternoon were suddenly silent. Lyle wiped the sweat from his brow and stepped forward for the second most important putt of his career – the first had been what turned out to be the Open winner from two and a half feet on the last green in 1985 at Sandwich. His grip on the putter was firm but not tight and when he made the hit, the ball never looked like going anywhere but into the hole. The line was inch-perfect, the pace just right. Sandy Lyle attempted a jig of delight but was almost too embarrassed to let himself go for fear it was all a dream.

He had completed one half of a Grand Slam. The U.S. Open and the U.S. P.G.A. Championship remain as golfing Everests to conquer and the chances are he will win those, too, as long as he gives himself enough chances to play the U.S. P.G.A! Curiously, Lyle has a blank spot when it comes to the fourth of the majors. Maybe when he is chatting next time to Jack Nicklaus, Tom Watson, Billy Casper, Arnold Palmer, Gary Player or Seve in that Masters locker-room he will be convinced that a player of his stature and ability must go for all four majors every year even if, usually, the weather at P.G.A. time does happen to be hotter and more humid than normal. Lyle, after all, is no ordinary golfer. He is an international performer with a unique talent and a superb temperament. The combination is deadly. In 1988 he became the first man to top a million dollars in career earnings in the States and a million pounds on the European circuit. For most of 1988, helped by wins at Greensboro and Phoenix in play-offs against Ken Green and Fred Couples, Lyle led the U.S. money list.

Only his decision to stick to a pre-arranged schedule and not go chasing the U.S. number one spot let in Curtis Strange. Personally I wish he had gone all out for glory although you have to admire his determination not to back down on contracts signed with sponsors to play in Europe.

I dwelt, at the start, on Lyle's greatest moment at Augusta because that was a major title he went out and won. In 1985 a fluffed pitch from an awkward lie just off and to the left of the last green and the subsequent one over par 5 just made things more awkward for him when he won the Open. All his rivals faltered that year and Lyle won but it was not nearly so cut and dried as at Augusta. Sandy Lyle is a genius, a laid-back one maybe, but a genius nevertheless with an on-course golf brain as shrewd as any successful City financier and with a hidden killer-touch lurking behind the smile. He may be easy-going but he knows where he wants to go and his rivalry with Nick Faldo and Severiano Ballesteros has served to sharpen his competitive teeth. Watching him you might just get the wrong idea. Lyle is a superb competitor even if it did take him five attempts to win the World Match-play Championship. In 1988 he finally won the title with a 2 and 1 win over his great rival Faldo. Mind you, one of the previous finals in which he took part went to the thirty-seventh in the rain before Seve won, two went against him on the thirty-sixth green and he lost the other at the thirty-fifth!

Lyle has every shot in his golfing locker and the ability to manufacture one or two that do not come with 'the standard model'. He has eradicated from his repertoire, it seems, the casually-missed two footer that used to prove so costly. The problem is simply finding the game too easy at times. His easy-going temperament sometimes allows mistakes, despite the solidity of a swing carefully tuned over the years by dad Alex and American teacher Jimmy Ballard in Florida. When others need to practise long and hard to keep their swings in shape, Lyle can warm up by hitting a few quick shots when others need a full half-hour to get themselves ready. He has a natural talent which is the envy of most of his colleagues. He has been swinging golf clubs, of course, since he was a curly-haired three-year-old. His father Alex, professional at Hawkstone Park, made small clubs for him and even a mini caddie-cart, and he hit his first shot 80 yards!

He won every Midland title there was to win as a youngster and, because it was financially expedient, played for England at boys, youths and senior level. He is, of course, Scottish and was eligible to play for England as an amateur on a residence basis. He was English when he first played in the Open as a 16-year-old at Lytham when Gary Player won. Sandy played three of the four rounds before missing the cut. Today he would have made it to the last day. There is only one cut now. It had been at Lytham in 1969 that Alex and Sandy sat in the stand around the greens and watched Jacklin win the Open. For Lyle it was an inspirational moment nearly made all the more sweet by the fact that Tony hurled his ball up into the stand in the direction of young Lyle. He did not know him at that point and anyway Lyle just missed catching it but it was, perhaps, an omen. Now Lyle is a stalwart of Tony Jacklin's Ryder Cup team.

By the time he had turned professional in 1977 he was a strapping six footer and had twice played in the final of the British Boys', won two English Strokeplay titles, the British Youths' Championship and had competed in Eisenhower Trophy and Walker Cup competitions. There was, therefore, every indication he

Sandy receiving the coveted Green Jacket (top) and in action (above)

would make the grade in the paid ranks although some golfers, admittedly less talented, have failed to cope with the transition. Lyle had no problem. He won the Qualifying School at the end of 1977 and in his first season took the Nigerian Open on the Safari circuit, creating in the process a record 18 under par 124 total at halfway that included a 61. In Europe he finished 49th on the money list behind Severiano Ballesteros but in his second and third years he had captured the top money spot and won three events, including the European Open at Turnberry in Scotland where he pulverised the field with a final round start in which he birdied six of the first seven holes to overhaul Mark James and Neil Coles. As he continued to improve he won regularly. By the time he headed for Hawaii late in 1984 he had won ten times in Europe but what happened at Kapalua would decide him to try his luck on the U.S. Tour. Lyle won the Kapalua tournament from a top quality U.S. field.

Sandy Lyle – now a Ryder Cup stalwart

Then there came the Royal St George's success in 1985 when he became only the fifth British golfer since the end of the Second World War to win the Open and the first British-based Scot since Willie Auchterlonie in 1893. He promised that his win would not change him as a person and that only his bank balance would show a dramatic increase. With that win he silenced once and for all those who had suggested he did not have a killer streak and that his putting was too weak for him ever to win a major! When he headed for Glasgow later that year he was given a hero's welcome. And he almost produced a hero's victory, but lost a play-off to Howard Clark. Still, he was number one again when in 1986 he made his first official U.S. Tour victory at the lively Greater Greensboro tournament in North Carolina where the fans enjoy a beer and speak their mind. The local papers screamed out 'Sandy conquers the World.' Well, not quite, but Craig Stadler, another Greensboro winner, said simply enough: 'He is a hell of a player.' The following year he holed a 35 foot putt on the last and went on to win the Tournament Players' Championship at the U.S. Tour headquarters at Sawgrass, Florida, in a play-off with Jeff Sluman, and the German Masters at Stuttgart. In 1988 he won three times in America and twice in Britain, including the World Match-play Championship.

Sandy is one of the new breed of European golfers who operate on a wider international stage. He competes not only in Europe and America but in Australia where last year he led the United Kingdom side to a first Test win against the locals beating Greg Norman in their personal singles duel, and in Japan where he has also been a winner. When pundits assess Lyle as a golfer they admire his great length off the tee, his overall competence with every club in the bag and pinpoint, too, his patience. Sandy himself is aware that the ability to remain calm when a crisis crops up on the course and never lose one's temper is a talent not everyone enjoys. The ability to remain patient when natural instinct might suggest otherwise is the fifteenth club in his bag and it really is a winner.

Father of two lively boys, Sandy Lyle, a broken marriage behind him, is a golfer with no airs and graces. He is not a high flier. When he won the Open he headed back home for a celebratory Chinese carry-out meal washed down, it is reported, by champagne. In fact he is

something of a Chinese restaurant expert. He could write a book about them. There is no stop in Europe where he cannot immediately go to the best 'Chinese' in town. After he had won in Greensboro and just two days before the U.S. Masters in 1985 Sandy, always popular with the press and sensible in his handling of the golf-writers, arranged a meal at the best Chinese restaurant in Augusta. After he won the Masters in 1988, the reporters took him, his proud parents, friends and caddie Musgrove to a victory meal at Hilton Head in South Carolina. The evening re-emphasised the close bond between players and press on the European circuit.

While most pro golfers relax by picking up a fishing rod and heading for a lonely stretch of river to help them get everything back into perspective Sandy Lyle prefers something more physical. He goes motor-cycle scrambling! Above all, and despite the personal disappointments he has had, he enjoys life and as he gets older is beginning to enjoy coping with stardom. He may not be as quick-witted as Lee Trevino or be as good as Supermex on the one-liners but he can come out with some beauties right off the top of his head.

To date he has won two majors. Predicting there will be more to come and that one day he will be the American number one is neither difficult nor stupid. He is hugely talented. There is no golfing target he cannot aim at without complete confidence in his ability to reach it. Whatever happens in the next few years, whatever titles he adds to his growing international collection Sandy Lyle – 'Lily' to his closest friends on Tour – knows how highly respected he is by his peers and by the general public. He never has been and never will be a golfing prima donna. He has his two size 11 feet far too firmly planted on the ground for that. He has had his form slumps but when he is 'on song' Sandy Lyle is an intimidating performer.

## *CAREER RECORD*

### Victories

| | |
|---|---|
| 1978 | Nigerian Open |
| 1979 | Jersey Open, Scandinavian Enterprise Open, European Open |
| 1980 | Coral Classic |
| 1981 | Paco Rabanne French Open, Lawrence Batley International |
| 1982 | Lawrence Batley International |
| 1983 | Cepsa Madrid Open |
| 1984 | Italian Open, Lancome Trophy, Kapalua International (U.S.), Casio World Open (Japan) |
| 1985 | Open Golf Championship, Benson and Hedges International |
| 1986 | Greater Greensboro Open |
| 1987 | U.S. Tournament Players' Championship, German Masters |
| 1988 | U.S. Masters, Phoenix Open, Greater Greensboro Open, Dunhill British Masters, Suntory World Match-play Championship |

### Did you know...

1. Sandy Lyle and Ian Woosnam played in Shropshire boys' golf teams together.
2. Sandy's first manager Derrick Pillage was so sure Sandy would win an Open that he put on £100 at 33-1 that he would do so within five years of turning professional. He lost. It took Sandy just over seven years to win!
3. Sandy Lyle was the first golfer to top a million dollars in America and £1 million in Europe.
4. Sandy Lyle relaxes by indulging in motor cycle scrambling. He is also an accomplished disc-jockey at disco sessions.

The 1985 Open champion

# MICHAEL BONALLACK

With an incredible short game, he was the best amateur in the world for a spell but now Michael Bonallack runs the most important golf championship in the world – the Open.

Michael Bonallack's distinguished amateur career began when he won the Boys' Championship in 1952. He was 17 and already showing the fighting qualities which were to give him a very special place in British golfing history. That Boys' title was the foretaste of an amateur career surpassed in British terms by only two men from, curiously, the same club – Royal Liverpool. They were John Ball and Harold Hilton. Ball won the Open in 1890 at Prestwick and eight Amateur titles in a 25-year spell from 1888 and might have taken that title more often had he not gone off to serve King and country for three years in the Boer War! Hilton was a double Open winner in 1892 and 1897 and won the Amateur title four times.

On the way to another Amateur title

Bonallack's record in more modern times – five Amateur titles and five English Championship wins plus an Amateur 'slam' in 1968 which also included victory in the English Strokeplay Championship and the winning of the silver medal as top amateur in the Open – is by any standards staggering. If it does not quite match Ball or Hilton remember it is much more difficult these days for an amateur to win the Open. Ball and Hilton did not have to cope last century with the in-depth professional talent from around the world that the modern amateur has to beat, although Bonallack did make a determined title bids not only in 1968 but in 1971 too when he finished leading amateur again.

If he failed to achieve his Open dream on the golf course, he has done the next best thing by taking complete control of the Championship administratively. Now as the respected secretary of the Royal and Ancient Golf Club of St Andrews, a post he took over from the charismatic Keith Mackenzie in 1983, he has the responsibility of running the Open each year! Modest and far more laid back than his ebullient predecessor who did so much to build the Open into what it is today Bonallack may have been a surprise choice as secretary but how well the appointment has worked out. Highly regarded around the world by amateurs and professionals alike, Bonallack has maintained the high traditions of the Royal and Ancient Golf Club superbly with a team of professional administrators second to none.

Of Cornish origin, Bonallack, a stalwart of golf in the county of Essex, may have thought twice of moving north with his wife Angela, herself a talented title-winner, but the challenge of the job and the lure of St Andrews quickly won him over.

The Old Course has a very special meaning to Bonallack because it was at St Andrews in 1971 that he led the Walker Cup team to victory over an American side packed with talented young men who would play such an important part in the professional scene later. The British and Irish were, as usual, the under-dogs. The Americans super confident!

Bonallack was at the famous seventeenth hole when, on the final day, with the match delicately balanced, he watched David Marsh, one up on Bill Hyndman, hit a 3-iron to 12 feet to clinch overall victory. It was for both men a magic moment!

It was a stroke of genius similar to many Bonallack himself played in his illustrious career. Not long after that team triumph Bonallack was awarded the O.B.E. It was richly deserved.

If Ireland's Joe Carr dominated amateur golf and, for a short time, the late lamented Scot Ronnie Shade reigned supreme, Bonallack nevertheless was the towering figure in the amateur game on this side of the Atlantic in the 60's and 70's. When finally Bonallack, 'The Duke' to his friends, met Carr in an Amateur final in 1967, it was the Englishman who won by 7 and 6. Irish fans insist that had they met ten years earlier the result would have been as decisive the other way! Carr did in fact, captain the British and Irish team that won the World Team championship at Olgiata in Rome in 1964 in which Bonallack played such an important part. For sheer golfing brilliance, however, his most impressive performance was against David Kelley in the English Championship of 1966 at Ganton. Kelley was round in 74 in the first round and lunched 13 down! Bonallack swept him cruelly aside with a 61, putting superbly. The final was over quickly. Bonallack was always a great competitor – he came from six down to beat Clive Clark in the British final at Porthcawl in 1965. Even when he was not playing well Bonallack could conjure up a way of getting up and down somehow. He has always been a magician around and on the greens even if his swing hardly has that classical look about it. Always gracious in defeat and even more so when scoring his innumerable victories, Michael Bonallack has served the game well with his adventurous, enthusiastic approach to the game and his impeccable behaviour both on and off the course!

Surveying the scene at the 1987 Dunhill Cup

## CAREER RECORD

### Victories

| | |
|---|---|
| 1952 | British Boys' Championship |
| 1961 | British Amateur Championship |
| 1962 | English Amateur Championship |
| 1963 | English Amateur Championship |
| 1964 | English Amateur Open Stroke-Play Championship |
| 1965 | British Amateur Championship, English Amateur Championship |
| 1967 | English Amateur Championship |
| 1968 | British Amateur Championship, English Amateur Open Stroke-Play Championship, English Amateur Championship |
| 1969 | British Amateur Championship, English Amateur Open Stroke-Play Championship |
| 1970 | British Amateur Championship |
| 1971 | English Amateur Open Stroke-Play Championship |

### Did you know...

1. Royal and Ancient Golf Club secretary Michael Bonallack is responsible, with the chairman of the Championship committee, for running the Open. In 1988 it cost £2.9 millions to stage the Championship.
2. In the English Amateur Championship final at Ganton in 1966 Michael Bonallack went round in 61 to lunch 13 up on the luckless David Kelley.

# *BERNHARD LANGER*

No top international player has suffered more from the putting twitch than Bernhard Langer but he still managed to win the U.S. Masters on the most frightening greens of all.

In the high-flying, big money, super-hype world of professional sport, Bernhard Langer stands out not only as a supreme golfer but as a man of tremendous personal dignity and a quite overwhelming modesty. The West German is without doubt in that small group of genuine stars who do not believe that they are God's gift to their sport. Perhaps in Langer's case it helps that he is in an even smaller group of successful men who believe in God in the first place.

No matter what prize he wins, which title he lifts, the German keeps his feet on the ground and his head out of the clouds. An abiding and devout belief in Roman Catholicism has given him not only a faith to follow, it has also bequeathed him a proper perspective of who he is, what he does and what his worth is in a world increasingly beset by problems of somewhat larger importance than how many putts it takes to get down from the edge of the green. When Langer says: 'I have not really done anything of any great importance in my life', he means it. This is not to suggest that golf is a trivial matter to him, far from it, but it does correctly infer that this serious man refuses to take himself, or the game he has graced for more than a decade, too seriously. It is also true that at different times in his glittering career Bernhard Langer has needed faith in something more than most. For the fact is that he has been tested more cruelly than any other golfer of his generation.

Celebrating in the 1987 Ryder Cup victory

Three times his ability has been challenged by spectacular attacks of the 'yips' or, in more precise terms, the mechanical inability to get his hands to do what his brain is ordering them to do when he stands over his ball with a putter. When he is suffering this strange affliction there is no sadder sight in the game. Sometimes in the last few years the problem has been so immense that he has approached greens with the stoicism of a man who is tired of life and is resolutely striding to the gallows. At the Open at Lytham in 1988, the suffering Langer four-putted the seventeenth on the final day!

Others would howl in despair at the beasts that are gnawing at their souls and their talent, but this is not Langer's style. In the end he overcomes his putting problems not by psychiatry or hypnotism. He conquers it by utilising the same qualities that have taken him to the very peaks of his chosen profession, sheer, undiluted and relentlessly hard graft. There is no

The 1989 Masters (top) and a possible new career? – on form at the European Open

more willing worker in golf than this slight and wiry German. And his other persona is that of a player attacking holes like a master swordsman cutting an opponent to shreds. He is a majestic long-iron player. His approach play is always immaculate.

His personality is a direct inheritance from his father Erwin who should have spent his life working happily enough on the family farm in Sudetanland. Unfortunately for Erwin this piece of land, now part of Czechoslovakia, was part of Germany in 1939 and Herr Langer was conscripted into the Germany Army as a courier. By 1945 Erwin was a prisoner-of-war. Worse, he was a prisoner of the Russians and in September of that year found himself with hundreds of his comrades on a train that was rumoured to be heading towards Siberia. At the border he jumped off the train and for four months lived in the woods before settling in Anhausen, a village 30 miles from Munich. Bernhard, his second son, was born there into a close-knit mountain community.

By the time he was eight Langer already had a deep interest in the game that was to make his name and his fortune. This interest is simple to explain – he needed the money that caddying at the Augsbourg Golf and Country Club brought him. Like many thousands of caddies before him, the young Langer filled in the periods between rounds by practising behind the caddie shed. Here he showed not only a natural ability to strike the ball but a ready willingness to work very hard indeed. It was a combination of talents that was to thrust him relentlessly towards his dream of a professional career.

In the spring of 1976 he bought a second-hand Ford Escort and headed for Spain and the European Tour. But after just three tournaments he was plunged into the first of his major putting crises as his stroke all but disintegrated. Ironically, as Langer's putting grew worse, his ability to hit the ball even closer to the flag from the fairway became even more impressive.

As his brittle putting stroke was restructured so that short putts no longer threatened his sanity, it seemed certain that Langer must one day break through from the ranks of the very good into the inner-circle of elite tournament victors. It happened in the 1980 Dunlop Masters when Langer beat off the challenge of one of the most glittering fields of the year to take this coveted title at the famed St Pierre Golf and Country Club in Chepstow. The following year he confirmed his emergence from the pack with wins in the German Open and the ill-fated Bob Hope British Classic.

Few, however, could have guessed where Langer's most thrilling victory was to be staged. For a man whose putting stroke could be suspect to even suggest he could win the U.S. Masters was close to being ridiculous. The Augusta National course in deepest Georgia has greens so fast they can test even the most confident of putters. Yet, in 1985, this is where Langer won his first and, so far, only, major title. To do it he had to beat off the challenge of his greatest rival, Seve Ballesteros, and, as usual, he did it with quiet dignity.

His wife Vikki, a former American air-stewardess, and their daughter Jackie travel with Langer everywhere. They are, he says, the most important people in his life. After his family and his religion comes golf. Despite the riches and the plaudits, and the 27 titles won worldwide, Bernhard Langer still has his priorities arranged in the correct order. In a sometimes bizarre sporting world, that comes as a pleasant change.

## *CAREER RECORD*

The 1987 Whyte & Mackay trophy

### Victories

| | |
|---|---|
| 1979 | Cacherel World Under-25 Championship |
| 1980 | Dunlop Masters, Colombian Open |
| 1981 | German Open, Bob Hope British Classic |
| 1982 | Lufthansa German Open |
| 1983 | Italian Open, Glasgow Golf Classic, St Mellion Timeshare Tournament Players' Championship, Johnnie Walker Tournament, Casio World Open (Japan) |
| 1984 | Peugeot French Open, K.L.M. Dutch Open, Carrolls Irish Open, Benson and Hedges Spanish Open |
| 1985 | Lufthansa German Open, Panasonic European Open, Australian Masters, U.S. Masters, Sea Pines Heritage Classic |
| 1986 | German Open, Lancome Trophy |
| 1987 | Whyte and Mackay P.G.A. Championship, Carrols Irish Open |
| 1988 | Epson Grand Prix |

### Did you know...

1. West Germany's Bernhard Langer practises with more clubs than anyone else on Tour. A trip to the practice ground can mean caddie Peter Coleman taking along four or five drivers for Langer to test, half a dozen wedges and a bagful of putters.
2. Bernhard Langer is almost as accomplished a skier as he is a golfer and when the European Tour players get together to have a soccer match with the caddies you can be sure Bernhard is a key man in the side.
3. Bernhard Langer is virtually a one-man golfing nation. He wins the German Closed Championship each year by huge margins.
4. Bernhard Langer has conquered the putting yips three times during his career. He has used a left-hand-below-right method on short putts and won the U.S. Masters!

# LAURA DAVIES

The Americans were not all that eager to allow Laura Davies to join their multi-million dollar tour but she made history by becoming the first British winner of the U.S. Open!

Laura Davies' triumph in America in 1987 was one of the sweetest acts of revenge in golfing history. It is also one of the most remarkable stories in Europe's modern-day swing to power over America. The big-hitting former supermarket check-out girl simply stunned the States by walking away with the U.S. Women's Open just four months after being told she was not good enough to play on the American circuit.

As leading money winner on the European Tour for the previous two seasons, Davies had approached the Ladies Professional Golf Association of America in February 1987 asking if she could compete in a U.S. tournament. In effect, the door was slammed in her face. She was informed she needed a LPGA players' card, and John Laupheimer, the women's tour commissioner, told her: 'Anyway, in recent history women from Great Britain have not made a great impact on the LPGA Tour'. Davies, driven away but undeterred, used the British Open title she had won the previous summer to gain entry in the U.S. Open at Plainfield, New Jersey. And the girl who had taken up golf only 9 years earlier, playing with her brother Tony, showed the Americans just how wrong they had been to reject her by becoming the first Briton to win the LPGA's most treasured piece of silver in its 41-year history.

Davies took the title the hard way, beating her childhood idol JoAnne Carner of America and Japan's Ayako Okamoto in an 18-hole play-off on day six of a gruelling tournament. The fourth round had been delayed for 24 hours following a violent thunderstorm. Yet even the storm's most spectacular moments were as nothing compared to the electrifying effect Laura's victory was to have on the golfing world. What stunned people most was the manner of the Coventry-born and Surrey-raised girl's triumph. Her prodigious hitting was allied to an unflappable temperament. Her holing out was fearless and she reduced the 509-yard seventh hole and 493-yard uphill 17th, both par 5's to virtual par 4's, feats of strength and accuracy which sent shockwaves throughout the field, most of whom were grateful to secure the sanctuary of the

Laura Davies in the sand at the 1988 British Open

Laura in 1987 – the year of her U.S. Open victory…

…but in a spot of bother in the 1988 British Open

green in the regulation three shots.

Laura has brother Tony to thank for stimulating her initial interest in a game which has secured her fame, fortune and an M.B.E. Tony, who shared her triumph at Plainfield where he acted as caddy, took young Laura with him when he played at West Byfleet. First she watched, then – at 13 – she began to play and once her fourteenth birthday had endowed her with her first set of clubs there was no holding her. Her handicap, starting at 26, quickly tumbled and by 1982 she had reached scratch. She was a county player and followed victory in the Surrey Girls' Open with her first major success in the Bristol and District Championship, where her victims included former English Ladies' champion and international player, Beverley New. She won the South-Eastern title the following year, which she successfully defended in 1984, and represented England in the home internationals. It was in 1984, too, that she won the highest representational honour in amateur women's golf, being chosen for the British side which faced America at Muirfield in the Curtis Cup. Britain and Ireland narrowly lost.

Laura had resolved to win a national title before taking what had become the inevitable step of turning professional. She had gone close in the 1984 English Amateur Championships, reaching the semi-finals before losing to experienced Linda Bayman, but at the end of the season, she changed her mind. It is a highly expensive business playing amateur golf at the top level and to subsidise her summer's activities Laura had had to work hard throughout each winter, in turn, as a supermarket checkout girl, a petrol pump attendant and a bookmakers' assistant. But the logical thing to do was to turn professional and this she did at the start of 1985 – with outstanding results. She won the Belgian Open on her way to topping the order of merit in her first season on the European Tour with prize money of £21,736. The Rookie of the Year award was procured as a matter of course. The following season Sweden's Liselotte Neumann led the money winners' list with five tournaments to play, by a healthy £11,000 from Gillian Stewart with Laura a further £2,000 adrift, Laura's victories in the Greater Manchester Open and the British Open closed the gap, but Liselotte entered the Spanish Open at La Manga, the final event, needing to finish seventh or better to win the order of merit. Laura amazingly made it three wins in five events while Liselotte finished well down the field, her total earnings for the season being pipped by Laura's £37,500 by just £494.

Despite increasing her earnings to £47,151 on the W.P.G.A. Tour in 1987 Laura slipped to second spot in the order of merit, but her £35,000 winner's cheque from the U.S. Open was a more than adequate solace. Her victory also shamed the American Tour officials into a belated sense of 'hospitality' and she earned an unprecedented invitation to play the American Tour without having to attend the pre-qualifying school. In 1988 she more than justified the decision by winning the Tucson Open, the Jamie Farr Toledo Classic and, in a closing adjunct to the season in Japan, the Itoki Classic. Her schedule was arduous, combining as it did tournaments on both sides of the Atlantic, but she still managed to annex three European Tour titles (the Ford Classic, the Italian Open and the Biarritz Open) in ten starts, and only once finished outside the top ten on her way to prize money of £41,871 and eighth place in the order of merit.

Her new-found wealth has allowed her to indulge in a passion for fast cars – she owns a BMW – and racing greyhounds, as well as enabling her to buy a cottage next door to her mother, Rita, in the Surrey village of Ottershaw. She spends most of what little free time she has, however, at the snooker table where her style, it is said, mirrors what she takes onto the golf course. It is bold, fast and very, very good. Throughout her albeit short career Laura Davies has conducted herself with grace and dignity. She is a modest winner and a gracious loser while still managing to be a determined golfing competitor with steel-like nerve and singular dedication.

# *CAREER RECORD*

## Victories

| | |
|---|---|
| 1985 | Belgian Open |
| 1986 | McEwan's Wirral Classic, Greater Manchester Tournament, British Open Championship, La Manga Club Spanish Open |
| 1987 | U.S. Open, Ford Classic |
| 1988 | Tucson Open, Toledo Open, Ford Classic, Biarritz Open, Itoki Classic (Japan) |

## Did you know...

1. Laura Davies was appointed a member of the British Empire (M.B.E.) after becoming the first British golfer to win the U.S. Women's Open in 1987.
2. Laura Davies employs her brother Tony as her full time caddie wherever she plays in the world. It was Tony who encouraged her to play more golf as a teenager by taking her to the West Byfleet Club in Surrey.
3. Laura Davies may well be the only international golfer who owns and runs greyhounds.
4. Laura Davies has won events in Europe, America and Japan but her most satisfying was the U.S. Open at Plainfield, New Jersey in 1987.

The 1986 British Open Champion

# *NICK FALDO*

Anything Sandy Lyle can do Nick Faldo can do equally as well. The rivalry between Britain's two most successful international players has helped them and the game.

If there is a more single-minded or determined golfer on earth today than 1989 U.S. Masters Champion Nick Faldo then such a man has yet to reveal himself. Who else but Faldo would have changed a swing reliable enough to have won him five European events in one year and to have established him as one of the best players of his generation simply because he wanted something better? His courageous decision to re-align his swing in order to eradicate an inconsistency in his game which he felt might prevent him winning majors sets him apart from the other European stars.

Nick Faldo in trouble at Augusta – three days later the Green Jacket was his

It is his hunger for success and recognition that drives him on when others are content to relax. It is a passion that has, at times, caused him to be much misunderstood. Tall, good-looking and naturally athletic, Faldo was born within 12 months of Seve Ballesteros, Bernhard Langer and Sandy Lyle. Yet unlike Lyle, whose father was a professional, and Langer and Ballesteros, who caddied as youngsters, Faldo grew up in the Hertfordshire town of Welwyn Garden City knowing little about golf. Cricket, soccer, cycling and athletics filled boyhood years until, one day, bored and alone in the house, the 13-year-old flicked on the television set and watched with increasing fascination as Jack Nicklaus played in the 1971 U.S. Masters.

Until then golf was a game played by old men as far as Nick was concerned, a pastime to be considered when the body grew tired or too wounded to participate in more active sports. That evening spent on his own at home, Faldo's attitude to golf changed. Overnight he was hooked. The bat, the ball and the bike were all consigned to the garage and Faldo set off to try to conquer a new peak. Right from the start he showed an instinctive ability to hit the ball. More than that, he was prepared to work hard to succeed. He quickly realised the only real way to make genuine progress within a game is to practise until it hurts and then to keep on practising. His appetite for work soon paid off and within a couple of years of discovering the game and with the full encouragement of his parents, Faldo was making a name for himself on the amateur scene. By the time he was 18 he had won both the British Youths' Championship

and the English amateur title. The Nick Faldo story had begun.

In his first year on the European Tour Faldo finished an impressive 58th on the money list. More importantly he was selected by Henry Cotton as Rookie of the Year. The old master could always spot talent, and he had noted the mark of greatness in the youngster. Twelve months later Faldo repaid Cotton's faith when he won his first tournament and his first win was no ordinary affair. Typically for a golfer inspired by the roar of the crowd, not overawed by it, Faldo became P.G.A. champion with a stirring performance over the toughest but fairest links in England, Royal Birkdale. Two years later he won the P.G.A. again and successfully defended his title in 1981. He should have won the same event at St Andrews in 1979 but the wind got up on the last day and he was caught and passed by Vicente Fernandez.

Faldo was by now a star, but he was not the popular figure he should have been. Instead, the cocoon of concentration that was the bedrock of his success isolated him from both general public and professional rivals alike. Faldo had the respect but not the affection of the fans. It was a situation that confused him, causing him to withdraw further into himself so that he sometimes saw slight and criticism where none had really been intended, particularly from the press with whom he had a running battle which

In action at Augusta (above) and (left) itching to get on with it

Faldo plays his part in the 1987 Ryder Cup victory

Another stylish shot in the World Match-play Championship

lasted more than four years. A messy and much-publicised divorce from his first wife, Melanie did not help his image and despite a phenomenal year in 1983, when he topped the European money list by winning those five titles, including a unique hat-trick of victories in early spring, Faldo's life was more often than not in some sort of turmoil.

In 1984 he won the Car Care Plan in Europe, and made a first breakthrough in America by taking the Sea Pines Heritage title at Hilton Head. It was about this time he also detected the first signs of real weakness in a swing that had looked almost perfect to almost everyone else. The realisation that not all was right had happened earlier that year when he strode into the last round of the U.S. Masters tied for the lead with Ben Crenshaw. While Crenshaw went on to win, Faldo dropped off the leader-board, his swing suddenly graceless and unreliable as it wilted under the pressure of competing in the final round of a major tournament with the chance of winning.

Instead of luxuriating in Europe he headed for Florida and a meeting with English-born golf guru David Leadbetter who systematically broke down the old Faldo swing and then helped him rebuild it. The process was slow and painful to watch. Even Faldo's main critics felt pity as his form slumped and his name slipped off the pages of newspapers that had carried daily bulletins on his career just a short time before. Faldo, however, refused to concede defeat. He believed in Leadbetter's teaching and he believed even more in himself. His self-made slump was made even harder to bear, however, when, just as his fortunes bottomed out in 1985, his long-time rival in Britain, Sandy Lyle, won the Open Championship. Looking back now, he admits Lyle's triumph was the toughest moment of all for him to handle especially as he had been British front runner in several Opens before 1985. 'I just looked at the pictures of Sandy with the trophy and thought "right, if he can win it, so can I".'

Two years later at Muirfield Faldo proved many things to many people when he, too, won the Open Championship. Now he had his own picture with the trophy to look at – and all because the new swing worked so well. He had also removed the monkey that had clung to his back for several years. At last he had approved of his own performance, which removed the pressure from himself and enabled him to relax. It meant a new Nick Faldo. He had not, in truth, evolved into a song and dance man or an easy entertainer, but at least he did allow the decent bloke inside to emerge. He also determined to enjoy the fruits of his win, which commercially were many. Since 1987 he has shown himself to be one of the top 10 golfers in the world. In 1988 he lost that play-off for the U.S. Open to Curtis Strange, finished second in seven other events and then ended the year in style with victory in the inaugural Volvo Masters at Valderama in southern Spain despite the close attention of Ballesteros and Lyle. But his greatest triumph was to come when he won the U.S. Masters at the start of 1989. The 'away' majors are always the most difficult to win. Nick won his second major in style, closing with a 65 which included four birdies in the last six holes. He may have had a 'life' when Scott Hoch, with whom he played off, missed from inside 2½ feet to win at the first extra hole – but it was always a difficult downhill left-to-right putt. When Faldo, who had dramatically recovered his 'feel' and 'touch' around the greens that week at Augusta, holed his winning putt on the next green minutes later he had again emulated Lyle! It was a moment to savour for British golf when Faldo had the Green Jacket put on his back by his great rival Lyle, the 1988 Masters Champion. Their rivalry keeps them both super-sharp.

They have had their differences in the past but a measure of their respect for each other occurred at Augusta in 1988. Lyle won the Masters and Faldo, commentating for the BBC, wasted no time in praising him. In 1989 the roles were reversed! The years ahead promise to underline Faldo's greatness. He has the talent and desire to gain maximum benefit from the hours of hard work he puts in on the practice ground. Nick Faldo will win more majors in the next five years – and that is his prediction!

## *CAREER RECORD*

### Victories

| | |
|---|---|
| 1975 | British Youths' Championship, English Amateur Championship |
| 1977 | Skol Lager Invitational |
| 1978 | Colgate P.G.A. Championship |
| 1979 | I.C.L. Tournament (South Africa) |
| 1980 | Sun Alliance P.G.A. Championship |
| 1981 | Sun Alliance P.G.A. Championship |
| 1982 | Haig Whisky Tournament Players' Championship |
| 1983 | Paco Rabanne French Open, Martini International, Lawrence Batley International, Ebel Swiss Open (European Masters) |
| 1984 | Car Care Plan International, Sea Pines Heritage Classic (U.S.) |
| 1987 | British Open, Peugeot Spanish Open |
| 1988 | Peugeot French Open, Volvo Masters |
| 1989 | U.S. Masters |

### Did you know...

1. Nick Faldo may be an honoured and respected member at Welwyn Garden City these days but when he started the members were not amused by his penchant for practising on the course.
2. Nick Faldo and Sandy Lyle were both offered scholarships to Houston University. Lyle never started, Faldo lasted only a few months.
3. In 1988 Faldo performed best of anyone in the four so-called golfing majors. He was tied 30th in the U.S. Masters, was runner-up in the U.S. Open, finished third in the Open at Lytham and fourth in the U.S. P.G.A. Championship in Oklahoma. He won the 1989 U.S. Masters.
4. Nick Faldo has shot three rounds of 62 – in 1983 in the Lawrence Batley at Bingley St Ives which he won; in 1986 at Sunningdale in the Panasonic European Open and in 1988 at the Peugeot Spanish Open at the Real Club de Pedrena near Santander.

The British Open Champion

# SEVE BALLESTEROS

Every ten years it is argued golf produces someone who is head and shoulders above the best of the rest and swashbuckling Seve fills the bill admirably.

Every so often in golf the game throws up a genius, a golfer so talented, so influential, so charismatic that he is inevitably head and shoulders above the rest. In the 1950's it was Ben Hogan, in the 60's Arnold Palmer, in the 70's, Jack Nicklaus and in the 80's it has been a former caddie from Pedrena near Santander in northern Spain. Seve Ballesteros.

The boom in European golf, especially on the Continent, can be attributed to the impact he has made on the national and international golfing scene with some help, of course, from Sandy Lyle and Nick Faldo and company. Of the three he has the strongest personality and has arguably the most shots in his repertoire. You might think he had been born, the youngest of four brothers of a farmer, simply to play golf. Any golf club looks so natural in his huge hands – large enough to hold 12 golf balls in each – that it seems just an extension of himself. He can work wonders with them all, the result of spending hours at the Real Pedrena course just a few hundred yards down the hill from the family farm overlooking Santander Bay hitting shots with 'borrowed' clubs. All his brothers had caddied before him and it was logical he should be drawn to golf for the extra money that was available. To have ignored golf would have been to look a gift horse in the mouth.

Seve just cannot believe his bad luck with this putt

Seve now earns millions a year from a host of lucrative contracts rationalised in the last few years by his American manager Joe Collet, who speaks fluent Spanish and moved from Los Angeles to Santander with his family to handle all Seve's corporate, financial and legal affairs. It was Collet who handled the delicate negotiations which led, after several years of legal wrangling, to the Ballesteros' break-away from his first manager Ed Barner, for whom Collet first worked. In fact Collet had been introduced by Barner to the dynamic golfer whose power off the tee is awesome, whose iron play can, at times, be Ben Hogan-like in its precision and who has the touch of an angel around the greens.

Seve Ballesteros, two times U.S. Masters winner (and it might have been four times), and with his name already engraved three times on the Open championship trophy, is the most complete golfer around. He does not have a weakness. When on song he is majestic and exciting to watch; when not he is still worth following. He is one of that rare breed of golfer with such a natural rhythm to his shots and with such a heart-on-his sleeve range of emotions that even on the rare occasion he does not play well (by his own high standards) he will still attract and captivate a gallery like a modern Pied

Piper. Genius is not too strong a word to use to describe Ballesteros because he is one. He walks the fairways proudly the way his father, whom he adored, had sailed and rowed the huge wooden boats in races around and across Santander Bay.

His father's death from cancer a few years ago left a gaping void in Seve's life. He recovered slowly from the sadness of being unable, despite having the money to pay for the latest treatment, to save him. Seve is, and always will be, a very private person unwilling to talk about those private family matters but there was clearly a very special bond between him, the baby of the family, and his strong, muscular, athletic father who was his son's greatest fan while always making sure to keep the family adulation well in control. By the very honesty of his

Augusta – the site of Seve's 1980 and 1983 victories (top) and with his Spanish World Cup team mates

upbringing Seve is very much a person with his feet very firmly planted on the ground. These days he may have residence qualifications, for obvious reasons, in Monte Carlo and mix with kings, princes and presidents but he still genuinely enjoys a glass of wine with the lads in the Pedrena equivalent of the local pub to talk not golf but football – he is a great admirer of Barcelona.

1987 – Muirfield Village, Ohio and a historic Ryder Cup victory

Comparisons are often made between Seve and Arnold Palmer. Both have had an immense impact on world golf and been responsible for thousands of men and women being attracted to the game. Both behave in a natural way that makes them easily identifiable with the public. When Seve makes a birdie or an eagle and smiles, the fans smile with him, just as they do with Palmer. When Seve looks glum or glowers and questions what could possibly have gone wrong when a shot comes up fractionally short of the target or his ball takes a cruel kick into trouble, the fans are unhappy for him. Just as they share his extrovert excitement, they suffer with him too. He has a magical rapport, just like Palmer, with the galleries wherever he plays – whether in Europe, Japan or America, where these days, sadly, he plays so seldom. He would argue that his heavy international schedule, essential because of his worldwide contractural obligations, prevents him from concentrating fully on the most important circuit of all, but maybe the long-time personal battle he has waged with Deane Beman, the U.S. Tour commissioner, is probably a more realistic reason. Special rules changes were made to make it easier for Seve and other Europeans to compete in America and still maintain their links with their home circuit but Seve asked for further concessions to which Beman and his Board felt unable to accede. Of course Seve is right. Players of his talent should be allowed to tee up where and when they want to. The American approach is more insular.

These days, despite the official dislike of appearance money, Seve can command almost what he likes in up-front payments even if he does not need it to keep the proverbial wolf from the door. It has become a symbol of prestige to him in the commercial world that embraces all sport these days. It is a symptom of the growth of the game. Millions have been invested in golf, millions are spent by golfers on equipment each year, millions of yen, dollars and pounds circulate among sponsors, managers, advisors, consultants, promoters as well as players, some of whom, like Seve, have a cupboard full of hats to wear at any time. Seve has a company, like Jack Nicklaus does, that runs and promotes tournaments and in which he is usually guaranteed to play. He has a golf course design and administration division, like Nicklaus and Palmer, Tom Watson and company. He has a golf accessories division making available high-profile, top-quality goods with the Seve label and, with his brothers, he has another company which arranges golf schools and coaching. Seve, his fortune safely and wisely invested often in property around the world, could be said to be like Palmer in a corporate sense. Both command huge empires. It is all a far cry from that period in Seve's life in the early 70's when, having graduated from the one club he had been given by brother Manuel to a full set, he was ready to tackle Europe if not quite the world. His keynote was attack. The course was his bull, the

fairways of Europe his arena. There is in his nature a determination to succeed which is why he has always had so much regard for the way Gary Player made his mark. Every round, even today, is a new challenge. Defeat is something to be avoided, victory something to savour.

Although as a raw 17-year-old he had very nearly won the Italian Open in 1974 at misty, rainy Venice, what really brought him dramatically into the golfing headlines was his electric performance two years later in the Open at Birkdale, the year the summer was so hot the course went on fire. It was the year Johnny Miller, who had three years earlier taken the U.S. Open title, completed the double but not before he had been uncomfortably aware of the virtually unknown Spaniard who spoke little English and seemed unafraid of even Jack Nicklaus. It was too early in his career for Seve to win the oldest and most prestigious Open in the world but he had a run at it, losing out only on the back nine of the final day when his natural aggression, not yet controlled, saw him drive into trouble. The exquisite pitch he played between the two bunkers to the left of the last green, however, to tie Nicklaus was a foretaste of what he had to offer in the years to come. A week after Birkdale he won his first title on the European Tour in Holland.

These days he has curbed his natural aggression but he will still gamble if he thinks it is worth it and the odds are even fractionally in his favour. Like the shot he played at the par 4 tenth at The Belfry one year in a match with Nick Faldo. The match was tight but the shot he wanted to play demanded inch-perfect precision. The hole dog-legs to the right and stretches 320 yards down the hill to a narrow green guarded in front and to the left by a wide pond and on the right by high trees. Seve reached for his driver and, shaping the shot expertly, faded the ball over the 300-yard carry and on to the green. There is a plaque on the tee today to commemorate the shot!

In the first five years of his career Ballesteros won 24 events in places as far apart as New Zealand, Japan, Kenya and at Greater Greensboro in North Carolina not far from the site of his first major win in America at Augusta in 1980, the year after he made history by becoming the youngest winner of the Open this century, the first Spaniard to do so and only the second European to take the title. The venue was Lytham and in practice Roberto de Vicenzo, the great Argentinian who had spotted Seve's extra special talent early when they had competed together, told him to go out and play 'from the heart'. He did and in the process broke the heart of that year's favourite Hale Irwin, who just a few weeks before had won the American title for a second

The Old Course in 1984 – Open Champion!

In trouble in the French Open

Seve finds his way clear of trouble at Muirfield Village (above) and Augusta (below)

time. In four rounds Seve sprayed his shots so dramatically that he hit only 14 fairways and just two on the decisive final day. He recovered brilliantly from areas of the course no other competitor knew about far less had visited. He was, at times, so wild he landed on the trampled down grass where spectators were walking. At the sixteenth he was even in an unofficial car park which led to him, somewhat unfairly, being described as the car park Open winner. Irwin could not believe it. Stunned, he fired a last day 78 while Seve, surviving his self-imposed torture, charged to an emotional success. When he had finally won he burst into tears when being hugged by his brothers behind the last green and had to be reminded he had not handed in his card. His seven-under-par winning score of 283 included a 65. Ten years later when he would win again at Lytham he did so with a tense, controlled closing 65 in which he hardly missed a fairway and closed out closest rival Nick Price with a 9-iron shot at the sixteenth from the middle of the fairway to just a foot. Compared to what had happened there in 1979, it was a measure of how he had matured. His second win at Lytham satisfied the fans, some of whom came hoping to cheer on Lyle or Faldo, Britain's most recent Open winners. But in the end they stayed to cheer Seve home. It was disappointing for Price, who played so gallantly, but the fact was had Seve not won in 1988, the fans would have gone away feeling cheated. That may have been his finest hour in Open golf had he not won an epic battle at St Andrews in 1984 with Bernhard Langer, his long-time Continental rival, and Tom Watson with whom, for most of the 80's he had been vying for the right to be considered Nicklaus' natural successor. That week at St Andrews, Seve 'killed off' the opposition. Putting superbly on those fast undulating Old course greens, concentrating magnificently, firing drives and iron-shots unwaveringly into the exact spot on the bunker-strewn fairways to have the right angle to attack the pin, Seve underlined that talent and courage, determination and flair are not enough in themselves. You must have self-belief and patience. He has both. With Langer and Watson playing as well as they could and coming to the line with him just the way Tom Weiskopf and Johnny Miller had with Nicklaus in that memorable 1975 U.S. Masters at Augusta Seve proved equal to the task. With Langer finally faltering and Watson hitting a crisp two-iron through the plateau green at the seventeenth hole and onto the road, Seve wrapped it all up with a last green curling birdie putt. The cheers echoed round the most famous and historic links in golf. Seve, releasing all the pent-up emotion he had kept so much in control for four pressure-packed days, clenched his teeth, punched the air and produced the broadest smile of his whole career.

To date he has not won a U.S. Open, although that remains his most cherished goal, but has twice won at Augusta, in 1980 and again in 1983. He loves Augusta with all its tradition.

Now a multi-millionaire, Seve still has golfing goals to achieve. He wants to prove to the world, but more importantly to himself, that he can win a U.S. Open on the tight type of courses used for this Championship each year. He has had his chances. More will come his way. He would like to become a member of that exclusive club of golfers who have won all four majors at least once – Gene Sarazen, Ben Hogan, Gary Player and Jack Nicklaus. That means he still needs to win the U.S. P.G.A. as well. In Europe he would like to be remembered as having won every national Open. He is still short of

Portugal and Italy!

He is fiercely patriotic and, curiously perhaps for someone not brought up or indeed aware of the Ryder Cup tradition and who, at one time, was dropped (or maybe more accurately snubbed for selection in 1981), he is a staunch supporter of the match which was opened to Continentals at Jack Nicklaus' suggestion in 1979. He is a loyal lieutenant, too, of Ryder Cup team captain Tony Jacklin and has not only been an inspirational figure on the course in recent matches but an invaluable adviser off it. It was Jacklin, who himself suffered a Ryder Cup disappointment in 1981, who won Seve round again – conscious that if Europe were going to emphasise their new found confidence and superiority over the Americans he could only do it with Seve's help. In 1985 the Europeans, supported by a partisan home crowd, won at The Belfry and two years later successfully defended at Muirfield Village, winning on American soil for the first time in a Cup history stretching back more than 60 years. Seve has won the World Cup twice for Spain, but has never managed to steer his country to success in the Dunhill Cup.

What further triumphs lie in store for Seve we shall just have to await patiently, but even if he were not to win another major he has already ensured his immortality as a golfer of immense talent, a competitor of great courage and determination, and a person of honesty and integrity who jealously guards his privacy.

In fact Ballesteros handles the pressure under which he plays and performs exceptionally well for 95 per cent of the time. He can be charming, he can be stubborn. He likes getting his own way. He is not a man who readily takes advice. He is Seve. Without the fire in his belly and without the ability to keep his cool when others fail to do so, he might not have made it to the top. As it is he has it all. Multi-winner Ballesteros is a giant personality who proudly and impressively graces the world scene, now with his wife Carmen, daughter of the Santander bank owner for whom he used to caddy proudly by his side.

# CAREER RECORD

## Victories

| | |
|---|---|
| 1976 | Dutch Open, Lancome Trophy, World Cup (team with Manuel Pinero) |
| 1977 | Japanese Open, Dunlop Phoenix (Japan), Otago Classic (New Zealand), French Open, Uniroyal International, Swiss Open, World Cup (team with Antonio Garrido) |
| 1978 | Martini International, German Open, Scandinavian Enterprise Open, Swiss Open, Kenya Open, Greater Greensboro Open, Japanese Open |
| 1979 | British Open, English Golf Classic |
| 1980 | U.S. Masters, Madrid Open, Martini International, Dutch Open |
| 1981 | Scandinavian Enterprise Open, Benson and Hedges International, Spanish Open, Suntory World Match-play Championship, Dunlop Phoenix (Japan), Australian P.G.A. Championship |
| 1982 | Cepsa Madrid Open, Paco Rabanne French Open, Suntory World Match-play Championship |
| 1983 | Sun Alliance P.G.A. Championship, Carrolls Irish Open, Lancome Trophy, U.S. Masters, Westchester Classic |
| 1984 | British Open, Suntory World Match-play Championship |
| 1985 | U.S. F. and G. New Orleans Classic, Carrolls Irish Open, Peugeot French Open, Sanyo Barcelona Open, Benson and Hedges Spanish Open, Suntory World Match-play Championship |
| 1986 | Dunhill British Masters, Carrolls Irish Open, Johnnie Walker Monte Carlo Open, Peugeot French Open, K.L.M. Dutch Open, Lancome Trophy, Sun City Million Dollar Challenge |
| 1987 | Suze Cannes Open |
| 1988 | British Open, Majorca Open, Scandinavian Enterprise Open, Lancome Trophy, Westchester Classic, Visa Taihneiyo Masters |

## Did you know...

1. Severiano Ballesteros averaged 28.25 putts a round in Europe in 1988 when he finished top earner for the fifth time. He finished the season 130 under par for 54 rounds.
2. Severiano Ballesteros first made the European Tour headlines when he came close to winning the Italian Open at misty, wet Venice in 1974. He was 18 and finished third.
3. Severiano Ballesteros built a green in his garden in Pedrena in Spain which matched the speed and undulations of a green at Augusta. It helped him with his pre tournament practice.

The 1988 Open Champion

# *GREG NORMAN*

Inspired by Jack Nicklaus, Greg Norman gave up the chance of flying for the Australian Air Force to chase birdies and eagles and must never have regretted that day.

The jury is still deliberating on the case of Greg Norman. So many questions have yet to be answered before the gifted but erratic Australian's abiding stature in the game is finally assessed. Can he, at 34, still become the Pavarotti of professional golf in the 90's, as seemed likely back in those incredibly golden days of 1986? Or will he be forced instead to accept contentment in a Sinatra-like role, entertaining fans inimitably, acquiring extraordinary wealth but falling short of the masterly status he covets.

The ultimate answer is surely in Norman's own hands because there is no doubt at all of the strapping, charismatic Queenslander's ability to hit the most fantastic golf shots. When Norman is in tempo and focussed on his task he can be unbeatable as he so graphically demonstrated with his rousing, runaway Open victory at Turnberry in July 1986. Already he has won more than 50 four-round tournaments around the world, most of them set up by at least one wondrous round in the low 60's. Yet his career has been littered, too, with a high number of near misses in the majors, some of them caused by the whims of fortune, others by a seeming vulnerability of temperament or method in the crisis. More recently, too, Norman has had to combat two other widely differing but equally debilitating impediments to his quest for greatness. The first is a chronic left wrist injury which forced him to withdraw midway through the 1988 U.S. Open at Brookline and subsequently take seven weeks away from the game. Eventually, it will need surgery to properly repair. But Norman feels he cannot take the time away from the game an operation would require. In the meantime he has often struggled to overcome the physical and mental constraints the injury inflicts on his ability to hit hard shots from the rough.

The second factor is far more pleasant but no less dangerous to any sportsman's career. In a nutshell, some believe Norman's massive personal wealth and rocket-fuelled lifestyle have unwittingly eroded his approach to the game. A consummate family man, devoted to his wife Laura and children Morgan-Leigh and Gregory, Norman is nonetheless consumed by peripheral goals and activities which seem to outsiders to capture increasing amounts of his time and energy. There are few challenges in life he seems unable to resist and none he cannot afford. Speed is a passion and the garage in his new 10 million dollar home in Florida is filled with sleek, luxury vehicles including a Ferrari F22, an Aston Martin

Greg Norman seeks respite in the shade at the 1988 Australian Open

DB5 and a Rolls Royce, numberplate AUSSI-1. He drives them swiftly whenever he can and among his closest friends is British Formula One ace Nigel Mansell who has fine-tuned Norman's considerable natural driving ability. There seems little doubt they will one day form a partnership in motor racing, Norman already having a considerable stake in the Brabham racing team.

In the Augusta sand (above) and (left) with daughter and son at the 1986 World Match-play

Fishing, scuba diving and hunting are his other great adventures and it was from the former he gained his nickname of The Great White Shark. Though he maintains, in the interest of accuracy, that he has never actually hunted sharks, only shot at them because they were stealing fish, New York columist Dave Anderson devised the name after hearing of Norman's deep sea exploits and watching his all-out style on the golf course. Indeed, when Norman is in full flight, the stark white hair of his Finnish origins flying and his mouth set tight in fierce desire, he almost resembles a vast Southern Ocean predator. His fascination with flying has led him to pilot Phantom jets and sit at the controls of Concorde. Indeed, but for a last second decision, his life's path may have lain in the sky rather than on the fairways of the earth. At 17 he went with his father, Merv, to seek a pilot's career in the Royal Australian Air Force. But as he neared the recruiting office the young Norman demurred. Though he had been playing golf for little more than a year he

knew in his heart he could master the game and was fascinated by it. Then and there he decided to seek a professional career.

Like all youngsters brought up on the endless beaches of the vast Queensland coast, Norman's sporting passion, had, until then, been surfboard riding. But at 16 he caddied one day for his mother, Toini, a five handicapper, and later borrowed her clubs to play a few holes. Instantly hooked, he progressed from a starting 27 handicap to scratch in two specatacular years, using as a bible Jack Nicklaus's two books, *Golf My Way* and *55 Ways to Play Golf* then coming under the tutorship of Royal Queensland's revered professional, Charlie Earp. By 1976, at 21, he was ready to attack the Australian Tour and after only a handful of tournaments he posted a spectacular, runaway victory over an imposing international field in the West Lakes Classic in Adelaide, South Australia. A glittering star had undoubtedly emerged, one who could hit the ball incredible distances from the tee and who instantly entranced galleries with his striking physical appearance and go-for-broke attitude.

Soon, under the influence of pipe-smoking Englishman James Marshall, Norman was campaigning and winning in Europe as well as Australia and titles fell to him like confetti, from Sydney to Stockholm. In 1981 he made a wondrous debut in the U.S. Masters, leading until a double bogey at the tenth in the final round and eventually finishing fourth. The spark to campaign in America had been lit, and so had an intense desire to win in Augusta.

By 1983 he had joined the U.S. Tour and a year later, after winning the Kemper Open, made his next serious drive at a major, tieing Fuzzy Zoeller in the U.S. Open at Winged Foot with a mammoth par putt on the final hole, which he coaxed in from the apron. It was all to no avail. Next day Zoeller waltzed away in the 18-hole play-off.

All this time Norman was refining his game, adding reliability to his short game and even more imagination through the influence of his friend, Severiano Ballesteros. And so he was ready for 1986, which will always be remembered as The Year of

The Shark delighted with one shot and in despair about another

The Shark but which, by his own tough standards, Norman now regards as a cavalcade of lost opportunity. In five stupendous months he led going into the last round of all four majors but came away with victory in only one, the Open at Turnberry. Despite a brilliant finishing charge at Augusta, a dropped shot at the last left him one short of Jack Nicklaus's epic, ordained Masters' victory. The next week he was second again, to Zoeller no less, in the Heritage Classic, before winning the National Panasonic Las Vegas million dollar event and the Kemper Open again.

Through all of this exalted run, Norman was battling illness, later diagnosed as 'walking pneumonia' but which he suspected, at the time, might have been a form of cancer. Though drawn and desperately worried, he led by a shot after three rounds of the U.S. Open at Shinnecock Hills but fell back in the ruck behind Raymond Floyd at the finish. He had better luck when he travelled to Scotland encouraged by the fact that a final medical diagnosis had removed his tumour fears and medication had controlled the bronchial problem. He tamed Turnberry with a majestic four days of touch and power. On a foully frigid and windswept Thursday, his opening 74 was adequate but it was a memorable record 63 next day which would give him a vice-like grip on the old claret jug. He missed a putt on the last for a 62 which would have been the lowest round in 130 years of Open history. A third round 74 in driving rain left him a familiar one shot clear in to the final round and that night a significant conversation took place in the Turnberry Hotel. Norman was dining with friends when Jack Nicklaus approached his table. 'Nobody wants you to win this more than me' the great man told his friend. 'Tomorrow, just concentrate on keeping your grip pressure light'. Norman committed the advice to memory and could not have had a better start next day. His closest rival, Japan's Tommy Nakajima, took four from the edge of the green and carded a double bogey at the first and when The Shark holed from a bunker for a birdie at the third the Open became a Sunday stroll in the park for the jubilant Australian. At last he had a major win under his belt.

A month later the U.S.P.G.A. was his for the taking at Inverness as he assumed a commanding four shot lead with nine holes remaining. But Bob Tway snatched it from the Shark's jaws with an 'impossible' holed bunker shot at the 72nd for a birdie and victory by a single stroke. Norman was left kicking himself for not taking earlier opportunities to clinch victory. If that was a quick reminder of the

A natty line in headgear and shorts (above) and clearing the sand expertly as usual (left)

game's capacity for retribution then what happended at Augusta next year was mind-blowing in its cruelty. Norman, Ballesteros and home-town boy Larry Mize went into sudden death and when Ballesteros went out at the first play-off hole and Mize missed the green with his approach to the next, the eleventh, the odds swung overwhelmingly Norman's way. He was on the edge of the green in two. As Mize stood over a 140 foot chip shot, the question was only whether he could get it close enough to salvage par. But seconds later the American was bounding exultantly around the green as the ball disappeared from sight, taking Norman's hopes with it and leaving only a sickening sense of total loss. Two majors had been snatched from him by two unlikely but superbly executed shots. No wonder it would have a lasting impression. He has rebounded from the double blow but the Augusta reverse took its toll on his confidence for weeks.

'I have to be honest and say that to this day, it is hard for me to really come to terms with how I felt then and after,' says Norman. 'I was stunned and it took me a good four months to get anywhere near over it. The next two years were probably the hardest of my life.' Yet, Norman maintained after his fifth Australian Masters triumph in 1989 that his best years may still be ahead. It is a view shared by Nicklaus, now not only a friend but a near neighbour in Florida. 'I feel I have not reached anything like my prime... that the best 10 years as a golfer are still to come. In truth, I sometimes feel that I'm almost only starting to learn,' Norman says.

To focus more sharply on the majors he has cut back on his commitment to commercial activity and the endorsements which have earned him a conservative £10 million since 1986. He will still chase adventure whenever he can and by his very temperament will lose some tournaments he ought to have won and capture some in which he seemed to have no chance. The opportunity is still there for him to assume the mantle of greatness and so, unquestionably, is the talent. History awaits the outcome.

# *CAREER RECORD*

The 1986 Open Champion

**Victories**

1976 West Lakes Classic (Australia)
1977 Kusaha Invitational, Martini International
1978 Caltex Festival of Sydney, Traralgon Classic, South Seas Classic (Fiji)
1979 Martini International, Hong Kong Open
1980 French Open, Australian Open, Scandinavian Open, Suntory World Match-play Championship
1981 Australian Masters, Dunlop Masters, Martini International
1982 Dunlop Masters, State Express Classic, Benson and Hedges International
1983 Kapalua International, Hong Kong Open, Suntory World Match-play Championship, Australian Masters, Stefan Queensland Open, National Panasonic New South Wales Open, Cannes Invitational
1984 Kemper Open, Canadian Open, Australian Masters, Victorian Open, Toshiba Australian P.G.A. Championship
1985 Toshiba Australian P.G.A. Championship, National Panasonic Australian Open
1986 British Open, Panasonic Las Vegas Invitational, Kemper Open, Suntory World Match-play Championship, Queensland Open, New South Wales Open, Panasonic European Open, West End Jubilee South Australian Open, National Panasonic Western Australian Open, Stefan Queensland Open
1987 Australian Masters, National Panasonic Australian Open
1988 Palm Meadows Cup, E.S.P. Open, P.G.A. National Tournament Players' Championship, Lancia Italian Open, M.C.I. Heritage Classic, Panasonic New South Wales Open
1989 Australian Masters Tournament, Australian Tournament Players' Championship

**Did you know...**

1. Greg Norman had a remarkable 1986. He won twice in America, three times in Europe and three times in a row in his native Australia. He made over a million dollars.
2. Greg Norman lists snooker, fishing and hunting as his main hobbies but another is collecting Ferrari sports cars. In 1988 he played in the Italian Open at Monticello when he received the guarantee he would go to No. 1 in the list for the newest Ferrari.
3. Greg Norman lives on the same estate in Florida as Jack Nicklaus and Mark Calcavecchia. Jack has advised him on his garden.

# G A R Y P L A Y E R

Fitness fanatic Gary Player of South Africa has always believed you get out of the game what you put in and for over 30 years has reaped rich rewards for his dedicated approach.

Another classic bunker shot from Gary Player

Gary Player had that intense look in his eye when he once admitted to me that because of a late night at the golfing banquet he had decided not to do his usual 100 (or more) push-ups before going to bed. Next morning, he felt so guilty that he got up extra early and 'punished' himself by hitting 200 shots in the cold morning air before a jog and a swim in the icy waters of the pool at his luxury ranch-style home just outside Johannesburg, in South Africa.

I re-tell the story not to embarrass Player but to underline just how dedicated the 'man in black' has been throughout his remarkable career. Superfit at 54, Player may no longer have eyes like a hawk and may even admit to the odd ache and pain, but he is fitter than most of the men he battles with each week on the Seniors Circuit and it shows. He is heading fast towards total earnings in five years on the old-timers league which will surpass what he won on the main U.S. circuit between 1957 and 1984.

Player, father of six and globetrotter extraordinaire, has, throughout his illustrious career shown the kind of commitment to his game and career that Ben Hogan showed after his car crash. Player is golf's tireless worker. He is golf's great enthusiast who never seems short of a goal at which to aim. His place in the record books is secure. Had Gary Player been an American or even operated full-time in America at the height of his power, he would have made an even greater fortune than he has from his base

One of the fittest players ever Gary is still going strong on the Seniors Circuit

in South Africa. Instead he chose to stay at home and carve out a second career for himself as a breeder of quality quarter-horses and race-horses. He would love one day to lead in his own horse as winner of the Epsom Derby. Indeed horse-racing and breeding would have been his compelling interest today had the Americans not started the Seniors Circuit and given all those golfers over 50 a golden opportunity to make the kind of money they never thought possible at a time when their careers would normally have been over.

'I always knew if I kept myself fit it would pay off in the end,' said Player who joined the Seniors circuit in 1985 and, somewhat typically, for a man with such a sharpened competitive edge, heralded his arrival by winning the very first event in which he played. During his main career in the States he won 21 times in just over 20 years and made 1,795,994 dollars. Since joining the Seniors Tour he had won 12 times by the end of his third full year and topped a million in earnings. One of only four golfers to have completed a modern Slam, Player has won three Opens in Britain in three decades, three U.S. Masters, two U.S.P.G.A. Championships and a U.S. Open. The others in the exclusive club to have won all four are Gene Sarazen, Jack Nicklaus (three times over) and Ben Hogan.

What Player has done would satisfy most golfers but the enthusiastic South African has always wanted to do even better. When joining the Seniors Tour, he decided his goal would be to complete what he calls a Senior Slam and he has! Only Gary Player, to date, has won the British Seniors at Turnberry, the P.G.A Seniors' Championship, the U.S.P.G.A. Seniors' event and the U.S. Tour's own Senior Championship title. It is an incredible performance by a man whose game these days is almost as good as it ever was. His average score in America in 1988 was 70.41 per round. Only Bob Charles scored better. 'These days,' Player told veteran *Golf World* columnist Dick Taylor, 'are the happiest and most enjoyable of my life. I have seen my family mature and now, without the same punishing schedule I once had, my wife Vivienne can travel with me much more.'

Player is no stranger to airports or

aeroplanes. No golfer has flown as much as him to win prize-money or supervise the building of the golf courses he has designed in every corner of the world. He reckons he has spent two years of his life sitting in aeroplane seats. He has flown over six million miles in notching up more than 150 victories, among them 13 South African Opens, seven Australian Opens including one in 1965 at Adelaide in which he shot two rounds of 62, and five World Match-play Championships. Those were at the West course at Wentworth, where he has co-operated with John Jacobs and Bernhard Gallacher to design and build an impressive new South course. In the Brazilian Open in 1974 at Gavea he shot a world record equalling round of 59.

By any standards what pocket-dynamo Player, just five foot seven inches tall and weighing less than ten stones, has done is incredible. It is as well he did not heed the advice given him by an experienced British professional when he first arrived to play the British circuit in 1955. He was only 19, his swing was unimpressive but he ignored Hugh Lewis' suggestion that he 'go home and get a job away from golf'. Lewis felt Player could not make the grade; Player, with much attention to his swing, knew he could. Two years after that, while on his way back to Europe with his swing in much better shape, Player, whose mother had died when he was 8 and whose gold miner father had saved hard to give his son the chance to play internationally, picked up the first of many first-place cheques by winning the Egyptian Open. He was off and running. Within a year he was finishing second to Tommy Bolt in the U.S. Open at Southern Hills in Oklahoma and just 12 months later was having his name engraved on the most famous golfing trophy in the world – the silver claret jug that has, since 1872, been the prize clutched lovingly by the winner of the British Open each year.

Player trailed the leaders by eight shots with two rounds to go on the final day but a 70 and 68 for 284 gave him the chance of emulating the South African hero of the day Bobby Locke, who had won the title four times between 1949 and 1957. Yet Player felt he had blown his chance by taking a two over par 6 after being bunkered at the last. He was firm in his view that someone playing later in the days before the leaders went off last would catch and pass him. He headed

Player with his usual gallery of admirers (top) in 1964 and (above) ten years later – still the fans' favourite

Sporting his favourite checked cap on the fairway and on the green

back broken-hearted to his hotel fearing the worst but, two hours later, wearing a natty white suit and a broad smile, the 23-year-old South African was stepping up proudly to receive the trophy as the youngest winner of the title this century. Since then, of course, there has been an even younger winner – Severiano Ballesteros was just 22 when he won at Lytham in 1979.

A first American major success came in 1961 at Augusta when he stole the title from Arnold Palmer who was poised to win for the third time in four years. Palmer led Player by one coming up the last, with both bunkered beside the green. Gary, one of the greatest bunker-players in golfing history, got up and down for his par, Palmer splashed out and, to the gasps of the crowd, three-putted to lose. Later Arnie would admit he lost it when, on his way to the last green a friend shouted to him and shook him by the hand congratulating him prematurely on his victory! In 1962 Player won the U.S. P.G.A. Championship at Aronimink in Pennsylvania and completed his set of four Grand Slam titles with a play-off victory over Kel Nagle of Australia in the U.S. Open in 1965. It would turn out to be his only American Open success.

Player had early on in his career been snapped up by the management team headed by Mark McCormack, the Cleveland lawyer, who, realising the earning potential of Arnold Palmer, had offered his services to Arnie and been given the job of looking after him. Jack Nicklaus was in the stable at that time as well and the trio would form a modern-day 'Big Three' playing television matches around the world. Together they did much to popularise the game. Player's second British Open win came in 1968 at Carnoustie in Scotland where Nicklaus had been favourite. Billy Casper led with a round to go but it was Player and Nicklaus, battling together on the final day, who captured the imagination of the intelligent Scottish galleries . . . and it was Player's three-wood shot at the par 5 fourteenth that would remain in most people's memories as he battled his way bravely to victory. It was an all-or-nothing shot and it came off brilliantly for the South African who would later claim he hit the ball so straight he had to lean sideways to see the flag. The ball finished just two feet from the stick and that eagle made all the difference.

In 1972 he won the U.S. P.G.A. again at Oakland Hills and in 1974 won two majors – the U.S. Masters by two shots from Dave Stockton and the Open at Lytham leading from start to finish. Peter

Oosterhuis, who for four years in a row was the European number one but who has now sadly retired from top-line golf, was second that year. Player had just one more major to tuck under his belt and it would come again at Augusta in 1978 when, seven shots behind with a round to go, he fired a record-equalling 64 to win in the most spectacular fashion. His attempt to make history by winning a major in each of four decades failed narrowly when he was pipped by Lee Trevino in the U.S. P.G.A. in the steaming heat of Shoal Creek in Alabama in 1984.

This disappointment is easily more than offset by a string of triumphs which have made him one of the most popular golfers of all time . . . a golfer with the heart of a lion and the courage of a tiger – qualities which were only too well displayed in the 1965 World Match-play Championship at Wentworth. After the first round he was six down to 'Champagne' Tony Lema, the former Open champion sadly killed in an air crash in 1966. When Player lost the first hole of the afternoon round it seemed as if the stylish Lema would win 'in the country' but the record books show Player won the match. Lema cracked as the South African, summoning every ounce of energy and concentrating as hard as he could, clawed his way back to draw level and then move ahead. That in a way sums up Player's refusal never to give-in until the very last hole.

No golfer has won more prize-money by making a series of closing birdies on the final day than Player. When other golfers, well aware that victory is beyond them, are content just to play their way despondently in, Player has always continued to compete as hard as he knows how in order to earn, quite simply, as big a cheque as he can. Maybe it stems from a family background in which everyone always had to work for everything they got but it has always been his way and will continue to be until the day he decides to retire. Happily the fittest grandfather in international golf has no plans to slow up just yet. After all he wants to become the first man to complete a Senior Slam twice over before he is 60!

## *CAREER RECORD*

**Victories**

| | |
|---|---|
| 1956 | Dunlop Tournament, South African Open |
| 1957 | Australian P.G.A. Championship |
| 1958 | Australian Open, Natal Open |
| 1959 | British Open, South African Dunlop Masters, Natal Open, Transvaal Open |
| 1960 | South African Open, South African Dunlop Masters, Transvaal Open, Natal Open |
| 1961 | U.S. Masters |
| 1962 | U.S. P.G.A. Championship, Australian Open, Transvaal Open |
| 1963 | Australian Open |
| 1964 | South African Dunlop Masters |
| 1965 | Piccadilly World Match-play Championship, South African Open, Australian Open, U.S. Open |
| 1966 | Piccadilly World Match-play Championship, South African Open, Transvaal Open, Natal Open |
| 1967 | South African Open, South African Dunlop Masters |
| 1968 | Piccadilly World Match-play Championship, South African Open, British Open, Natal Open, Western Province Open, Wills Masters |
| 1969 | South African Open, Australian Open |
| 1970 | Australian Open, Dunlop International |
| 1971 | Piccadilly World Match-play Championship, South African Dunlop Masters, Western Province Open, General Motors Open |
| 1972 | South African Open, South African Dunlop Masters, U.S. P.G.A., Brazilian Open, Western Province Open, Japan Airlines Open |
| 1973 | Piccadilly World Match-play Championship, South African Dunlop Masters, Rothman's Match-play |
| 1974 | U.S. Masters, British Open, South African Dunlop Masters, Australian Open, Brazilian Open, Ibergolf Tournament, International Classic (South Africa) |
| 1975 | South African Open, Lancome Trophy, General Motors Open |
| 1976 | South African Open, South African Dunlop Masters, General Motors Open |
| 1977 | South African Open, I.C.L. International |
| 1978 | U.S. Masters |
| 1979 | South African Open, South African Dunlop Masters, South African P.G.A. Championship, Johannesburg International, Sun City Classic |
| 1980 | Chile Open, Ivory Coast Open |
| 1981 | South African P.G.A. Championship, South African Open |

# *DAVID GRAHAM*

Australian David Graham began playing golf left-handed, switched to right-handed, and highlighted his career with a stylish victory at Merion in the U.S. Open.

There can't be any more arduous journey from oblivion to the pantheon of world golf than that undertaken by David Graham. Nor have many of the game's ruling class encountered so many pitfalls or worked harder than the Dallas-based Australian with the military style walk and supremely competitive nature. At 21 years of age, Graham was 6,000 dollars in debt, all but friendless, and was battling to master a golf game which could make him competitive on the hardly-lucrative Australian circuit. Already he had switched from playing left-handed to right, had split irrevocably with a father who opposed his golfing ambitions, had spent time as a club pro at a tiny course in the Tasmanian town of Burnie and had been forced to take a job packing golf equipment in Sydney.

Yet, only 14 years later, Graham stood bursting with pride and emotion on the eighteenth green at Merion Golf Club in suburban Philadelphia knowing he had become the first Australian to win the United States Open championship. He had done so with a final three under par 67 which will be recalled whenever great rounds in the majors are discussed. Somehow, on such a supremely tight and tough layout, he had hit every green in regulation and every fairway bar the first when his tee shot rolled just eight inches into light rough. No wonder Bill Rogers, joint runner-up with George Burns, said of Graham: 'To do what he did in the last round of a U.S. Open is absolutely unbelievable.'

David Graham at the 1985 Open

Unbelievable is almost the right word to describe Anthony David Graham's life. Someday, no doubt, someone will make it into a film. Born in Windsor, Victoria, in 1946, his boyhood was filled with acrimony and loneliness until one day, cycling home from school, he saw a man hitting golf balls in a suburban paddock. Graham was fascinated and, after a time spent hitting a tennis ball with a hockey stick, he was able to borrow a rudimentary set of clubs. Only trouble was they were left-handed and Graham was a natural right-hander.

Soon he was working at John Green's pro shop at nearby Wattle Park Golf Club at weekends and practising whenever he could, a lifetime habit which was to play the greatest role in his rise to eminence. At 14, he was offered a full-time assistant's role with the well-respected George Naismith at Melbourne's sand belt Riverside course. But it meant leaving school and his father forbade him. Graham went anyway and the pair have not spoken since save for one occasion in America when a

man approached the Australian claiming to be his parent then disappeared as quickly and mysteriously as he had arrived. It was Naismith who convinced Graham he had to become a right-hander to succeed in tournament play. The youngster struggled for 12 agonising months before he got the hang of the game again. When Naismith left Riversdale, Graham took the post as pro at nine hole Seabrook Golf Club in Tasmania so he could support his mother. But in three years he had acquired business debts of 6,000 dollars.

Typically, he made himself a hermit for 18 months to pay them off, eating sparsely, never spending money on entertainment and all the time working on the golf secret he knew was within touching distance but could never quite grasp. By now he was working for the PGF equipment firm in Sydney, packing clubs, delivering messages but also having time off to hone and experiment with his game. And suddenly, in the 1967 Queensland P.G.A., everything clicked into place. He won, with a 10 under par total of 282. A great career was off and running.

Sun, sea and 'sand' – Turnberry (above) and Augusta (left)

A year later, he was fighting Jack Nicklaus, Arnold Palmer and Gary Player for the Australian P.G.A. title in the third round when he rolled in a 20 footer for what should have been a birdie and a share of the lead. Instead it would become a heartbreaking bogey when Bill Dunk's caddie could not remove the flagstick before the ball struck it, invoking a two shot penalty. Shocked, Graham dropped to his knees and covered his face with his hands

In 1981 Graham became the first Australian winner of the U.S. Open

so the gallery could not see the tears of dismay running down his cheeks. It would be the last time he would ever cry on a golf course but the intense desire to succeed would never vanish.

Graham finished sixth and the next week flew north to Cairns to marry Maureen Burdett, a local bank clerk he had met and fallen in love with during a pro-am tour stop. Together they dreamed, planned and saved so Graham could eventually tackle the American circuit. The opportunity came in 1970 after a tumultuous year in which the determined Graham won the Tasmanian, Victorian, Thailand, French and Yomiuri Opens and committed himself to the management of colourful American, Bucky Woy. He was to miss his U.S. Tour card at the first attempt, however, and then had to fly almost immediately to Buenos Aires where he was to partner his great friend, Bruce Devlin, in the World Cup for Australia.

The organisers had wanted Bruce Crampton as Devlin's partner but the Australian P.G.A. stood firm and Graham repaid their loyalty. Graham and Devlin won by ten shots with a record low score and Graham finished just behind local hero Roberto de Vicenzo who won the individual title. That should have banished any self doubts forever but when Graham made it onto the U.S. Tour the following year he was dismayed at the disparity of his game compared to that of most of his opponents. 'I couldn't spin the ball . . . didn't know how to hit a high, soft shot. Right away I knew I would have to start all over again or go crazy trying to win with what I had,' he recalled recently. So the learning process started for a third time. Once more he endured hours of rigid discipline and physical pain and by 1976 it was all paying off.

He captured the Cleveland Open, the American Classic, the Chunichi Crowns and finally the Piccadilly World Matchplay, defeating Hale Irwin at the 38th hole in the final. His worldwide earnings of almost 290,000 dollars were topped only by Jack Nicklaus who had also become a friend, intrigued by Graham's unbridled knowledge of club-making and the mechanics of the game. Graham's temperament had undertaken the same change as his game. Once surly and unapproachable, he dropped his guard as success followed upon success and he allowed his store of intelligence and warmth fuller play. In 1977 he realised his life's ambition, closing out Nicklaus and a star-spangled field to win the Australian Open. By now he was being talked of as a majors contender and that was to become graphic reality at venerable Oakland Hills in the 1979 U.S.P.G.A. event.

With only the 72nd hole to play, Graham had a two shot lead over Ben Crenshaw and the engravers were poised to add his name to the trophy. Instead, he took a double bogey for a 65 and went to a sudden death where Crenshaw appeared to have it sewn up at the first when

Still going strong in 1987 these days he plays for fun and for himself

Graham found heavy rough from the tee. As the tension mounted the Australian, somehow, sank a 25 footer for his par then holed another 10 footer at the next to match Crenshaw's birdie and keep the play-off alive. The third hole decided it. With Crenshaw bunkered and spectators racing in all directions, Graham struck a superb four iron to the 202-yard par three and watched as it settled six feet away. When he knocked it in for his ninth birdie of the tumultuous day, he had become the first Australian winner of a major since Peter Thomson's 1965 British Open.

Yet what took place at Merion two years later would dwarf even the P.G.A. title. Starting the last round of the Open three shots behind Burns, he unveiled an epic cavalcade of iron play and rock solid putting which simply ground down his opponents. Though Rogers, Crenshaw and Nicklaus variously threatened, Graham's wondrous birdies at the fourteenth and fifteenth took him two clear of Burns. When he walked, filled with emotion, down the eighteenth fairway, he knew the Open was his.

Inevitably, comparisons with Hogan, who had also won at Merion, were made. Their style, personality and determination were similar and so, it had been proved, was their execution of great shot-making when it was needed. Graham was able to turn the Open success into lifetime financial security for Maureen and his sons, Andrew and Michael, and this, more so than any expiration of his powers, is probably why the once-hungry Australian has not added to his majors tally in the intervening years. He might have won the British Open at Sandwich until Sandy Lyle came rushing past and he has shown on the U.S. Tour and in events such as the Dunhill Cup that he can still trade shots, if not putts, with the best of the new generation.

'These days I play for fun and for David Graham. I'm not saying I won't be competitive again but I have to agree that my priorities now lie in other aspects of golf, notably designing, and with my family,' he says. Nobody could blame him for that. Most assuredly David Graham has earned a less hectic schedule!

## *CAREER RECORD*

### Victories

| | |
|---|---|
| 1970 | World Cup (with Bruce Devlin), French Open, Thailand Open |
| 1971 | Caracas Open, J.A.L. Open (Japan) |
| 1972 | Cleveland Open |
| 1975 | Wills Masters |
| 1976 | Westchester Classic, American Golf Classic, Chunichi Crowns Invitational (Japan), World Match-play Championship |
| 1977 | Australian Open, South African P.G.A. |
| 1978 | Mexico Cup |
| 1979 | U.S. P.G.A. Championship, West Lakes Classic, New Zealand Open |
| 1980 | Mexican Open, Rolex Invitational (Japan), Brazilian Classic, Memorial Tournament |
| 1981 | Phoenix Open, U.S. Open, Lancome Trophy |
| 1982 | Lancome Trophy |
| 1983 | Houston Coca-Cola Open |

### Did you know...

1. David Graham became a right handed golfer despite starting the game playing with a set of left-handed clubs.
2. In the last round of the U.S. Open on the Merion course, one of the most tight and demanding used for the Championship, David Graham hit all 18 greens in regulation.
3. David Graham is not just a tournament golfer. He designs clubs and courses around the world.
4. Australian David Graham won over 100,000 dollars in six straight seasons in America from 1979.

The 1976 World Match-play Champion

# 'JUMBO' OZAKI

He rarely ventures from Japan to play the game but when he does 'Jumbo' is assured of a large following – he is a showman supreme.

'Jumbo' Ozaki is to Japanese golf what Severiano Ballesteros, Sandy Lyle or Nick Faldo are to Europe, what Greg Norman is to the Australian circuit and what Curtis Strange is to the U.S. Tour.

All play internationally, and all made a million dollars or came close to it in 1988. Yet Ozaki, of that group, gets little international publicity because he hardly ever ventures far from his Chiba home.

Called 'Jumbo' because he is much bigger than most Japanese golfers, Ozaki has been and indeed still is to Japanese golf what Arnold Palmer was to American golf 20 years ago. He has had a galvanising effect on the game. He is one of those golfers in the rare category of proven crowd-pullers. People will pay to watch Jumbo play even if he is not at his best.

'Jumbo' in action in the World Cup – It's a mystery how that one did not drop!

Jumbo burst on the scene as long ago as 1971 after deserting major league baseball for a more lucrative golfing life. Initially he played like a baseball slugger and certainly has always capitalised on his enormous length off the tee even if the ball does not always fly as straight as it should. The uncertainty of it all is, in fact, one of the reasons people flock to watch him play. He is a cavalier of the links, ready to smile at adversity in the full knowledge that even if he does run up one high number he will birdie and eagle other holes before the end. It is a happy position to be in. If he is a legend in his own lifetime it is because the Japanese golf fans are totally in awe of his unbridled talent.

Unfortunately in his first season it would not be unfair to suggest that his raw, exuberant, downright erratic play let him down. He hit out of bounds 41 times and sometimes at crucial points in a round. Yet he still finished second in the prize-money list! In fact he is part of the most successful golfing family ever in terms of earning power. His two younger brothers, Tateo ('Jet') and Naomichi ('Joe'), are also top players.

He learned quickly, just as Seve Ballesteros did in the late 70's, that if he was to be really successful he would need to be more consistent off the tee. His out of bounds tally in the second year was one shot and he has never looked back. If he is now too careless at times, if his smile when he lands in trouble is even bigger, then it is only because he has made his name and his money. He can afford to play in a manner which suggests he is just out to have a bit of fun and the obvious enjoyment he gets from it all is infectious.

A 'big' favourite at home but only an occasional performer away – here at the U.S. Open

He is, in short, a showman supreme.

Most of the time these days, of course, he drives long and straight, using a metal driver with a seven degree loft and placing the ball on tall tee pegs specially made for him. They are three inches high and look as if they might have been manufactured for a trick-shot artist. Few other golfers could use them effectively but they work for Jumbo who, when he connects, can almost literally hit out of sight. In 1988 in his own country Jumbo won eight times. He topped the money list with ease and most importantly won the Japanese Open again. It was his year in Japan in just the way Seve dominated Europe.

At Melbourne during the revitalised World Cup of Golf, Jumbo entertained spectators at the driving range by trying to hit the flat roof of a greenkeeper's shed 302 yards away. He did after some near misses. That is how prodigious a hitter he is. It is his style of play and the manner of his successes that have made him a golf multi-millionaire in Japan where he plays most of the time. He has had just one win 'away from home', and that was in New Zealand in 1972 . . . 16 years ago. He nearly won top honours at the World Cup in Melbourne but, carelessly missing some short putts on the glassy greens, he lost out narrowly to Ben Crenshaw in the individual and Japan went down by a slender shot to the Americans in the team event.

Jumbo loves his golf and he lives the lifestyle of a sporting god. When I covered the Kirin Cup in Tokio in 1987 I was amused to see him being picked up in a Rolls Royce. Like Greg Norman he has a passion, too, for Ferraris, and Lamborghinis and Mercedes, and like Norman can afford to buy them. He says he does not travel because he cannot speak English . . . but when he wins so much at home he knows he does not need to bother although his 'stay-at-home' attitude has robbed millions around the world of watching a true sporting extrovert at close hand! In fact he speaks better English than he likes to admit.

When an Australian reporter wanted to speak with him on tape on one occasion Jumbo bowed and very politely declined. In perfect English he told the radioman: 'I'm sorry. My English is just not good enough. I do apologise.' He went off smiling with his henchmen. Like all Japanese he has a strong back-up team of advisers and friends, some of whom he will enjoy visiting the casino with. He is a great gambler off the course which is why he sometimes gambles on it too. If the challenge is there it is in his nature to try to beat it, yet he has shown enough control in recent years to prove that sometimes sense prevails.

The Spaniards may stick together in Europe and the Scots and the Irish are regular golfing buddies, but nothing can compare with the close-knit relationship of Jumbo's 'family'. He has surrounded himself with 12 or 15 top players including his brothers Jet and Joe and they keep themselves very much to themselves. It is a 'mini' golfing clan.

Jumbo's incredible success has made him a true sporting hero who, it seems, can turn his hand to anything and be successful at it. Just like Tony Jacklin, who made a record several years ago when he was U.S. Open champion, Jumbo has used his singing talents to good effect and is particularly good at mimicking the late Elvis Presley. It helps that although 42 he

In trouble at the British Open

looks a chubby but boyish 29! A room in his house an hour's drive from Tokio is filled with his collection of electric and acoustic guitars! He has a real fascination for them.

Graham Marsh, who plays regularly in Japan, points out that the analogy of Jumbo, or to give him his proper name Mashashi Ozaki, to Palmer is a fair one. Marsh says: 'Jumbo shows his emotion on his sleeve the way Palmer used to do. He gets angry when things are going wrong but laughs a lot. He is genuinely a fascinating character.' Jumbo was photographed in 1987 playing golf with a member of the Japanese 'mafia' and did not go to Augusta to play the Masters after worried American officials withdrew his invitation. The matter was grossly unfair and damaging to Jumbo who was completely innocent of any dealings with the underworld. Hopefully he will take his rightful place at Augusta in future.

Greg Norman considers Jumbo one of the greatest players in the world and certainly his participation in tournaments is a key factor with sponsors in Japan. If Jumbo is not playing there is every chance the television ratings will drop dramatically to the deep chagrin of those involved in the sponsorship. Mind you he has had his rough patches. Graham Marsh recalled recently that at one point a few years ago he missed eight or maybe even nine half-way cuts in a row. It was crisis time for the big fellow.

Then he made through to the last two rounds and that night Marsh came upon the Jumbo family celebrating in a bar drinking beer, wine and sake as if they were bringing in the New Year. It was, said one of the group, a 'Jumbo Half-way Cut' party. Yet most of the parties in recent years have been 'Jumbo win parties' and there is no indication he is losing his appetite for competition or for the game. The hope is that before he gets too old he might just take time off from his financially rewarding home circuit to play internationally for one season at any rate.

Jumbo is a golfer not to be missed if he is around at the time of the Open or World Match-play. Whatever your schedule try to go along and join in the 'Jumbo fun' if he is in town. I can assure you he will not be disappointing.

Trying to keep warm in chilly Britain (right)

## CAREER RECORD

**Victories**

| | |
|---|---|
| 1971 | Japan P.G.A. Championships, Japan Series, Golf Digest, Setonaikai Circuit |
| 1972 | Wizard, Sapporo Open, Asahi Kokusai, Chiba Open, Kanto Open, First Flight, Japan Series, Grand Monarch, New Zealand P.G.A. |
| 1973 | Kanto Pro, Tokai Classic, Taiheiyo Club Masters, ANA Sapporo, Toboku Classic |
| 1974 | ANA Sapporo, Tohoku Classic, Japan P.G.A., Japan Open, Suntory Open, Japan Series |
| 1975 | Tohoku Classic |
| 1976 | Kanto Open, Chiba Open, Hiroshima Open, Sanpo Classic |
| 1977 | Pepsi Wilson, Kanto Open, Tokai Classic, Japan Series |
| 1978 | Pepsi Wilson, Hiroshima Open |
| 1980 | Dunlop International, Fuji Sankei, Japan Series |
| 1982 | Kanto Open |
| 1983 | Jun Classic |
| 1984 | Kanagawa Open, Hiroshima Open |
| 1985 | Kanagawa Open |
| 1986 | Fuji Sankei, Nikkei Cup, Maruman Nihonkai Open, Jun Classic |
| 1987 | Chunichi Crowns, Fuji Sankei, Jun Classic |
| 1988 | Dunlop Open, Nikkei Cup, Maruman Open, Japan Open, Golf Digest, Bridgestone |
| 1989 | Fuji Sankei Classic |

# ISAO AOKI

Japanese golfer Isao Aoki may have a most unusual putting style but it has always worked superbly well for the most internationally aware of the Far Eastern contingent.

Isao Aoki in the Augusta sand in the '86 Masters

Isao Aoki celebrated 25 years as a professional in 1989 with his game in fine shape and his desire and determination to win as razor-sharp as the crease he always has in his slacks.

The 46-year-old Japanese golfer is a stylish-looking man with a very unorthodox and highly individual swing and technique which works so effectively for him that he has become golf's elder statesman in his country. Unlike most Japanese players, who are content to play a home circuit which offers as much prize-money and as many tournaments as the European circuit, Aoki has been prepared to adopt a more international image and has benefited hugely from it.

If a Championship is worth winning you can be sure that Aoki, often accompanied by his wife Chie, is a regular competitor. Unlike many Japanese golfers he is as well known in America, Europe and Australia as he is at home. Early in 1989, for instance, he held off a strong challenge from a host of younger lions to win a tournament at Royal Melbourne which was sponsored essentially by Japanese money. It was yet another example that week of Aoki, temperamentally well suited to the game in that he is calm, cool and confident on the course, displaying his exemplary iron-play. He gets his approach shots or short-hole tee-shots usually very close. Indeed sometimes into

the hole itself to his financial benefit!

In Monte Carlo in 1985, for instance, he won an authentic replica of a vintage car for an inch-perfect iron and a classic ace even if Sam Torrance beat him for the title. Five years earlier at Wentworth he won a fully-furnished holiday home at the fashionable Gleneagles development in Perthshire, Scotland for his second hole ace with a 7-iron in the World Match-play. He later gifted the house to charity.

No less a judge than Gary Player has suggested, without a dissenting voice being heard, that Aoki has no peer from 50 yards and in but then this was always the department the Japanese golfers, frequently playing on hilly courses and to plateau greens, have got to be good at to win. What is so unusual about Aoki's style, however, is the way he positions the club at address for putting in particular but for short irons as well. The toe of the club is several centimetres off the ground and the strike appears to be made with the heel of the club rather than the centre of the blade. Few golfers could use such a technique. Aoki uses it brilliantly.

Like most of the Japanese circuit stars, Aoki began his golfing life as a caddie at the Akibo Club, which was not far from his school, and he always had a better chance than most of getting a bag. For his age, he was bigger than most of the other lads and stronger too. They called him simply 'The Tower'. It suited him well but he was not just an inch or two taller than the others. He was a cut above them in the way he approached the game, what he knew about it and what he planned to do in it when he finally left school. He would practise in the very early morning and again at night when the course was empty. He would try out shots, experiment, in a bid to prepare himself fully for the day when he would turn professional and start playing golf full-time.

As well known internationally as at home Aoki came closest to a Major victory at the 1980 U.S. Open – losing out to Jack Nicklaus by two shots

When Aoki began his pro career in 1964, the Japanese circuit was not as well organised as it is today but such events as there were on the calendar promised rich pickings for the slim six-footer. His breakthrough, however, was not just slow in coming. It looked, for a time, as if it would not happen at all and he did not win for seven years. Aoki's first major success was the Kanto P.G.A. Championship in

Eastern Japan in 1971 but now no Japanese golfer has won more events than him. To date he has picked up close to 60 first prize cheques worth millions of yen and when he turns to the U.S. Senior circuit in four years time he will be ready to make even more rich pickings.

He is eligible for that circuit because of his dramatic U.S. Tour win in the 1983 Hawaiian Open at Waialae Country Club. American Jack Renner, who would go on to win the title the following year, was in the clubhouse with a 19 under par total being congratulated by friends on his success when Aoki, the only man who could catch him, unleashed a monster drive and second shot up the par-5 last. He had only 128 yards left for his third shot from longish grass but he spoiled Renner's premature celebration! Aoki holed out for a winning eagle!

If winning the World Match-play title at Wentworth in 1979 and the Panasonic European Open in 1983 had given him particular pleasure, that American triumph in Hawaii was the victory that gave him even more delight. Any foreigner winning in the States feels an extra special sense of achievement. It is after all the toughest circuit to win on in the world.

Aoki would have loved to have been the first Japanese golfer to win a major but as the years roll by this is less likely to happen. Perhaps his chance came and, sadly for him, went in 1980 in the U.S. Open at Baltusrol. Aoki shot three straight 68's for a new 54-hole aggregate record of 204 but could not shake off the man who has won more majors than anyone else. Right up there with him was Jack Nicklaus, who had won the Open three times before, including 1967 at Baltusrol. Nicklaus had equalled the Championship record with an opening 63 and his 36-hole total of 134 was also a record. After three rounds he, too, was on 204, but the pundits in the press-tent had noted that Nicklaus, although winning the Open at St Andrews in 1978, had not taken a major in America for five years since the U.S. P.G.A. of 1975. He had gone 12 American majors without winning so was this going to be Aoki's week? Was Nicklaus flattering to deceive? They should have known better than to write off the Golden Bear. Aoki certainly had no illusions about how well he would have to play on the last day to win.

He did play well but it did not happen for him. The Japanese golfer stuck like a limpet to Nicklaus all day but when the Golden Bear holed across the green at the seventeenth, Aoki knew he would have to content himself sadly with second place despite a last round 70. Nicklaus shot a brilliant 68 under pressure and pipped Aoki by two.

Surprisingly for a man of his calibre, Aoki has won only two Japanese Opens, one of them in a play-off with Terry Gale in 1983 at Rokko-Kokusai but that win was long overdue. He had shown incredible patience and coped well with the frustration of having been runner-up four times.

Like so many golfers, Aoki, a very private man on Tour, enjoys nothing better than to relax with a fishing rod in his hand. By planning his schedule carefully, keeping himself fit and watching his diet, Aoki has remained at the top years enjoying a well-deserved reputation as Japan's leading golfing globetrotter.

## *CAREER RECORD*

**Victories**

| | |
|---|---|
| 1971 | Kanto P.G.A. |
| 1972 | Kanto P.G.A. |
| 1973 | Coldbec, Chunichi Crowns, Pepsi Wilson, Sapporo Tokyu, K.B.C. Augusta, Japan P.G.A. |
| 1974 | Kanto P.G.A., Kanto Open, Sanpo Classic |
| 1975 | Kanto Open, Chunichi Crowns |
| 1976 | Tokai Classic |
| 1977 | Tohoku Classic, Jun Classic |
| 1978 | Chunichi Crowns, Japan Pro Match Play, Sapporo Tokyu, Kanto P.G.A., Japan Series, World Match Play (Eur) |
| 1979 | Chunichi Crowns, Japan Pro Match Play, Kanto P.G.A., Japan Series |
| 1980 | Chunichi Crowns, Yomiuri Open, K.B.C. Augusta, Kanto Open, Jun Classic |
| 1981 | Japan P.G.A., Japan Pro Match Play, Shizuoka Open |
| 1982 | Japan Pro Match Play |
| 1983 | Kanto P.G.A., Sapporo Tokyu, Japan Open, Japan Series, Hawaiian Open, European Open |
| 1986 | Sapporo Tokyu, Japan P.G.A., K.B.C. Augusta, Kanto Open |
| 1987 | Dunlop International (Asc), A.N.A. Open, Japan Open, Japan Series |
| 1989 | Coca Cola International (Aus) |

The 1983 European Open Champion

# BOB CHARLES

He started his working life counting other people's money as a bank clerk but Bob Charles ended up making money for himself on all the international golf circuits.

It is typical of quiet Kiwi, Bob Charles, that when he described himself in his instructional book, he wrote: 'I see myself as an everyday guy who also happens to be the luckiest left-handed golfer in the world.' The Luckiest? 'Charley's' view has to be respected, but as everyone else knows full well, luck has rarely had anything to do with the fact that he has been and remains the best left-hander the game has known.

Yet even that accolade short changes him, disguises the true extent of the one-time bank clerk's influence and standing among his peers. For the truth is that Charles has been among the finest players – right or left-handed – for the past 30 years, and has certainly been among the most peerless exponents of the art of putting ever known. Nobody knows better than Charles himself, however, that his abiding fame will be that he became the first left-hander to do just about everything in professional golf. The first and only left-handed winner of the British Open. The first left-handed winner of a U.S. Tour tournament. The first left-hander to dominate the money list on the Seniors Tour. The list could go on forever.

In action at Turnberry in the 1986 Open

The left-hand syndrome dominates though Charles might just as easily have played the 'right way' round because he does everything right-handed except games requiring two hands. He started as a leftie because both his parents played that way, and very well too. His father, Ivor, was a two handicapper and winner of many district titles while his mother Phyllis got down to a 6. So it was no surprise that the young Charles was on the golf course, albeit in a pram, from the time he was born.

There were only nine holes of primitive fairway on the course in the tiny town of Hinekura where Ivor was the local school headmaster. Yet they were to produce in Charles a fine champion and a thoroughly decent fellow who would be warmly welcomed all over the world. A scratch player at only 16, Charles became an instant household name in his native New Zealand in 1954 when he captured the N.Z. Open, beating the great Peter Thomson who had won three of the previous four titles and would go on that year to capture the first of his five British Opens. It was an astounding performance from a youngster who had never been given a formal golf lesson and it instantly established his future life pattern. He was further encouraged when, after an exhibition with Bobby Locke, the South African maestro told him he had the game to reach the top and insisted he realised that being left-handed would not inhibit his progress.

By 20 he had moved to Christchurch with the bank, was a permanent fixture in N.Z. amateur teams and had come under the instruction of Harry Blair, the well-

respected professional at Christchurch Golf Club. He enjoyed a tour of the United States, during which he took an inspirational look at the style of Ben Hogan and Sam Snead, and had the bonus of an invitation to the U.S. Masters at Augusta, which he quickly found did not suit the left-hander's fade as much as a right-hander's draw. In 1960, facing a transfer from Christchurch by the bank and having finished fourth at Merion in the individual standings of the Eisenhower Cup, Charles took the plunge and turned professional, leaving almost immediately for South Africa. As he wrote later in *The Bob Charles Left-Hander's Golf Book*: 'In my pocket I had a round-the-world air ticket and a few hundred dollars. This was not a trip to gain experience . . . it was the real thing. If I failed, and spent the dollars, I knew I would have to catch the first plane back home.'

He did not fail. Nine months later he was home again from South Africa and Britain with his pockets full of money. So too was his heart full with love for Verity, the beautiful South African who would soon become his wife, and through whom he met George and Brenda Blumberg, who would steer Charles to Mark McCormack and a contract handshake which would guarantee his business and financial security for life. So it was with a fine sense of purpose that Bob and Verity Charles attacked the U.S. Tour in 1963 in what would be the fulcrum of his career.

He did well at Augusta, Greensboro, New Orleans and Houston but even better when he headed to Britain to play the Open at Royal Lytham and St Annes. It was a tiring week. He had to play 108 holes – four rounds of the tournament and 36 additional holes of a play-off with Phil Rodgers – but he won. Charles had made his move in the Championship with a third round 66 which edged him clear of Peter Thomson in second place and Jack Nicklaus and Rodgers two behind. While Nicklaus and Thomson faded, the slim Kiwi and the chubby American tied.

Their play-off will be long remembered for the putting skills which eventually made Charles an eight shot victor despite an out-of-bounds tee shot in the

His only Major was the 1963 Open but Bob Charles is still enjoying his game on the Seniors Circuit more than 25 years later

afternoon which inspired Rogers to draw back to just one down with 12 to go. Pat Ward-Thomas described it thus: 'His putting tortured and destroyed Rogers with a merciless finality that was almost inhuman. In the morning he had only 26 putts, single-putting no fewer than 11 greens, having played them less accurately than Rogers. If ever putting was the name of the game it was for Charles that day.' It is little wonder Bob Charles rates Lytham one of his favourite courses. In 1969 he was second to Tony Jacklin and, at 52, he played superbly to finish joint 20th behind Seve Ballesteros in 1988.

Surprisingly, that Open would be Charles' only victory in a major though he was beaten by only one shot in a U.S. P.G.A. title and was twice third in the U.S. Open. Yet he continued to thrive firstly on the U.S. Tour and then in Europe during the 70's. He won the 1965 Tucson Open, the '67 Atlanta Classic after changing his swing radically to fade rather than draw the ball, and had a superb 1968, finishing second with Nicklaus in the Open at Carnoustie, being runner-up to Palmer in the U.S. P.G.A. and then downing Nicklaus in a thrilling final round duel for the Canadian Open. His winning shot was a seven iron approach at the last which finished only nine inches away to pip Nicklaus and Bruce Crampton. He also won the World Match-play title in 1969, Charles beating Gene Littler at the 37th with a four iron to 30 inches for a birdie after saving a half at the 36th with a 27 foot putt.

When his attention switched to Europe during the 70's he had five Top 10 finishes in the Order of Merit while winning the Dunlop Masters, John Player Classic, Swiss and Scandinavian Opens. And in 1983, at the age of 47, he returned to the U.S. Tour and captured the Tallahasee Open. It was the forerunner of great things to come on the Seniors Tour. Playing these days in glasses but with greater length than ever and with his putting skills undiminished, Charles has become the man to beat in every tournament, setting a money-making record in 1988 after finishing seventh and third on the list in his first two seasons.

## CAREER RECORD

### Victories

| | |
|---|---|
| 1954 | New Zealand Open |
| 1962 | New Zealand P.G.A. Championship, Swiss Open |
| 1963 | British Open, Houston Open |
| 1965 | Tucson Open |
| 1966 | New Zealand Open |
| 1967 | Atlanta Classic |
| 1968 | Canadian Open |
| 1969 | Piccadilly World Match-play Championship |
| 1970 | New Zealand Open |
| 1972 | Dunlop Masters, John Player Classic |
| 1973 | New Zealand Open, South African Open, Scandinavian Open |
| 1974 | Greater Greensboro Open, Swiss Open |
| 1978 | Air New Zealand Shell Open |
| 1980 | New Zealand Open, New Zealand P.G.A. Championship |
| 1983 | Talahassee Open |
| 1986 | Mazda Champions |
| 1987 | Vintage Chrysler Invitational, G.T.E. Classic, Sunwest Bank Charley Pride Golf Classic |

### Did you know...

1. Bob Charles is a sheep farmer in his spare time. He lists farming as one of his hobbies but it will become a full time occupation when he finally retires from golf.
2. Bob Charles is considered to be one of the finest putters in the game. He has had more tap-in second putts after long, raking first putts than anyone else on either the American or European Tours.
3. Bob Charles does everything right handed except playing games which require the use of two hands.
4. Bob Charles made almost as much on the 1988 Senior Tour in America as he did in his whole career on the main circuit of which he was a member from 1962.
5. Bob Charles now happily divides his time between homes in New Zealand, Florida and South Africa.

# Roberto De Vicenzo

Multiple title-winner Roberto de Vicenzo remains one of the game's superb strikers of a golf ball but will never forget his disappointment at the U.S. Masters in Augusta.

Roberto de Vicenzo in 1967 – the year of his victory in the Open at Hoylake

Stylish, elegant, warm-hearted Roberto De Vicenzo celebrated 50 years as a golf professional in 1988. During that time he has won more than 200 tournaments including, most notably, the Open Championship on the last occasion it was played at Hoylake in 1967. His place in golfing history, however, was ensured by a sad incident at the U.S. Masters at Augusta in 1968.

Roberto signed for a 66 instead of a closing 65 in the U.S. Masters and by that mistake cost himself the chance of going back the following day for an 18-hole play-off with Bob Goalby. The error meant De Vicenzo, then at his most confident and after a flawless final round, had to accept second place. The huge green and white scoreboards at Augusta showed De Vicenzo had made a birdie three at the seventeenth hole. Twenty-five million viewers around the world had watched him take three but, when it came to signing his card, to authenticate the score, De Vicenzo failed to notice that Tommy Aaron, later to win the Masters himself, had inadvertently marked the proud Argentinian down for a par four.

Always very stylish he will perhaps be most remembered for the tournament he didn't win – the 1968 Masters

It was De Vicenzo's responsibility, of course, to cross-check the individual scores but in the rush to get him from the last green to a television interview, he had failed to do this. He had hardly started the interview when he was asked, dramatically, to return to the last green where tournament director Colonel Homer T. Shields told him his Masters dream had become a nightmare on, of all things, his 45th birthday. It was one of the saddest moments in international golf. Naturally De Vicenzo took it like a man. One of the game's great sportsmen, Roberto knew the rules and appreciated that the incident, which left Goalby a somewhat hollow winner and marker Aaron deeply saddened, was of his own making. He should have checked the card more carefully, refused to be hustled by TV producers until he was satisfied everything was in order.

It was the grimmest moment in the illustrious De Vicenzo career which began as a lad when he and four other brothers, who also turned professional, began to caddie at the golf club 200 yards from his home in Buenos Aires. Self-taught because no one in the family had any connection with what was an elite game in Argentina, Roberto was so captivated and so good at golf he had turned pro by the age of 17 and carved out a glittering international career. It had to be international. The opportunities to make a lot of money from it in Argentina were limited.

De Vicenzo is one of that rare breed of gentlemanly golfers loved universally for generosity of spirit and natural humility. He constantly down-plays his triumphs and shrugs off the admiration heaped on him over the years for his majestic, free-flowing, rhythmical swing. It is one of classic simplicity and beauty. He has always been a delight to watch. In 1966 he was being talked about as the greatest of the international challengers never to have won an Open in Britain but he was to end all that talk a year later when golfing aficionados around the world cheered him to victory by two shots from Jack Nicklaus.

If Augusta was the nadir of De Vicenzo's career – he took a long time to fully recover from that disappointment – Hoylake was the high spot. That week in Liverpool was the final realisation of a dream by a man who later was to be given the rare privilege of being offered honorary membership of the Royal and Ancient Golf Club of St Andrews. Aged 44 at the time, he remains the oldest winner of the British title. Second once and third five times in ten previous Opens, De Vicenzo was the people's choice to win that week.

Throughout the week he played relaxed golf, not forcing the way he had in 1966 at Muirfield when finishing well down the field. If there had been talk overnight of his temperament under pressure – after a record-equalling third round 67 he had a two shot lead with a round to go – letting him down it was not to be. He was always in control with the Championship developing, latterly, into a duel between him and the defending champion Jack Nicklaus. When De Vicenzo birdied the fourteenth he had moved four ahead but he dropped a shot at the fifteenth and Nicklaus birdied the treacherous sixteenth hole where the long approach shot for someone trying to reach the green in two is played over the corner of the out of bounds. De Vicenzo himself then hit a full-blooded three-wood over the trouble to the heart of the green and at that magic moment he knew the title was at last his. Later, after the speeches and the celebrations were over, De Vicenzo left Hoylake not in luxury but in the van belonging to his Scottish caddie Willie Aitchison. In the excitement of it all they forgot to take the trophy!

Over the years the big, broad-shouldered, gentle man has represented his country 17 times in the World Cup – winning the team title with Antonio Cerda in 1953, the inaugural year. He was twice individual title winner. Hugely respected wherever he plays – and sadly these days it is seldom in Britain – Roberto was among the first to spot the extra-special talent of a raw young teenager by the name of Severiano Ballesteros.

The last ever Open Champion at Hoylake – the course just cannot handle the present-day crowds

The Spanish language gave them an additional affinity and it was De Vicenzo's advice to Seve in 1979 that helped Ballesteros to the first of his Open triumphs. De Vicenzo advised Seve to go out that week and 'play from the heart'. He did and no one was more delighted than the golfing genius from Argentina who epitomises in his character and demeanour all that is best in the Royal and Ancient game.

## *CAREER RECORD*

### Victories

| | |
|---|---|
| 1951 | Palm Beach Round Robin, Inverness Four-ball Tournament |
| 1953 | Mexico City Open |
| 1957 | Colonial National Invitational, All-American Tournament |
| 1965 | Los Logartos Open (Col) |
| 1966 | Dallas Open |
| 1967 | British Open |
| 1968 | Houston Champions Tournament |
| 1974 | U.S. P.G.A. Seniors |
| 1979 | Legends of Golf (with Julius Boros) |
| 1980 | U.S. P.G.A. Senior Open |
| 1983 | Doug Sanders Celebrity Pro-Am, Legends of Golf (with Rod Funseth) |
| 1984 | Merrill-Lynch Golf Digest Commemorative Pro-Am |

### Did you know...

1. Gary Player said that had Roberto de Vicenzo been a better putter he might have become the greatest golfer of all time.
2. Robert de Vicenzo will be for ever the last man to win an Open at Royal Liverpool's course at Hoylake. The course is no longer on the Open list.
3. The Argentinian, who has won national titles in 14 different countries, is a former winner of the Bobby Jones award for sportsmanship. The citation stated that "he has always been noted for his fair-play, self control, self denial and generosity of spirit and that he has always shown respect for the game and the people in it".

# *INDEX*



---

**Picture acknowledgements**

The Publishers wish to thank the following sources for their help in providing the illustrations. Where there is more than one acknowledgement on a page the credits start with the top photograph and then run down the page.

*Allsport Photographic* 47a, 48a, 62, 65, 66a, 68, 69a, 73a, 79, 80a, 83b, 95b, 101b, 101c, 113a, 117b, 119a, 125, 128, 130, 138b, 142a, 143a, 146, 147, 155b, 159b, 161b, 165b, 167b, 171, 174, 176a, 177, 179b, 180a, 182a, 185a, 186, 187, 188, 189b. Simon Bruty 87a, 89, 90b, 91, 93, 95a, 118, 129, 133, 136, 139, 142b, 162a, 168. David Cannon 43, 44, 69b, 70, 80b, 81a, 86, 87b, 88, 90a, 94, 96, 97, 98, 99, 100, 102, 103, 104, 105, 106, 107, 108, 110, 111, 112, 113b, 114, 115, 116, 117a, 119b, 120, 121a, 122, 123, 124, 127, 131, 134, 137, 138a, 140, 141, 144, 145, 148, 149, 150, 151, 152, 153, 154, 155a, 156, 157, 158, 159a, 160, 161a, 162b, 163, 165a, 166b, 169, 170, 175, 176b, 179a, 180b, 181, 182b, 183, 184, 185b. Tony Duffy 101a. David Leah 178. Mike Powell 82. Steve Powell 109, 121b, 126, 132. Peter Read-Miller 40. Dan Smith 92, 143b, 164, 166a, 167a. Pascal Rondeau 135.

*Mary Evans Picture Library* 18.

*Golf Illustrated* 10, 19, 20a, 22, 29, 30, 35, 36, 37a, 38, 39, 41, 50, 52, 54a, 55, 60a, 63a, 64a, 77a, 83a, 84b, 85a, 172.

*Michael Hobbs Golf Collection* 11, 12, 13, 14, 15, 16, 17, 20b, 23, 26, 27, 28, 31, 32, 33b, 33c, 34, 37b, 45, 61, 71b, 72, 75, 78, 189a.

*Bob Thomas Sports Photography* 56, 57, 58.

*Topham* 21, 24, 25, 33a, 42, 46, 47b, 48b, 49, 51, 53, 54b, 59, 60b, 60c, 63b, 64b, 66b, 67, 71a, 73b, 74, 76, 77b, 81b, 84a, 85b, 173.